THE
LAST
DAYS
OF
MARILYN
MONROE

A list of titles by James Patterson appears
at the back of this book

JAMES PATTERSON

& IMOGEN EDWARDS-JONES

THE
LAST
DAYS
OF
MARILYN
MONROE

CENTURY

Century

UK | USA | Canada | Ireland | Australia
India | New Zealand | South Africa

Century is part of the Penguin Random House group of companies
whose addresses can be found at global.penguinrandomhouse.com

Penguin Random House UK,
One Embassy Gardens, 8 Viaduct Gardens, London SW11 7BW

penguin.co.uk
global.penguinrandomhouse.com

Penguin
Random House
UK

First published in the UK by Century 2025
001

Printed and bound in Great Britain by Clays Ltd, Elcograf S.p.A.

The authorised representative in the EEA is Penguin Random House Ireland,
Morrison Chambers, 32 Nassau Street, Dublin D02 YH68

A CIP catalogue record for this book is available from the British Library

ISBN: 978–1–529–92847–1 (hardback)
ISBN: 978–1–529–92848–8 (trade paperback)

Hollywood is a place where they'll pay you a thousand dollars for a kiss and fifty cents for your soul. I know, because I turned down the first offer often enough and held out for the fifty cents.

—from *My Story* by Marilyn Monroe

THE
LAST
DAYS
OF
MARILYN
MONROE

PROLOGUE

ONE

Los Angeles, California
August 5, 1962

HOUSEKEEPER EUNICE MURRAY wakes suddenly, fear lodged in the pit of her stomach. It's the middle of the night. She is worried, unsettled without knowing why.

It could be the stifling heat, or the cheap bedsheets that need changing. She gets out of bed, fumbling for her padded pink slippers and matching terry cloth dressing gown.

Opening her bedroom door, the housekeeper shuffles out into the vaulted hall of the home where she lives and works. The Spanish Colonial–style hacienda is tucked away at 12305 Fifth Helena Drive, a wooded cul-de-sac in Brentwood.

It belongs to her employer, movie star Marilyn Monroe.

Boxes are everywhere, half unpacked, the sideboard and spare chairs piled with papers and movie scripts. Unhung framed pictures sit on the floor, turned toward the wall to protect the glassed-in images.

The house is a relatively recent purchase, made on the advice of Marilyn's psychiatrist, Dr. Ralph Greenson.

"Marilyn, you need to put down some roots," he'd advised her. "Get yourself a house of your own."

It's true that after a childhood that included stints in eleven foster homes, two years in an orphanage, and a mother locked up in a mental asylum, Marilyn has always felt deprived of a real home.

So she had bought this house. But even after six months, she still hasn't really moved in, hasn't found the time to arrange things in the main house, much less the big backyard, the swimming pool, and the citrus grove. Half her furniture is still on order.

Mrs. Murray crosses the corridor to Marilyn's bedroom. The door is shut, but the telephone cord wedged under the door attracts her attention. It's the white telephone.

Marilyn has two lines. The white telephone is for personal calls. Marilyn often telephones her friends in the evenings, one after another. She lies in bed, cracks open a Nembutal capsule, adds a chloral hydrate tablet, drinks a champagne chaser, then gives them all a call. How she keeps track of what she says to whom, Mrs. Murray has no idea.

The other telephone, the pink one, is her general line, and it often rings during the night. Marilyn usually muffles the pink telephone and leaves it in the next room, smothering it under some cushions so it doesn't wake her. She's a light sleeper. An insomniac who's obsessed with sleep.

It's been over ten years since Marilyn has gone to bed without sedation. Barbiturates. Nembutal. Powerful drugs. Sometimes they make her forgetful. When she can't remember if she's taken the pills, she rolls over in bed, cracks open another bottle, and pops some more.

Mrs. Murray looks at the telephone cord again. Lamplight seeps out from the crack between the carpet and the door. She puts her ear to the door and listens. The silence concerns her. No giggles. No breathy whispers. Something isn't right.

She tries the door handle, but the door is locked. That's unexpected. Marilyn is fearful of locked doors. Her bedroom door is only locked when she's with a gentleman friend. Tonight she went to bed alone.

Eunice tries again, but she can't get the door opened. Starting to panic, she runs into the next room, throws the cushions off the pink telephone, and dials Dr. Greenson.

She knows the number by heart. Not only has Ralph Greenson been Marilyn's personal psychiatrist for the past two years, he's also the person who first hired Mrs. Murray to work with Marilyn. He treats Marilyn at home because she is too famous to visit his clinic. He lives nearby and was over to the house earlier that day.

The phone rings and rings.

"Come on!" begs Mrs. Murray, pulling her dressing gown tighter around her. "Pick up! Pick up..."

"Hello?" Dr. Greenson answers sleepily.

"It's Marilyn," she blurts. "Her door is locked. I can't raise her."

"Eunice?"

"Please..."

"I'm on my way."

Marilyn's bedroom overlooks the front lawn. Mrs. Murray hurries through the living room and out the front door. Along the way, she grabs a metal poker from the fireplace.

Outside on the lawn, she stops in front of Marilyn's bedroom. Her light is on, but the curtains are drawn. One window is slightly ajar. Standing on her tiptoes, Mrs. Murray pushes the poker through the crack and jabs at the top of the curtains, edging one aside along the rail, exposing an eerie scene.

There she is.

Marilyn Monroe.

The most famous woman in the world.

TWO

"MEN DON'T SEE ME. They just lay their eyes on me."

Mrs. Murray never understood what Marilyn meant by those words—until now. The housekeeper can't scream, she can't shout, she can only stare.

Has Marilyn overdosed again? Is she simply asleep? Or is she actually dead? There have been other nights Marilyn took too many pills. Times she's been rushed to the hospital to have her stomach pumped, only to return, phoenix-like, hours later, like nothing had happened.

She looks so peaceful. Her eyes shut, her lips slightly parted. Lying on the bed. Naked. The alabaster skin. The bleached-blond hair in loose curls around the famous face. The sheets are wrapped around her calves. Her hand still clutches the telephone, which hangs off the hook.

The silence is oppressive. There's no wind blowing through the trees, no cars driving this secluded lane. It feels like the world has stopped spinning. Surely, its brightest star, and its most photographed, cannot be dead at only thirty-six years old.

Where is Dr. Greenson?

The silence is broken by the high-pitched sound of Marilyn's dog barking from the guest house. *Maf normally sleeps in the main house. How did he get out?*

Mrs. Murray listens to his anxious barking. *Can the dog sense what's going on?*

A car comes screeching down Fifth Helena Drive. The front gate slides open and a man dressed in a dark suit and open-collared shirt—no time to put on a tie—runs across the lawn. "Is she breathing? Has she moved? Can you see her?"

Dr. Greenson sees the poker in Eunice's hand. "Give me that," he orders, using the tool to smash the bedroom window. The sound of shattering glass makes Maf bark even louder.

"I'm going in," Dr. Greenson announces, swinging his leg over the windowsill. "Get Dr. Engelberg! I need to know what drugs he's given her."

Dr. Hyman Engelberg is Marilyn's personal physician. He and Dr. Greenson have been coordinating Marilyn's care.

Dr. Greenson hauls himself through the window and into the bedroom. He stops in his tracks at the bed, where Marilyn lies on her back. His patient, whom he adores. So beautiful. So young. So talented. The scene is almost too painful to witness.

He leans over her. He presses gently on the side of her slim white neck. *Please, God, let there be a pulse.* He presses harder. The flesh feels tepid, not as warm as he would like. *Maybe there is something? There! A little . . .*

Then he realizes his error. It's his own pounding heartbeat that he feels.

"We've lost her!" he cries out, his knees buckling beneath him.

What to do? Who to call? An ambulance? The hospital? Where's Engelberg?

The dog barks. Eunice weeps, removing her spectacles to dab her eyes with a handkerchief. Ralph Greenson has unlocked the door. His face is white with shock as he counts the pill bottles on the nightstand. Eight. Ten. Twelve. Some fifteen. All opened. There's a trail of white pills scattered across the carpet, but there's a fifty-capsule bottle of Nembutal that is completely empty.

Is this what she wanted? Greenson can't believe it.

She was in a low mood when she called him yesterday evening. She complained about her personal life, she complained that she couldn't sleep. But she wasn't suicidal. He's sure of that.

The front door slams. Running feet hammer across the terra-cotta tiles in the hall. "Where is she?!" demands Dr. Engelberg as he bursts through the bedroom door.

"Is she breathing? Have you checked for a pulse?" he asks Greenson, bending over. "Are you sure she's not still alive?"

"She's gone," replies Greenson, with a slow shake of his head.

Dr. Engelberg inserts the earpieces of his stethoscope and places the instrument on Marilyn's chest to listen for breathing sounds. He pauses. He then checks the pulse points at her wrists and listens to her lungs.

"There's no sign of foul play, no blood or wound," he declares, examining the body. "But she is gone. Most certainly." He sighs, removes his stethoscope, and picks up the empty bottle of Nembutal.

The customary dose is one tablet per night.

"I gave her that prescription only three days ago," Engelberg says. "And only after she begged me."

"I thought we agreed that we were weaning her off medication?" Greenson raises his voice for emphasis. "That's what we said. No more drugs. No more. Enough."

"We had," acknowledges Engelberg. "And we were doing well. I'd got her usage right down. Until her last appointment when she wouldn't let me leave without prescribing fifty capsules." He starts picking up the bottles on the nightstand, his eyes scanning the labels. "Chloral hydrate. Jesus," he whispers. "Knockout drops...Where did she get fifteen bottles of medicine?"

"I thought it was you," Greenson says, glaring at Engelberg.

"Me? No. I'd never prescribe that. Mix it with alcohol and Nembutal..." He looks down at Marilyn on the bed and checks the empty bottle again.

"Fifty..." He shakes his head. "I think we should cover her up, don't you? Or at least roll her onto her front?" He looks around the sparsely furnished and frankly inelegant room of the world's most famous movie star. "Give the place a little decorum."

"I can't face it," Greenson replies, his voice barely audible, "but shouldn't we call the police?"

It is 4:25 a.m. when Engelberg makes the call.

THREE

"MARILYN MONROE HAS DIED. She's committed suicide."

Sergeant Jack Clemmons is a homicide investigator with the Los Angeles Police Department. He immediately presumes the call is a hoax. Drunks call the police department, making ridiculous claims, at every hour of the day.

"Who did you say was calling?" he asks.

"I'm Dr. Hyman Engelberg, Marilyn Monroe's physician. I'm at her residence. She's committed suicide."

"I'll come right away."

It is almost 5 a.m. when Sergeant Clemmons arrives. He's already radioed for backup. He hopes they won't be long. It's never pleasant attending a suicide.

The one-story bungalow with a tiny front yard is smaller than he expected. *Don't they make millions in Hollywood?* He knocks on the front door.

It takes a while for someone to answer. *Weren't they expecting him?* He can hear the constant yapping of a dog. And from the inside, whispering and shuffling sounds.

Finally, an elderly woman answers. She's neatly dressed in a maroon skirt and a buttoned-up baby-blue cardigan.

"Sergeant Clemmons."

"Eunice Murray," she replies, smiling briefly. "I am Marilyn Monroe's housekeeper. Or I was ... She's committed suicide."

"She has?"

"I found her. Lying on her bed, naked, still holding the telephone. It was the telephone cord that first alerted me," she continues in an odd monotone. "I woke and left my bedroom," she indicates across the corridor. "And I saw the cord and the light under the door."

"What time was this?"

"Three a.m. I remember it as I looked at my watch." She lifts her wrist by way of demonstration. "Over here."

He follows Mrs. Murray through the hall.

She points toward the open bedroom door. "Forgive me if I don't come in. But I have a lot to do."

In the half-lit bedroom, Clemmons finds two men, who introduce themselves as Marilyn Monroe's attending physicians. Dr. Greenson sits with his head in his hands, while Dr. Engelberg paces the cream-colored carpet. He glances at the broken window and the pinking dawn, like he is waiting for something.

Clemmons surveys the small bedroom. There's no glamorous padded headboard, no glittering chandelier, none of the spoils of stardom. There are pills and handbags and clothes on the floor, which is now also covered with shattered glass. He looks down at the bed. Marilyn's body is covered in a sheet. She is lying on her front. One arm hangs off the bed, her hand in a claw. Her unpolished fingernails are bitten to the quick.

This isn't right. Clemmons furrows his brow. Marilyn's legs are perfectly straight. Her face is buried in a pillow. He'd like to get a look at her mouth, check for signs of foam or vomit. Suicides are usually messier than this. The normal signs of distress or struggle are not present.

"Where's the drinking glass?"

"The what?" replies Dr. Engelberg.

"Her glass of water." Clemmons nods toward the nightstand. "If you're going to take a lot of pills, you need a lot of water."

"I don't know," Dr. Engelberg sounds irritated. "Maybe the housekeeper does."

"So, this is not the crime scene?" The sergeant looks from one doctor to another.

"It is," declares Dr. Engelberg. "But there's no crime."

"So, where's the glass?"

"There wasn't one," says Greenson. "Not when I broke in through the window anyway."

"No glass," confirms Clemmons, taking out his notepad.

"Not that I saw," says Dr. Greenson. "But then I wasn't really looking. I was more worried about, um, the patient."

"You broke in?" asks Clemmons.

"Through that window." Dr. Greenson glances over his shoulder at the shattered windowpane.

"And did you try to revive her?"

"It was too late," replies Dr. Engelberg.

"We were all too late," adds Greenson.

"Do you have any idea when she took the pills?" Neither doctor meets his eye.

"No," they both reply.

"Do you mind if I take a look?" he asks, indicating the bed.

"Go ahead," replies Dr. Engelberg.

Clemmons pulls back the sheet. There are the distinctive blond curls, the smooth curves of her shoulders, the luminous white skin of her back. He pauses. It feels almost indecent to carry on. There's a slight purple discoloration over her buttocks. Her smooth legs are aligned, her toes turned inward. She has a dried-up blister on her left foot. He covers her quickly. It feels intrusive.

"Any idea who she was calling?" he asks.

"Calling?" Dr. Engelberg looks surprised.

"The housekeeper says she was holding the telephone?"

"Oh? Did she? Maybe she realized what she had done and was calling for help?"

"But the housekeeper's bedroom is less than ten feet away. Why wouldn't she just shout out?"

There's another knock at the front door. *This is my case now,* Clemmons thinks as he strides to answer it, determined not to leave the two doctors alone at the scene any longer than necessary.

"Who are you?" asks the sergeant.

Standing on the doorstep is a scrawny young man with a small chin and a large Adam's apple, dressed in workman's dungarees and carrying a toolbox.

"Norman. Norman Jeffries. I came as quickly as I could. My mother-in-law called and asked me to come and fix a broken window."

"Your mother-in-law?"

"He's married to my daughter," Mrs. Murray says. "He does all the odd jobs around the house."

"And you called him?" Clemmons is astonished. *Who comes to mend a broken window at 5:15 in the morning?*

"He lives locally. And it needs to be done." Eunice looks at the detective. "It's dangerous."

Clemmons takes a step back to allow the handyman in.

"There are newsmen outside the house," Jeffries tells the sergeant. "And a few of the neighbors."

"Newsmen?" asks Clemmons.

"That's right," he confirms. "They asked what I was doing here. I said I was here to fix a broken window. Has something happened?"

Was his call for backup intercepted?

"How many people are outside?" asks Clemmons.

"Twenty, thirty," replies the handyman. "I didn't stop to count."

FOUR

THE SECRET IS OUT. Hollywood's screen goddess is dead.

Sergeant Clemmons's radio call was overheard and beamed around the world. Newspaper editors are waking their reporters, demanding that they get over to Brentwood. *Time, Life,* and the *New York Herald Tribune* already have writers stationed outside Marilyn Monroe's gate.

More reporters arrive. Cameras. Lights. News trucks park up along Fifth Helena Drive.

Inside, the police set up an office in the kitchen as more officers join the investigation. A police photographer documents Marilyn's bedroom, popping off flashbulbs.

Marilyn's lawyer, Milton "Mickey" Rudin, marches in, as does her personal publicist, Pat Newcomb.

"This must have been an accident," Newcomb says, but she is overcome with grief and quickly dissolves into sobs. "When your best friend kills herself, how do you feel? What do you do?"

In the chaos, a gossip columnist manages to get into the house and take photos of Marilyn lying dead on the bed. Pretending to be from the coroner's office, he's only removed when the real team arrives at about 5:45 a.m. The mortuary van navigates the crowds, barely clearing the gate.

Everyone wants a glimpse. A glimpse of what? The body? A curl of blond hair hanging off the back of the stretcher?

Guy Hockett, director of Westwood Village Mortuary, walks into the bedroom along with his son, Don. The younger Hockett has been working with his father to earn money for a trip to Mexico at Christmas. Together, they begin to pick up some of the drugs and place them in plastic evidence bags.

Next, it's the body. This is only Don's third corpse. The first two, both elderly men, didn't bother him much. But this is Marilyn Monroe, and he can't bear to look.

"Get the gurney, son," says his father, sensing Don's discomfort. "I can deal with this."

Don walks back through the house packed with police officers and doctors all talking over each other. He walks past the housekeeper doing the washing and goes out into the front yard. He pulls the gurney out of the back of the van and sets it up on its wheels. It's old and stained. It doesn't seem good enough for her.

By the time Don returns to the bedroom, his father has prepared the body. Marilyn's arms are crossed over her chest and she's covered in a pale blue blanket. Together they lift the corpse and use two leather straps to secure it on the gurney.

Dr. Engelberg accompanies the somber procession. At the

entrance to the house, they pause. The young man straightens the blanket. The doctor looks down at tiles set into a flagstone. One bears a small coat of arms and two words in Latin.

"*Cursum Perficio*," he says, then translates the inscription: "My journey's end." He sighs as he watches father and son wheel the gurney toward the van. "Oh, Marilyn. Dear, dear Marilyn."

"So, I have fixed the window," announces Norman Jeffries, holding his toolbox. "I think I'll be off then. Nothing more for me to do here."

The bewildered doctor is not really listening. He watches the van disappear through the gate to the explosion of a thousand flashbulbs.

"I can take the dog if you want," Jeffries says, nodding over at the guest house. "Poor little thing hasn't stopped barking. I wonder if he knows his mistress is gone."

Maf's stuffed toys, a tiger and a lamb, are strewn across the backyard.

As Engelberg gathers up his things, he watches Mrs. Murray walk across the front lawn toward where *Life* magazine entertainment correspondent Tommy Thompson is waiting outside, his microphone at the ready.

"She was nude...totally nude when I found her," Mrs. Murray begins, "lying in bed, clutching her white telephone. Her bedroom light was on and the telephone cable under the door alerted me..."

Eunice Murray would stick to her story, but everyone who crossed the threshold that night would say something different.

How do you go about writing a life story? Marilyn once asked a journalist. *Because the true things rarely get into circulation. It's usually the false things. It's hard to know where to start if you don't start with the truth.*

But nobody was interested in that.

1939

CHAPTER 1

HER BUST IS the first thing her classmates notice. What the hell happened to Norma Jeane the Human Bean over the long, hot summer of 1939?

Thirty or so students at Ralph Waldo Emerson Junior High School watch, open-mouthed, as thirteen-year-old Norma Jeane Mortenson rushes into morning math class in Westwood, California. A whirling dervish of books, auburn curls, and a tight sweater.

She's late. She's always late.

Without a nickel for bus fare, it's more than a two-mile walk from Sawtelle, where no one who's anyone lives, to the school in prosperous Westwood. Norma Jeane never has a nickel, so every school day she walks the nearly five-mile round trip there and back to the intersection of Corinth and 11348 Nebraska Avenue.

Come rain or shine, she always walks alone, singing as she goes down the road, or in the school corridors, or on her way to the lunchroom. She sings, *"Jesus loves me, this I know,"* which is lucky, because no one else loves her.

Norma Jeane boards with Ana Lower, who she calls "Auntie" Ana. But Ana is no real relation; she is the aunt of Norma Jeane's legal guardian, Grace McKee Goddard.

Grace is her mother's best friend, and has been watching out for Norma Jeane since she was born on June 1, 1926, in the charity ward of Los Angeles General Hospital. When Norma Jeane's mother, Gladys Monroe Baker, was institutionalized in 1934, she signed her daughter's care over to Grace—and now Grace has passed the teenager on to Auntie Ana, a safe spot after years spent shuttling between foster homes and the orphanage.

Like Grace and Gladys, white-haired Auntie Ana is a devout Christian Scientist. As a local landlord and a church advisor, Ana is compassionate yet practical. She tries to teach the thirteen-year-old about sex. Warn her.

The lesson comes just in time. On the first day of school that year, Norma Jeane discovers that she has outgrown her two county-issued dresses. She goes next door to borrow a little blue sweater. And it is a little *too* little, and too blue, and the whole class can see the bounteous gifts that Mother Nature has bestowed on the formerly skinny waif.

When I walk into the classroom, Norma Jeane realizes, *the boys suddenly begin screaming and moaning and throwing themselves on the floor.*

At recess, Norma Jeane is surrounded. There are six boys, all of them smiling.

"What happened to you?" asks one freckle-faced jock, his hand cupping his chin as he looks her up and down. "You've gone from String Bean to hubba-hubba in one summer."

"Hmm," purrs Norma Jeane. The buzzing "hmm" noise is the one all the girls at school make to sound like Jean Harlow in the movies.

The other kids in her class used to whisper. They pointed their fingers and crossed to the other side of the street. No one wanted to be seen with the girl who stuttered when she spoke and dressed in clothing from the Los Angeles Orphans' Home Society. No one wanted to be friends with the girl whose mother is institutionalized. No one wanted to invite Norma Jeane home after school.

Now the boys are much more attentive.

"You're the Hubba-Hubba, Hmm Girl, that's what you are."

The boy's voice isn't teasing. He's paying her a compliment, which might be the very first she's ever had. Norma Jeane doesn't quite know how to react, so she smiles sweetly and bobs a little curtsy.

"Why thank you, sir."

Norma Jeane is excited to tell Aunt Ana the news. "They know my name now. I'm no longer the Orphan," she says, breaking into an imitation of her schoolmates' taunts—'*Orphan 3463 with no friends and a mumma in the madhouse.*'" She smiles. "The world is a much friendlier place now that I'm the Hubba-Hubba, Hmm Girl."

When Norma Jeane finds some old ruby lipstick and a pencil to darken her brows, the world gets even friendlier. Drivers honk their car horns when they pass her on the way to Westwood and every boy wants to walk her home from school.

Her stutter begins to disappear.

She chooses a boyfriend. He's more than old enough to know better, but maybe he doesn't care that the girl sitting in his passenger seat, laughing at his bad jokes, is only thirteen years old.

Norma Jeane and her new boyfriend drive to the beach. It's a beautiful day for a stroll on the sand overlooking the largest and deepest ocean on earth.

She's been practicing a new walk, a sophisticated, languid movement with pointed toes and swinging shoulders. Point and swish. Point and swish. Just like the divas on the silver screen.

"Shall we dive in?" asks her beau.

"In the ocean?"

"Of course, the ocean," he laughs as he strips off his shirt and shorts and runs toward the foam.

Norma Jeane peels off her shirt and her cheap old slacks, leaving her clothes in a neat pile on the sand. She can feel the warm sun tapping her shoulders, the wind whipping her curls, sticking a strand to her lips.

In a swimsuit borrowed from a friend, she walks toward the water's edge. In the too-small suit, she's nearly naked, but there's no turning back.

A young man wolf whistles. There's another whistle and another.

Who are they whistling for? she wonders.

No one ever whistled for Norma Jeane the Human Bean. They are whistling for this new girl. What a thrill.

She stretches in the sun and walks slowly up the beach.

I'll remember this afternoon forever. Today I became a girl who belongs to the world . . .

CHAPTER 2

JOY NEVER LASTS.

That's the lesson young Norma Jeane learned when she lived with her mother, Gladys Baker, in Hollywood. Back then, Norma Jeane went to the cinema every Wednesday, all on her own. For ten cents, she would sit in the front row and watch a film over and over. Beautiful women in beautiful clothes who walked like tigers in the forest, full of power and purpose, especially Claudette Colbert in *Cleopatra*.

It was more than a whole new world. It was her whole world.

Though the little girl often stayed past sundown, she was always careful to mind her mother and stay on the sidewalk walking home.

Theirs was a little white two-story house, where Norma Jeane and her mother lived with lodgers. For a while, it was a dream. Gladys even buys an out-of-tune, second-hand grand piano that had once belonged to Oscar-winning actor Fredric March.

"You'll play the piano over here, by the windows," Norma

Jeane's mother tells her. "And here on each side of the fireplace there'll be a love seat. And we can sit listening to you. As soon as I pay off a few other things I'll get the love seats, and we'll all sit in them at night and listen to you play the piano."

But these domestic dreams are soon shattered. Gladys's mental health deteriorates, just as it had when Norma Jeane was born, and she's sent away to yet another hospital.

When those few months of happiness end, Norma Jeane feels the pain.

Now her heart is breaking again, because Aunt Ana's heart is giving out. She's over sixty now and suffering from cardiovascular disease. Far too infirm to look after a teenager.

Norma Jeane returns to live with her guardian, Grace McKee Goddard. In the 1920s, Grace and Gladys worked together cutting and splicing negatives at Consolidated Film Industries, back when Grace drank a little less and Gladys could stick with a job.

In her younger years, Grace dreamed of becoming an actress, a passion she instills in young Norma Jeane. "One day you'll be just like Shirley Temple. You'll see," Grace tells her.

Yet Grace's own personal life is tumultuous. She marries and divorces three times. Her fourth husband, Ervin "Doc" Goddard, has his own teenage daughter, Eleanor "Bebe" Goddard, with whom fifteen-year-old Norma Jeane shares a room when she moves in with the family at 14743 Archwood Street in Van Nuys.

The girls also share a love of clothes and makeup. When they enroll in Van Nuys High School in September 1941, they tell everyone they're half sisters.

For rides home after school, they rely on the kindness of a neighbor.

James Dougherty is twenty-one years old, with sapphire eyes, dirty blond hair, and a wide grin. The former football captain and class president of Van Nuys High School is dressed in coveralls, just coming off his shift at Lockheed Aircraft in Burbank. The assembly lines are making P-38 Lightning fighters and Hudson bombers as the United States gears up to join the war that started when Germany invaded Poland in 1939.

"Normie?" he asks one afternoon, spotting the five-foot-five Norma Jeane standing alone, her hair in braids and with freshly applied scarlet lipstick. "Where's Bebe?"

"She's home sick," shrugs Norma Jeane. "So, it's just me today." She gets into the front seat of his flat-nosed blue Ford coupe and shuffles close to him.

"I wish I knew how to drive," she says. "Will you teach me one day, Jim?"

Dougherty collects Norma Jeane every day from school. They drive through the Hollywood Hills, and park up at that spot on Mulholland Drive where all the teens end up on a Tuesday afternoon.

"Can I call you Daddy?" she asks, as he kisses her neck.

"You can call me whatever you want," he mumbles.

Norma Jeane doesn't know her father. She's only seen his photograph once before. Gladys, in one of her more lucid moments, showed it to her. There was a sparkle in his eye, a curl to his lips, and a devilish mustache. He looked just like Clark Gable.

31

She thinks Dougherty looks a bit like her father, too. She talks about her father. Endlessly. Or her lack of one. She was born illegitimate, she explains. Dougherty doesn't mind, so long as he can carry on kissing her.

"What a daddy," she smiles, pushing him gently away.

CHAPTER 3

ON DECEMBER 7, 1941, the Japanese bomb Pearl Harbor and terror rips through Los Angeles. They are next, surely? The City of Angels is not only the peddler of dreams, but also the center of US aircraft production.

Lockheed gets every available aircraft flying. Fighters and bombers come west to protect the coast from potential kamikaze attacks. Others patrol inland. There are blackouts.

In the spring, the blow comes.

"You'll have to go back to the orphanage," explains Grace, over a cigarette and a glass of warm gin. Her husband is being transferred for work. "Doc can't turn down a new job across the country. There's nothing I can do." She grinds her cigarette into the ashtray.

"But you promised...You p-p-promised." Norma Jeane's cheeks are burning red. She cries silent tears over the injustice of it all.

What has she ever done to deserve any of this? She's been a good girl. She babysat all those foster kids. She only ran away from the orphanage once, but barely got as far as the end of the drive before realizing she had nowhere to go and turning back.

When Mr. Kinnell, the lodger at her mother's house in Hollywood, locked her in his bedroom, she kicked and screamed and whacked him. But when her mother explained that they couldn't afford the house without him, Norma Jeane stopped making a fuss. Mr. Murray Kinnell. She would never forget his name.

And now here she is being returned to the orphanage, like an unwanted present that's shop-soiled.

She rocks back and forth in her chair and starts to sing under her breath. She wraps her arms tightly around herself, digging her fingertips into her upper arms until it hurts.

"Jesus loves me, this I know. Jesus loves me, this I know."

She closes her eyes. She rocks some more.

"Stop it," snaps Grace. "Stop it right there! I have an idea."

The idea is this: Norma Jeane will marry Jim Dougherty. Grace has arranged it all.

"He's said yes," she tells her ward, who doesn't have much choice in the matter. "We have to wait until you're sixteen, but that's in a couple months. You'll have to drop out of school, obviously. But who needs that now?"

Grace doesn't wait for an answer. "Anything but the orphanage, right?"

"Anything but the orphanage," agrees Norma Jeane.

* * *

Norma Jeane is standing at the top of a spiral staircase in a long-sleeved dress handmade by Aunt Ana. The white embroidered lace gown is topped with a sheer veil.

Eighteen days ago, Norma Jeane celebrated her birthday. Today, June 19, 1942, is her wedding day.

By the fireplace stands the sharp-featured minister in an even sharper suit. But next to him, grinning with delight, is Jim Dougherty. He is sure and solid and reliable.

Everyone looks up at the bridge at the top of the stairs. Norma Jeane smiles through the sickly sweet scent wafting from her bouquet of white lilies.

There is no music. Just a nod from the pinched-faced preacher.

And one long, deep breath.

There is no backing out now.

CHAPTER 4

THERE IS A WEDDING NIGHT—"Don't worry, you'll learn," is Grace's advice—but no honeymoon.

Dougherty goes straight back to work at Lockheed. On his lunch break, he clicks open his carefully packed black metal Victory Thermos lunch pail.

Norma Jeane delights in choosing home furnishings, but she's no cook. Along with dry and tasteless sandwiches, she sends handwritten notes at the bottom of the container.

Dearest Daddy—when you read this, I'll be asleep and dreaming of you. Love and kisses, Your Baby.

She cooks green peas and orange carrots together "because the colors look nice" and puts salt in his coffee because she read about it in a magazine. He doesn't mind.

Nor does he mind the piles of encyclopedias Norma Jeane buys from the door-to-door salesmen, or the dolls and stuffed animals she lines up on the chest of drawers "so they can see what's going on." She even tries to bring a cow into their tiny house in Van Nuys. It had been lowing in the rain and its plaintive voice had upset her, so she'd enticed it inside to keep it warm.

His friends at work pass around her photograph and ask him what it's like to be married to a sixteen-year-old girl.

"She's insatiable," he boasts. When they go out for weekend drives, she makes him pull the car to the side of the road, to make the sex even *more* exciting than it already is. "You should hear me. 'Honey,' I say, 'honey, you do know we've got a home and a beautiful bed we could go to.' But she won't stop." He chuckles. "She leans on my chest and looks up at me with those big baby blue eyes, 'Pull over, pull over, baby, pull over right here.'" He laughs. They all laugh. "You should see what she looks like without any clothes on."

"Lucky Jim" his friends call him. None of them would mind that view.

But none of them have any idea that Dougherty is only telling stories. Norma Jeane makes men think of sex but is herself not at all interested.

Yet Norma Jeane spends hours in the bathroom making herself look nice when Dougherty invites the guys from work over for a beer. His friends can't keep their eyes off her. She starts out all quiet at the beginning of the night. Perched on a chair, just listening, but toward the end of the evening, a whole new person erupts. The result is hypnotic.

"Dance with me, Norma Jeane," pleads one friend. "Dance with me, you beauty queen."

She's like an enchantress, all hips and swings, with her wide, pretty smile and her auburn hair. She insists on rolling up the carpet to dance and show them how it's done. She sits on their laps. Her husband looks on. But all he wants is for her to stop.

After his friends leave, they have a fight. Norma Jeane runs off into the darkness in her nightgown.

"Come back!" shouts Dougherty. "Come back!"

He looks out into the empty street. It's past midnight. He turns out the lights and pulls up a chair, staring out of the dark window. An hour passes. Maybe more. His nose is pressed against the window. His cheek is pushed up against the cold glass. Then suddenly, he sees her coming back, a white flash, sprinting toward the house as if being chased by the devil.

Norma Jeane hammers on the door. Dougherty opens it. She tumbles in.

"He's after me. A man is chasing me. He was in the street, then in a tree, behind a car. He's everywhere." Her eyes are wide with panic. "He's there, he's in the street, go and look in the street."

Dougherty is skeptical, but goes up and down the street, looking left and right, then comes back to the house.

"It's fine, honey, there's no one there."

"He's there, I tell you!"

Norma Jeane won't let it go.

"You're CRAZY," he finally yells, grabbing her by the shoulders. "You're one crazy bitch!"

The word hangs in the air, sucking up the silence. *Crazy.*

"And you're a brute!" she whispers.

"And you're a *little* girl."

CHAPTER 5

JIM DOUGHERTY JOINS the Merchant Marine.

He's first sent to Catalina Island, twenty-two miles off the coast of Southern California, to teach ocean safety. The couple lives in a boarding house above the Marlin Club and Norma Jeane gets a job working at Lloyd's Candy Store.

To qualify for sea duty—he'll see the world, earn some money, and get away from his wife of thirteen months—he trains at base camp. She misses him terribly. She has no relatives or friends to visit. When he telephones her, she answers with a yelp. When is he coming home?

By the time he ships out in December 1943 aboard the *Julia S. DuMont* bound for the South Pacific, she's worked herself into a panic. He's signed up to be away for over a year, and she'll have to go back to living with her mother-in-law.

There is a scene. There's always a scene with his wife.

She's on her knees, clutching his legs. Her mascara-streaked face is crumpled in misery. "I'm so lonely when you're gone."

"I'm coming back," he keeps saying. "I promise. And when I get back, we'll have a baby."

Have a baby? His seventeen-year-old wife shudders at the thought. *I can see it only as myself, another Norma Jeane in an orphanage. Something will happen to me. Jim will wander off. And there would be this little girl in a blue dress and white blouse living in her "aunt's" home, washing dishes, being the last in the bath water on Saturday night.*

Norma Jeane lies awake at night, crying and feeling lonelier than ever.

CHAPTER 6

"HAVE YOU EVER modeled before?"

Private David Conover of the Army's First Motion Picture Unit wears a camera around his neck as he casually questions the attractive female factory worker.

"Just clay," she replies.

Conover's assignment today is a 1944 variation on the "We Can Do It!" campaign popularized by the 1942 hit song "Rosie the Riveter." It's so important that his commanding officer, Captain Ronald Reagan, has requisitioned a rare commodity: color film.

Yank magazine, the Army weekly, is planning a morale-boosting piece titled "Women in Industry" for its December 22, 1944, issue documenting these "busy patriots" on production lines "doing their bit for the war."

Norma Jeane Dougherty is dressed in her uniform, overalls she wears cinched in at the waist and unbuttoned at the front.

I was surprised they insisted on putting us girls in overalls.

41

Putting a girl in overalls is like having her work in tights, particularly if she knows how to wear them.

Norma Jeane certainly knows how to wear them.

At the Radioplane factory specializing in drone warfare, Conover can't believe his luck. Right here in Burbank is the worker elected "queen" of the company picnic. She has a smudge on her face and her hair's tied up in a scarf, but her eyes have more soul than he has ever seen.

"You don't belong here," he declares.

"Where do I belong?" she asks.

"On the cover of a magazine!" he says. "You're a cover girl, that's for sure."

Her mother-in-law, Ethel Dougherty, got her this job. She works at the Radioplane factory, too, as a nurse. Though Norma Jeane starts off as a typist, "I only did thirty-five words a minute and didn't do them very well, so they gave me a job inspecting parachutes," she says. Now she works ten-hour shifts inspecting and spraying parachutes with flame retardant. Though she won a $50 war bond at the picnic, her regular salary is $20 a week.

With Conover's encouragement, Norma Jeane takes off her head scarf and clips up her auburn curls, then smooths down her shirt and reapplies glossy red lipstick.

She poses, smiling, with a propeller. She is a natural in front of the camera. Exuding life from every pore. What a paradox—so unconfident in real life and yet so vibrant on film.

She's intrigued to discover that the army private also has a stutter, the same speech impediment she's had to overcome.

Conover invites her to visit his photography studio on the Sunset Strip.

"But I am a married woman," she says.

"So much the better," he replies with a wink. "Strictly business."

Conover manages to negotiate for her to be allowed a few days leave from the factory. Keen to learn, Norma Jeane squints over every print, asking about lighting and positioning and why one photograph works better than the other. His earlier photo of her didn't make it into *Yank* magazine's issue on women in industry, but he's eager to have another shoot. Norma Jeane writes to Bebe Goddard that Conover tells her "I should buy all new clothes to go into the modeling profession....He said he had a lot of contacts that he wanted me to look into."

He photographs her in the Hollywood Hills wearing a white romper, a blue and white striped top, and a red sweater. The camera loves Norma Jeane. Conover snaps away, his hands shaking with excitement.

"How am I doing?" she asks, shielding her eyes from the sun. "Am I photogenic?"

"Hell, yes!"

CHAPTER 7

I HAD BEEN a sort of child bride and now I was a sort of child widow. Sundays were the loneliest. I would go to Union Station and watch people. You learned a lot watching them. You learned that pretty wives adored homely men and good-looking men adored homely wives.

Norma Jeane's been lonely. Anyone can see that, her wistful thoughts so plain on her face, almost as if she's speaking them aloud.

Three days before Christmas, Norma Jeane stands on the platform of the Glendale Transportation Center waiting for the Amtrak from San Francisco. Like one of the women she's watched all those Sundays, she scans the approaching crowd.

"Jim!" she yells. "JIM," she yells, and waves. "Jim!"

She runs toward her husband, weaving her way through the people, and hurls herself into his arms. While her husband's been away, Norma Jeane's modeling work has taught her how good it can feel to dress up in someone else's clothes. Why not try on the role of a married woman in love?

"Darling!" She kisses his neck and runs her hand over his prickly buzz cut. "Welcome home!"

When they get to the motor lodge they've booked for the night, she puts on a silky black negligee. "What do you think?" she asks, standing in the doorway to the bathroom.

"I think you look mighty fine," Dougherty replies. "Come right over here!"

"Did I tell you I've been modeling?" she asks, leaping onto the bed. "I'm really enjoying it. I think I might actually be quite good."

"So my mother tells me," he says. Ethel's not a fan of her daughter-in-law's new aspirations.

"She told you?" Norma Jeane wrinkles her nose. "It was supposed to be my little secret to surprise you."

"If you're enjoying yourself it doesn't bother me much," he tells her, laughing.

"What's funny?" she asks.

"All this modeling business is fine, honey, but when I get out of the service, we're going to have a family and you're going to settle down." He kisses her. "You can only have one career, and a woman can't be in two places at once."

The country is at war, and there's no point in arguing. Norma Jeane doesn't mention her modeling aspirations for the rest of his leave. Instead, they watch movies at Grauman's Chinese, picnic at Pop's Willow Lake, and go to the Cocoanut Grove for meals. At the twenty-four-acre nightclub in the Ambassador Hotel on Wilshire, they eat a steak dinner.

But a familiar unhappiness presses down on Norma Jeane. With her husband back out to sea, she'll have nothing left but terse conversation with his mother in the evenings and Sundays at Union Station.

"I think I'm going to call my father," she announces, out of the blue.

"Your father?" asks Dougherty, astonished.

Norma Jeane has been learning some family history. While her husband was away, she blew most of her savings on a visit to Chicago, where Grace McKee—no longer Grace McKee Goddard since splitting from Doc—has been living and working in a film laboratory.

After four or five gins, Grace told some revealing stories. Norma Jeane learned a lot about her mother, Gladys, and her extended family. Not only does it turn out that Norma Jeane has an older half sister from her mother's first marriage named Berniece Baker, she's now learned the identity of the Clark Gable look-alike man in the photo Gladys had once shown her. It wasn't Martin Edward Mortensen, Gladys's estranged second husband, whose name the twenty-four-year-old mother had misspelled as "Mortenson" on her newborn daughter's birth certificate.

The man with the debonair mustache and a glint in his eye was Stan Gifford—her mother's former supervisor at Consolidated Film Industries, and Norma Jeane's real father.

She tells Dougherty that she has Gifford's number and she's going to call him.

"Honey," he says. "I am not sure that is the best idea."

But she telephones anyway.

"This is Norma Jeane," she says, her voice trembling, as she sits on the edge of her bed, her hand gripping the pillow. "I'm Gladys Baker's d-d-daughter."

The voice on the line is cold and utterly devoid of emotion. "I have nothing to say to you." Stan Gifford pauses. "Don't ever call me again."

He hangs up.

And she collapses back onto the bed.

Dougherty watches as his wife cries uncontrollably, pummeling the pillows with her fists.

"I'm not sure what's worse," she says between sobs. "To have no daddy, or to have a daddy who doesn't love you at all."

CHAPTER 8

"WE'LL HAVE TO GET RID of the wiggle," Miss Emmeline Snively says.

The Blue Book Modeling School is headquartered in the Ambassador Hotel on Wilshire Boulevard. The agency's director sits bolt upright behind a large leather-topped desk, reviewing her latest prospect.

Norma Jeane Dougherty, in a freshly ironed white sharkskin dress and white suede shoes, walks up and down in front of Miss Snively, hips swinging left and right over her double-jointed knees.

Miss Snively watches the young modeling hopeful with an inscrutable gaze, her white kid-gloved hands resting on her lap. She opines, "The wiggle *and* the hair."

With only twenty girls in her agency bluebook, Emmeline Snively is particularly choosy. She promises to groom those select few "for careers in motion pictures, photographic modeling and fashion modeling" via "personalized instruction in charm and poise, success and beauty and personalized development." It's all in the brochure.

California blonde, notes Snively about Norma Jeane's hair. *Fair in summer and dark in winter, bleached on top by the sun. Too dull for photographs, it looks flat in the light. And far too thick, and far too curly.* She sets down her fountain pen and leans across the desk. "Do you really want to be a model, dear?"

"I'd really like to try. I have some photographs," Norma Jeane gestures toward her bag lying on the leather-topped desk.

"Yes, yes...we've seen your snaps."

A photographer shooting a local beauty contest had already sent over Kodachromes of Norma Jeane.

No one turns up to a modeling audition in a white dress that turns transparent in the sun. And yet, here she is, as clean and white and shining as her dress.

"Oh, those girls are so pretty," Norma Jeane says, looking at the agency photo board.

Snively likes the looks of this pleasant-faced girl. Her teeth are nearly perfect, though she'll need the small lump taken off her nose and maybe a bit more of a point to her chin. But she has charm. Lots and lots of charm.

What a wonderful little doll she would be on the cover of a magazine someday, the modeling agent thinks. *She has that girl-next-door look. She is irresistible.*

"You have to have the know-how to model," explains Snively. "We offer a three-month course for one hundred dollars."

"B-b-but I don't have one hundred dollars."

The poor child looks so dejected, so downcast, that Snively makes her a rare offer. "Then you can pay me out of your future earnings. Do you want to start working immediately?"

"Yes, please!"

There's one more thing.

"Your smile. It's too high, and that makes wrinkles," Miss Snively tells her. "Lower that smile."

"Lower my smile?" Norma Jeane's top lip is quivering with the effort.

"Lower than that..."

Emmeline Snively has never seen a girl work as hard as Norma Jeane. She attends fashion modeling classes with Mrs. Gavin Beardsley, makeup and grooming with Maria Smith, and posing instruction with Miss Snively herself. Norma Jeane, despite always being late for the airplane factory, is never once late at the Blue Book. She is attentive, she takes notes, and she studies her photographs, finding her good and bad angles.

She's started out with less than any girl I've seen, but she wants to learn, she wants to be somebody. She has real drive, Snively thinks. *If I teach her how to pose, how to handle herself, she'll go far.*

For her first, informal assignment, Miss Snively sends Norma Jeane to Hungarian-born photographer Andre de Dienes.

At the sight of her, he thinks, *It was as if a miracle had happened to me. Norma Jeane seemed to be like an angel. An earthly, sexy-looking angel!*

The following week Norma Jeane is booked as a hostess at the Los Angeles Home Show in Pan-Pacific Auditorium. She's a hit with the clients, the other models, everyone. She earns $10 a day for ten days, which is a lot more than the $20 a week she earns at the factory. Had she not had to eat, drink, and pay Ethel some rent, the job would have earned her almost enough to pay back the Blue Book Agency.

By the spring of 1946, when postwar optimism has made everything seem a little more possible, Norma Jeane Dougherty has appeared on the cover of thirty-three magazines. From *Glamorous Models* to *Peek and See,* she is everywhere, perhaps even a little overexposed.

"The problem," says Emmeline Snively one afternoon, "is your figure."

"My figure?"

"You're not really a fashion model, you're not someone who just shows the clothes. Someone who sells an outfit. The dresses and the shirts and the bathing suits are always that bit too tight on you. No one is looking at the clothes, they are looking at you! 'To hell with what she is wearing! Who's that girl?'"

"And that's a bad thing?"

"If you want to be model, it is."

"It's a funny old business, isn't it?" says Norma Jeane. "I asked a photographer the other day why I was wearing a bathing suit for a toothpaste ad, and he looked at me as if I was some kind of crazy!"

Emmeline Snively laughs. She likes Norma Jeane. "Make sure you keep that bathing suit on! A young lady should never model undraped."

"Undraped?"

"Nude. Nude photography is the kiss of death for a model. The kiss of death, let me tell you."

Miss Snively has a lot of ideas about what's best for her model's career. For instance, in Snively's expert opinion, Norma Jeane's thick, curly dark blond hair doesn't frame her face properly. It doesn't move when she moves. It sits on her head like a stiff little hat.

After much coaxing and persuading, Snively finally convinces her to agree to an appointment at Frank and Joseph's Salon on Hollywood Boulevard, where her hair is bleached and straightened.

The transformation takes some getting used to.

"This isn't the real me, I'm not a platinum blonde," Norma Jeane laughs along with Sylvia Barnhart, the stylist in charge of her makeover. She turns her head left and right, moves her chin up and down. "But I like it."

"And so will all the boys!" replies Sylvia, holding up the mirror so she can see the back. "*All* the boys."

CHAPTER 9

CAPPED SMILES, FIXED NOSES, dyed hair, legs as smooth as alabaster: 1946 Los Angeles is awash with show-biz hopefuls. They all want one thing—to make it in the movies.

Their dreams in their backpacks, their longing written all over their overly made-up faces, these hopefuls trawl the streets of West Hollywood, exuding hope and desperation. Weighed down with their headshots and well-thumbed scripts, they wait at bus stops and queue at diners for temporary jobs—just until their big breaks hit. They talk about the times they were "an extra on Broadway," how they can do "tap and jazz and can sing like an angel," or how they were voted "Miss Teen Texas three-years-in-a-row."

Norma Jeane lies in bed at night, listening to the staccato snoring of Ethel Dougherty through the paper-thin walls of the two-bedroom house in Van Nuys, and dreams of escape.

The war is over, the economy is booming, and everyone else seems to be getting on with their lives, except for her. She feels trapped, living with her disapproving mother-in-law, writing letters to her husband, who never seems to reply. She's heard no news from him in weeks. Though the war is over, he's been recalled to help transport men and supplies back to Europe and the United States after the Allied victory.

She'd tried to impress him with her modeling career, that she was working, earning a living. The last time she'd seen him, she'd shown him the magazine covers, piled high on the small table in Ethel's living room. She'd waved about the adverts and fashion spreads.

He'd cared only about the bills. "You took all the money we had in savings and bought clothes with it," Dougherty accuses her. She'd written him about her new blond hair. He wasn't interested. She'd known, as he'd shipped himself off yet again, full of promises of a speedy return and fidelity, that the most important promise had already been broken.

She could no longer ignore the splendid beauty of Hollywood.

All actors and actresses were geniuses sitting in the porch of paradise — the movies. Acting became something golden and beautiful. It wasn't an art. It was like the bright colors I used to see in my daydreams — like a game that enabled me to step out of a dark and dull world, into worlds so bright they made my heart leap just to think of them. From time to time, I took drama lessons when I had enough money. They were expensive. I paid ten dollars an hour, and I often used to say my speech lessons out loud as I was walking around... The idea of the movies kept going through my mind.

Emmeline Snively believes Norma Jeane might have what it takes to make it in the movies. She recommends the girl to her friend Helen "Cupid" Ainsworth—a comedic actress who now works out of the West Coast office of the National

Concert and Artists Corporation and refers to herself as the "biggest agent" in Hollywood. Charmed by the sweet-natured, bottle-blond Norma Jeane, Ainsworth puts her straight on her books, with Harry Lipton as her special "motion-picture" representative.

In May 1946, Norma Jeane heads down to Schwab's Pharmacy at 8024 Sunset Boulevard.

Part diner, part drugstore, Schwab's sells cigarettes in one corner and cigars in the other—and has a newsstand up front and a pinball game at the back.

It's *the* place to be, where the actors gather to hear about who's who, and what's what. It's where movie star Lana Turner was discovered, so they say. Now it's full of hundreds of girls in tight sweaters, sucking on cream sodas and trying not to smear their lipstick.

The noise, as Norma Jeane swings through double doors, is overwhelming. The steaming coffee machines, the clatter of knives and forks, the thunderous laughter, the ping-pong of gossip. It is difficult to know where to put herself.

She glances up and down the counter.

"Do you mind if I sit here?" she asks a young man with slick hair and a shiny suit, hunched over a notepad.

"Sure," he says looking up and pushing his heavy-rimmed glasses back up his long nose. "Go ahead, it's not taken."

"That's really very sweet of you," she replies with her not-too-high smile, as she climbs up onto the leather stool in her tight black pencil skirt and places a folder of headshots onto the counter. She sighs. "So, what does a girl drink in here?"

"Well, it depends," replies the young man, stubbing out his cigarette and looking her up and down.

"On what?"

"On what sort of a day you've had."

"Well, honestly, it's not been great. I've been sitting on a hard bench so long in the sun, along with all the other hopefuls, waiting for a part, any part, a walk-on role, an extra, a chance...I think might have burnt my nose." She taps the end of her nose with the tip of her index finger. "I feel it must be quite pink."

"Let me see," asks the man, bending over to take a closer look. *She smells of talcum powder and pears,* he thinks. "It looks perfectly fine to me."

"You're just saying that to be sweet."

"No one calls me sweet."

She sits back to look at him. "But you do look sweet with your thick glasses and your smart tie."

"I'm a journalist, ma'am."

"But that's so brave."

"I specialize in gossip."

"That's so fun!"

"I'm Sidney—Sid—Skolsky. I write a newspaper column called 'From a Stool at Schwab's' for *Photoplay* magazine."

"And here you are, on a stool in Schwab's!"

"Here I am indeed. What can I get you?"

"Hmm."

"Did they ask you to come back after sitting in the sun? Or did they say, 'See you around'? Or worse, 'We can't see you today at all'?"

"We can't see you today at all."

"Then you, my dear, will be needing a bourbon."

"A bourbon-bourbon?"

"A 'We can't see you at all' bourbon."

She smiles and extends her hand. "I'm Mrs. Norma Jeane Dougherty."

"Well, in all my life I have never heard a more terrible name for such a beautiful young woman."

Turns out that Sid Skolsky is quite the guy. He knows everyone, everything: all the deals, the casting directors, the producers, the directors, who's up and coming, and who's on their way down.

The reason he works mostly out of Schwab's—or "the Schwabadero, the wannabes' Trocadero," as he calls it—is because he doesn't know how to drive. He has a phobia of cars, to go along with his phobia of cats, dogs, germs, and children. Others put forward the uncharitable explanation that Skolsky's legs are too short for his feet to reach the pedals of an automobile.

Norma Jeane listens, her mouth slightly open as she soaks up his every word.

"Say," he says, pointing the end of his lit cigarette in her general direction. "You do know that no major studio will put you under contract?"

"Why not?"

Is it her nose? Her hair? What?

"No one wants a girl who's married," he declares. Movie studios don't employ married women. Why waste time and money promoting a girl who's going to leave and have babies when there are so many single girls in this town who are desperate to work?

CHAPTER 10

HARRY LIPTON, NORMA JEANE'S new agent at the National Concert and Artists Corporation, quickly confirms what his client has heard.

Faced with the choice between a movie contract or a marriage contract, she doesn't hesitate. "My marriage didn't make me sad, but it didn't make me happy either," Norma Jeane says. "My husband and I hardly spoke to each other. This wasn't because we were angry. We had nothing to say. I was dying of boredom."

On May 14, 1946 — two weeks before she turns twenty — Norma Jeane files for divorce from James Dougherty after less than four years of marriage.

Legally, she's supposed to live in Nevada for four months until the divorce is granted, but she spends most of that time on modeling photo shoots in California, while staying in the apartment downstairs from her beloved "Auntie" Ana Lower at 11348 Nebraska Avenue.

Ethel Dougherty is not surprised or disappointed to see

Norma Jeane go. *That* girl, with her poor institutionalized mother, was bad news from the start. Now Ethel has the blissful satisfaction of being proved right.

Yet Jim Dougherty is blindsided. He's on a ship in the Yangtze River getting ready to go into Shanghai when he's served with divorce papers.

Furious, he paces the boat deck, demanding the captain send word that Norma Jeane gets "not one more cent" of his allowance money. She is, however, allowed to keep his car. He's not a monster. He'll give her something.

Norma Jeane ends the summer of 1946 with newfound freedom and a 1935 Ford coupe, the same car Dougherty used to ferry her to and from school, not so many years ago.

Not that Norma Jeane thinks or cares about that. She is on her way, straight to the offices of Ben Lyon, former silent movie star and now talent director for the 20th Century-Fox Film Corporation.

Wartime was good to Fox. Americans on the home front, in desperate need of distraction, packed movie theaters. The studio — product of the 1935 merger between 20th Century Pictures and the Fox Film Corporation — capitalized on William Fox's pioneering theater chain and the Fox Studio Lot in Century City, with its fifteen sound stages and outdoor sets depicting scenes from western towns and the Sahara Desert to cabaret theaters and New York City skylines.

Norma Jeane is fascinated by Lyon, who starred in seventy-two movies and was idolized for his roles on the silent screen.

On her first visit to Lyon's office, she trips in the reception area. Catching her heel on the door frame, she takes a tumble, scattering headshots and modeling photos all over the linoleum floor. As she scrambles about on all fours, an Ohio State University journalism student named Robert "Bob" Slatzer lowers himself to the floor to assist her.

"Thank you so much," she keeps saying, through a mass of blond curled hair. "So very sweet of you."

She's what the dreams of a slightly overweight boy from Marion, Ohio, are made of. He immediately falls in love.

Slatzer is scheduled to interview an actor, but he drops the story and instead asks Norma Jeane out to dinner. He borrows a friend's car for the night, pulls up outside her apartment on Nebraska, and takes her to a little place on Malibu overlooking the Pacific Ocean.

Helen "Cupid" Ainsworth, Norma Jeane's agent at the West Coast office of the National Concert and Artists Corporation, is determined to make a more consequential match.

It's well known that Howard Hughes, millionaire industrialist and president of California Pictures, has been bedridden since July, when he crashed a prototype Hughes Aircraft XF-11 spy plane in Beverly Hills. Hughes miraculously survived, but his recovery is arduous. He's immobile in a full-body cast and restless — until he sees Norma Jeane in a bathing suit on the cover of *Laff* magazine. Her sweet smile brightens his days and gives him purpose. He is determined to find out who she is and sign her to a movie contract.

Ainsworth is smarter than most, and she understands the power of the press and generating a little heat. She tips off her friend, the gossip columnist Hedda Hopper, and plants an item about Hughes's interest in her client: "Howard Hughes is on the mend. Picking up a magazine, he was attracted by the cover girl and promptly instructed an aide to sign her for pictures. She's Norma Jeane Dougherty, a model."

She then telephones Ben Lyon and tells him that Norma Jeane has yet to sign with Howard Hughes. But Lyon's window of opportunity is slim.

Norma Jeane is at home with Aunt Ana on the July day when she gets the call. She jumps into her 1935 Ford coupe and speeds to the studio lot, as fast as the engine will allow.

"It's Jean Harlow all over again!" Lyon exclaims when Norma Jeane walks into his office.

The risk-averse executive recklessly bypasses studio procedure for screen-testing talent and organizes an unauthorized shoot.

A skeleton film crew captures Norma Jeane's every movement as she performs on a darkened soundstage. She lights a cigarette, smokes it, walks back, sits down, and crosses her legs. She has no lines to recite. No need, when her essence is lighting up the room, and the screen.

On the makeshift set, no one makes a sound. Those few who are present stand stock-still, just staring. Lyon feels a chill run all the way down his spine. Whatever it is, whatever that magical *something* is, Norma Jeane has it.

Now he has to convince his boss, 20th Century-Fox chairman and co-founder, Darryl Zanuck.

The well-oiled operation springs into action when it's time to watch the next round of dailies. Lyon's secretary calls the projectionist to warn that the Boss is on his way, and the Fox staffers leap to their feet as the big man enters the projection room and takes his place next to Lyon.

The talent director's mouth is dry. His hands are clammy. His heart pounds in his ears with the knowledge of the sneak attack he's engineered for Zanuck, a man who dislikes surprises.

Today, after the dailies finish, instead of the lights coming up, the projector keeps rolling, playing an extra bit of film on the end of the reel. Norma Jeane's screen test.

"What the hell..." says Mr. Zanuck, sitting up in his seat, opening his mouth, and slowly removing his fat cigar. Ben Lyon closes his eyes, waiting to be fired. "Did I authorize this test?"

"No, sir," mumbles Lyon.

"What's her name?"

"Norma Jeane Dougherty. She's a model."

"It's a mighty fine test," he says, rising from his seat. He snaps his fingers. "Sign her up."

Norma Jeane is offered a six-month contract that pays $125 a week. But as a twenty-year-old woman in 1946, she's still considered a minor.

As her legal guardian, Grace McKee is thrilled to oblige. "I was the one who believed in you. I was the one," she crows.

The two women dress in their Sunday best to co-sign the contract alongside a 20th Century-Fox executive and a notary public. Norma Jeane will start work two days from now, on August 26.

While they wait to see Ben Lyon, Norma Jeane remembers how, when she was nine or ten, Grace would come to the orphanage and take her out sometimes. "I would put on your lipstick," she muses softly, "then you would take me to have my hair curled. Things like that meant a great deal to me."

"Mr. Lyon will see you now," says the talent director's secretary, opening the door.

"Come in, come in..." Lyon is out of his seat, his hand extended, smiling. His office is spacious. The sofa is soft, the walls are covered in large framed film posters, and his view onto the back lot is splendid.

Norma Jeane cannot stop smiling her not-too-high smile.

"Now," he begins. "About your name. Dow-erty. Dock-a-tee. Dock-a-tee-tee. How do you pronounce it?" He waves his hands. "Don't answer that. It's gotta go."

Norma Jeane shrugs. Fine by her. She feels no attachment to it.

"And the first name too. Norma Jeane. It's too old-fashioned. Norma. Or Jeane. One or the other."

Mmm, she thinks. *Who am I? A Norma? Or a Jeane?*

"Marilyn Miller, that's who you remind me of. You're a Marilyn!" Lyon suddenly snaps his fingers and points straight at her. "Bingo! But we can't use the same last name."

"There's always Monroe," suggests Grace. "Her mother's maiden name."

"That could work." Lyon nods. "Marilyn Monroe, Marilyn Monroe. It rolls off the tongue."

"Marilyn Monroe..." Norma Jeane smiles. "I think I could be her."

CHAPTER 11

"MY MOTHER IS actually dead...as is my father."

The newly minted Marilyn Monroe sighs and looks out the window, pausing her interview with Roy Craft. Twentieth Century-Fox has assigned the former *Life* magazine correspondent and RKO Pictures publicist to be Marilyn's press agent.

"I was brought up in an orphanage, where I shared a room with twenty-six other girls. It was a terrible place. For birthdays, they brought out a wooden cake with one slice cut into it. One small piece of cake for the birthday boy or girl. I went to many, many foster homes. Too many to count."

"That's so sad," replies the young man sitting opposite. He's bent over his notepad, scribbling down every word.

"Isn't it?" agrees Marilyn.

It was Grace's idea to lie to Roy Craft. Having dead parents evokes sympathy. Being the illegitimate child of a mother whose paranoid schizophrenia had her cycling in and out of institutions risks judgment, shame, and public humiliation —

especially if a reporter were to track down Gladys at the hospital.

"So?" Craft is waiting, pen poised. "How did they die? Car crash? Drowning? Spanish flu?"

Marilyn panics behind her fixed half smile. She and Grace McKee had not settled on a cause of death, only that the deaths had occurred.

"Mmm, I find it too upsetting to talk about," she mumbles, rubbing her left eye as if to hold back tears.

"Of course," he nods.

"But my childhood was very poor. I used to stand in line outside Helms Bakery at the end of the day to buy bags of stale bread for 25 cents and I'd eat the bread, I'd dunk it in milk for dinner. Stale bread and milk. I had one blue dress, that was it..."

"One blue dress." The young man is taking copious notes. "Do you have any brothers or sisters?"

"I am all alone in this world." Marilyn smiles again.

"So how were you discovered? How did you land your contract?"

"Oh, that's such a good story!" She leans forward. "I was babysitting for a Fox executive, and he found me in his living room looking after his daughter. So, he didn't really have to go far, not even to Schwab's where they found Lana Turner."

"Lana Turner wasn't discovered in Schwab's." Craft looks up from his notepad. "That's just one of those Hollywood myths."

"Oh. But I like that story." She pauses. "It's just a shame for all those pretty girls sitting in Schwab's right now, staring at the door, hoping for lightning to strike twice."

"Well, that's Hollywood for you!" The press officer laughs. "Full of lies."

Marilyn laughs too. Little does Roy Craft know, as he is drafting his press release, that he is adding to the list of lies. There was never a babysitting job with a Fox executive, and the fact that the Helms Bakery story was told to her by her foster sister Bebe doesn't really matter. It's her story now. She tells it over and over to any reporter who will listen. With each telling, she adds more detail: the line lengthens, the bread hardens, the milk sours.

I have a new name, Marilyn Monroe. I have to get born. And this time better than before.

Such is her determination to outrank the other half-dozen starlets newly contracted by the studio in September 1946 that every day Marilyn arrives at the Fox lot early.

Dance classes, acting classes, voice coaching: Marilyn attends every lesson offered. She hangs out in the lighting department, dressed in her uniform of a tight sweater and snug-fitting pants, swinging her legs on the chair, asking endless questions. She visits the editing rooms and sits in the hairdressing department. She has nowhere else to go, no husband to cook for, no children to nurture, no family at all. She has only the studio and its staff. Technicians become her closest friends.

"You're desperate to absorb all you can, aren't you?" asks Allan "Whitey" Snyder as he spins her around in the makeup chair.

They've been sitting together all afternoon while he tries different makeup looks on her. He's working on a film on the lot, but he's already fond of the "orphan from nowheresville."

She makes him laugh and she's smart, so between takes he paints her face—a light base, sharp pointed eyebrows to expand the forehead, and a pale eyeshadow and a black kohl flick on the eyes. Only the lipstick color varies.

"This is your 'look,' " he says. "You shouldn't change it."

Marilyn looks at her newly made-up face in the mirror, her arched black brows and heavily lined eyes.

She knows that this city is full of boys and girls lying in bed, looking at the stars, hoping that one day they will be among them. But surely she's dreamed bigger, hoped harder, and prayed longer than *all* of them.

"I do get a terrible case of the doldrums sometimes," she declares to Snyder. "I do try and snap out of it." She laughs. "When you're young and healthy you can plan on Monday to commit suicide, and by Wednesday you're laughing again."

"Well, I, for one, am thankful that it's a Friday," he replies.

Fridays. "They put the call list up on Fridays and that's when you look down and you find your name and beside it, they've written—'No call,' " she pouts. "And I've had a 'no call' again today. I've had 'no calls' for months. No auditions, no call-backs, no work. All I want to do is work, Whitey, work! Is it too much to ask?"

I know I'm a third-rate actress. When the lights and the camera face me, I feel myself to be clumsy, empty and uncultured. I am a sullen orphan with a goose egg for a head! I can actually feel my lack of talent. But my God, how I want to learn! To change! To improve. I don't want anything else. Not men. Not money, not love, but to act!

CHAPTER 12

AS A FREELANCE JOURNALIST, Bob Slatzer has almost as much free time as Marilyn. The two have remained friends ever since their accidental meeting in the Fox talent director's office.

In between attending auditions or taking classes at the studio, she and Slatzer travel around Los Angeles in Jim Dougherty's old car. They visit Hollywood landmarks while Slatzer talks about books and films, music and art. Topics he knows more about than is reasonable — and that Marilyn, having left school at fifteen, is eager to learn about.

Her thirst for knowledge is insatiable. She reads all the books Slatzer recommends. Every time he starts a story, she stares at him with big blue eyes, prompting as if on cue, "And then...?"

He loves how she gives him her complete attention.

One afternoon in December 1946, Slatzer takes Marilyn to a dilapidated house that once belonged to John Barrymore, the late silent film star known as "the Great Profile." His estate is up for auction. All fifty-five rooms and everything in them.

Slatzer thinks it might be amusing to have a look around, but the place feels uneasy, even grotesque. It's full of taxidermy animals, totem poles, and suits of armor. Marilyn shudders as they drive away through the rusty, poorly oiled gates.

To make up for the miserable Barrymore mansion visit, Slatzer offers to bring Marilyn along to a party in Beverly Hills. "All the stars will be there," he tells her. The party is hosted by Charles Feldman, a producer and agent.

Feldman is the kind of self-invented man celebrated in Hollywood. Orphaned as an infant, he moved with his adoptive family to Los Angeles, later working as a postman to pay his way through University of Southern California law school. On the basis of his charisma and personal connections, Feldman founded Famous Artists Corporation and built it into a top motion picture agency.

Now he lives at 2000 Coldwater Canyon Drive, a Spanish-style home in Beverly Hills, where an army of caretakers spritzes the lawn to keep it green and white-gloved waiters serve hors d'oeuvres artfully arranged on silver trays.

It's 9 p.m. when Slatzer and Marilyn step into the opulent home that celebrity decorator Billy Haines has designed in *chinois* style to accentuate Feldman's famous art collection.

Marilyn's hair and makeup are perfectly done, just as Whitey Snyder has taught her. But her nails are bitten to the quick, and her inexpensive dress, mended stockings, and scuffed pair of heels betray her humble origins.

"I swear I feel as frightened as if I'm breaking into a bank!" she whispers.

"Food's in the other room," says Slatzer. He'll never pass up an opportunity for free canapés. "Come on!"

Within seconds, he's disappeared. Marilyn stands on her own, staring at the throng. And what a glamorous throng it is. Dinner jackets, diamonds, long gowns, white evening gloves, circling trays of champagne, sparkling crystal glasses, vast arrangements of white roses. It is another world, filled with stars from 20th Century-Fox.

In one corner there's Gene Tierney, with her dark hair and her pale blue eyes. The star of Otto Preminger's 1944 murder mystery *Laura* is wearing a low-backed dress possibly created by her husband, the designer Oleg Cassini.

Sitting on a couch is Jennifer Jones. Marilyn can't take her eyes off the slim brunette. Jones is the real deal. She's been nominated for Oscars every year since first winning the Best Actress Academy Award for her title role as a pious young woman in 1943's *The Song of Bernadette.* Her latest movie, *Duel in the Sun* with Gregory Peck, could not be more different; it just came out last month and folks are already calling it "Lust in the Dust," but Marilyn prefers the much sexier part Jones plays in that one.

And who's that sipping a glass of champagne? Oh, gosh, it's Olivia de Havilland, the actress Oscar-nominated for MGM's 1939 epic *Gone with the Wind*!

Marilyn is about to approach the waiter carrying a silver platter of flutes when she spots a party guest holding a highball. Party host Charles Feldman is reputed to look remarkably like Clark Gable. Is it him? Or could it *actually* be Clark Gable? She can't breathe at the prospect of a real-life encounter with the star that so reminds her of her daddy. Her father, with the rakish mustache and a glint in his eye.

He looks so familiar it makes me dizzy.

Clark Gable — or his double — raises his cocktail and smiles at Marilyn as he walks past.

Another handsome man approaches, this one wearing a sharp suit and holding out a glass of champagne. "Would you like a drink?" he asks Marilyn, his blue eyes twinkling.

"Who, me?"

"I brought it for Gene, but it appears that somebody beat me to it." He gestures over to where Gene Tierney stands, the actress already holding a flute.

"Why thank you," replies Marilyn, accepting the slender glass with all the elegance she can muster. "Thank you, Mr. . . . ?"

"Kennedy," he smiles again, revealing perfect white teeth. "Jack Kennedy."

I could never be attracted to a man who had perfect teeth, Marilyn thinks. *I don't know what it is but it has something to do with the kind of men I have known who had perfect teeth. They weren't so perfect elsewhere.*

The newly elected Massachusetts congressman's Hollywood ties date back to his financier father, Joseph Kennedy Sr., who famously made millions in the late 1920s by consolidating movie studios — and wooing stars like Gloria Swanson.

"Charlie throws a great party," Kennedy says, clinking her flute with his own, then returning to stand by Gene, who smiles up at him as he runs a finger down her naked back.

Marilyn stands on her own, uncertain where to turn.

"My dear young lady," comes a plummy English accent. "Do come and sit by my side."

Perched on the stairs, a large glass of bourbon in his hand, is a distinguished-looking gentleman. "Pardon me if I don't rise. My name is George Sanders," he says.

"How do you do." Delighted to be spoken to, she takes the seat he's offered her, next to him on the staircase.

"I presume you also have a name?"

"I'm Marilyn Monroe," she says.

"May I have the honor of asking you to marry me?" the man asks. "The name, in case you have forgotten, is Sanders."

Crossing her legs to cover the runs in her thrice-darned stockings, Marilyn takes a sip of her champagne and prepares a diplomatic response to the man's proposal. Before she can say a word, Sanders continues.

"You are naturally a little reluctant to marry one who is not only a stranger, but an actor," he says, gesturing with his bourbon. It's clearly not his first of the evening. "I can understand your hesitancy—particularly on the second ground. An actor is not quite a human being—but then, who is?"

From across the room, Marilyn notices a woman staring daggers at her and gesturing furiously to guests nearby.

"Blond, pneumatic, and full of peasant health. Just my type," Sanders is saying. "Think it over, Miss Monroe. I can promise you only one thing if you marry me. You'll become one of the most glamorous stars in Hollywood. I'll help you. Word of honor."

After a moment of silence, Marilyn turns to look at George Sanders—and realizes that he's fallen fast asleep.

CHAPTER 13

EVERY FRIDAY MARILYN STANDS in front of the bulletin board and runs a red-lacquered fingernail down the list, and every Friday, there's still "no calls."

Bob Slatzer returns to Ohio, so Marilyn needs a new companion. She begins driving Sid Skolsky around town, ferrying him to interviews and waiting for her luck to change.

Continuing the Pygmalion game Slatzer had begun, Skolsky opens an account for Marilyn at a local bookstore on Sunset Boulevard. Her enthusiasm is contagious, and the way she reads, with her tongue sticking slightly out of her mouth, is worth the fifty cents he's paid for the novel.

Marilyn requires no lessons when it comes to courting attention. She's on the Fox lot daily, whistling up to the second-floor window of the press department and asking if there's anything she can do. Studio photographers start to use her for publicity. She does shoots in bathing suits, giggling in the cold.

Publicists manage to plant a few simple stories about the

aspiring actress in the *Los Angeles Times*. **BABYSITTER LANDS IN FILMS** perpetuates the myth they'd created the year before, that she'd been discovered while watching the children of a Fox executive. They take two years off her age, claiming she's eighteen years old, and illustrate the article with a large photograph of Marilyn in a tiny white bathing suit.

Skolsky also slips snippets about her into his columns, some making it into the *New York Post*, and yet...still there are no parts.

Marilyn calls the talent director Ben Lyon. All the time. To the point that sometimes he asks his secretary to pretend he's out.

She corners him in his office, picking his brain for hours, asking him questions he can't answer, like *Are there too many blondes on the lot?*

"There's Betty Grable, she's *the star* of the Fox lot. There's June Haver and Vivian Blaine, and then there's little old me. Should I change my hair? Dye it black? Do something else?"

"Marilyn, you have to be patient. I've been in this business a long time, in front and behind the camera, and you're putting in the work, going to class, there's not much more you can do," replies Lyon.

"There's always *more* you can do."

"I know you've set your heart on being queen of the lot."

"I've set my heart on much more than that!"

"And I know the folks on the lot are like family to you. Be patient and study."

"Mr. Lyon, might I suggest that the lot is full of bit-part players who have all been patient, and who have all studied hard. And where has that got them? They're curled up on the cutting room floor. Or they're still sitting on the hard bench in the sun, next to me. There are those who strike gold overnight, and those who don't."

Marilyn is worried. Her contract is almost up. "Who knows if they will renew my contract? I haven't worked a jot, and it's been nearly six months."

She walks out of Ben Lyon's office, striding off in her heels. The white sun is shining, and she can't see a thing. She shields her eyes, taking a deep breath. She *is* going to be the girl who strikes gold overnight. She's just got to keep being strong.

"Hey!" comes a shout, followed by the long honk of a car horn. "Look out, lady! Watch where you're going!" The chauffeur leans out the window of a stretch limousine. "I coulda killed you!"

"I'm sorry, sir," she replies, leaning over to look into the window of the back seat. Her bright blond hair glints in the sun. "I wasn't thinking, I was running my lines." She half smiles and glances toward the elderly gentleman perched on the leather seat at the back. "My apologies, sir." A blond curl falls forward, and she tucks it back behind her ear.

"Say, what's your name?" demands the man, removing an unlit cigar from his mouth. He's dressed in a slick pearl-gray suit; his hair may be thinning, but his eyes are sharp and bright.

"Marilyn." Her voice is breathy. "Marilyn Monroe."

The man looks familiar. She squints, certain she's seen his face in the newspapers. Is he the man who's been in prison for paying off the Theatrical Stage Employees Union? She's not quite sure. Wasn't he pardoned in 1945 by President Truman himself?

"Joe Schenck." He sticks out his small hand. His accent is American via Rybinsk, Yaroslavl Oblast, Russia.

That's him. She smiles again. A founder of the Academy of Motion Picture Arts and Sciences and 20th Century-Fox, Schenck is currently serving as production chief. He has a Mediterranean-style mansion in the exclusive Holmby Hills area on the west side of Los Angeles. He regularly fills the lavish estate with "Schenck's Girls"—young lovelies whom he invites over for cocktails, dinner, screenings, and card games. It is desirable to leave before the cards.

It's worth listening to Sid Skolsky's ramblings, she realizes. On their drives around town, her gossip columnist friend is always telling stories about who's who and what's what— including all about Schenck and his sleazy parties and his demanding friends.

Thankfully she does listen, most of the time.

The sixty-eight-year-old man knows everyone. He counts among his friends "the meanest man in Hollywood," co-founder and president of Columbia Pictures Harry Cohn, and producer Sam Spiegel, whose recent film *The Stranger* starring Orson Welles has Oscar buzz. Bugsy Siegel, the Mafia-hitman-turned-hotelier who'd recently been acquitted of the murder of fellow mobster Harry Greenberg, is also in Schenck's circle.

"Very lovely to meet you, Mr. Schenck," she replies, reaching through the window to shake the tips of his sweaty fingers.

"Are you a new actress on the lot?" he asks. "I haven't seen your face before...And I never forget a face."

"I'm a contract player." Marilyn purses her lips.

"Well, you must be starving," he laughs. "Contract players are always starving. You guys never have enough money to eat."

"I wouldn't say that, sir! I have a very generous contract, and I do a lot of modeling."

"I bet you do." He looks her up and down. "Any parts yet?"

"Not yet."

"You should come to my house," suggests Mr. Schenck, handing her his card. "I'm having a party."

"You are?"

"And we always need beautiful girls."

CHAPTER 14

FOX MAKEUP ARTIST Whitey Snyder is doing Marilyn's hair and makeup.

She's bought a bright-red low-cut evening gown, "the loudest one I could find," she tells Snyder.

"Your arrival in that's going to infuriate half the women present," Snyder jokes.

But Marilyn is taking a serious approach to the evening that lies ahead. *I'm going to Mr. Schenck's mansion because he is one of the heads of my studio,* she reasons.

To Whitey Snyder, she says, "I am sorry in a way to do this, but I have a long way to go and I need a lot of advertising to get there."

Joe Schenck's limousine picks Marilyn up from the Fox lot and drives her to the Owlwood Estate, at 141 South Carolwood Drive, in Holmby Hills. Through the imposing gates, she can see the mansion lit up against the night sky.

She steps out of the car, her heels crunching on the gravel of the sweeping driveway. Water flows from a decorative fountain, but her mouth is dry with fear.

They say I'm whistle bait, could be, but I'm forever meeting guys who don't stop at a whistle. I've learned to handle them all.

The double doors open to reveal a large glimmering chandelier illuminating a wide, curving staircase with a wrought-iron balustrade.

"Norma Jeane, is that you?" a woman calls from across the foyer.

Standing at the foot of the stairs is a girl Marilyn knows from her Blue Book Modeling days.

"I am Marilyn Monroe now," she smiles.

"Well, I'm still June! You look marvelous," the woman says, coming toward her with outstretched arms. "I love what you've done with your hair. The blond suits you." June links arms with Marilyn and walks her through the hall paneled in dark wood. "Have you ever been here before?"

"Never," replies Marilyn.

"It's a gorgeous house!" June squeezes her arm. "They say the property spans ten acres and I believe it. There's a tennis court and a theater, where Mr. Schenck shows films that haven't even played in the movie houses yet!" She points toward the sound of laughter and through an open door. "Out there's a swimming pool."

"I didn't bring a suit," Marilyn says.

"Next time," June says. "I've been invited back more nights than I can count."

They approach a large rectangular pool full of attractive young women cavorting in the water — some in bathing suits and others in various states of undress — as well as a few men.

Four or five other men are seated at a long poolside table, sucking on cigars.

Marilyn recognizes the man from the back of the limousine. "Mr. Schenck!" She waves. She sucks in her stomach and sways her hips, picking her way across the wet flagstones toward Schenk.

What a face, she thinks, as she nears him. *It is as much the face of a town as of a man. The whole history of Hollywood is in it.*

When she reaches the table, another man beckons her over.

She smiles at the handsome, well-dressed man patting the cushion next to him. His shiny gold watch glints in the lamplight.

"Come and sit, my darling," he says. "I'm Ben Siegel. Would you like a highball?"

Marilyn happily obliges, sipping her drink and listening as Mr. Siegel talks about his new project, the Flamingo Hotel in Las Vegas, Nevada.

There are important people here, she realizes. *These aren't party figures but Mr. Schenck's personal friends.* She knows better than to ever use Mr. Siegel's hated nickname — Bugsy — to his face.

"Come to the opening," he tells her. "Jimmy Durante's the headliner. It's going to be a swell party."

"Opening the day after Christmas," Marilyn says. "What a marvelous idea."

"Do you like gambling?" Siegel asks. He drops a mention that he also owns the Agua Caliente Racetrack in Baja, California. She's always welcome to be his guest.

Three highballs later, the noise from the swimming pool

has become increasingly raucous. Empty cocktail glasses are abandoned on lounge chairs and wet bathing suits are piled on the pool deck. Marilyn glances across and spots a nude girl in the water. Her dark hair is wet, her makeup smudged, her bare breasts bouncing with the motion of throwing a beach ball across the shallow end of the pool. In the dim pool lighting, she cannot be sure, but it looks an awful lot like her friend June.

When I started modeling, she reminds herself, *sex was part of the job. All the girls did. They weren't shooting all these sexy pictures just to sell peanut butter in an ad or get a layout in some picture magazine. They wanted to sample the merchandise, and if you didn't get along, there were twenty-five girls who would. It wasn't any big dramatic tragedy. Nobody ever got cancer from sex.*

Joe Schenck slips his arm around Marilyn's shoulders, interrupting her thoughts. "Would you like to come inside and play cards?"

"Cards?" she asks.

"Sure," he nods. "We're all going in."

The pool crowd is meandering across the lawn, back toward the house. They've paired off into couples, each man with a girl by his side. Some are barefoot, swigging from a bottle of champagne.

"Mr. Schenck, I am not very good at cards." Marilyn wrinkles her nose.

"Call me Joe," he says, wrapping his arm around her waist. "You don't have to play. You can just watch. And fix me some drinks."

Around a green baize table, a game of gin rummy is in full swing, its players sipping cocktails and smoking cigarettes.

Marilyn sits on one side of Schenck. On the other is a naked redhead who's intent on the game. The redhead's playing to win, and when she does, she squeals with delight, throwing down her hand of cards and kissing Schenck hard on the cheek.

"Well done!" he laughs. "Here we go!" He takes a $50 bill out of his wallet. "You won that fair and square."

"Thank you, Joe!" She plants another kiss. "You are the sweetest."

"Say, Marilyn? Aren't you working tomorrow?" Schenck asks. "Let me call you a limousine."

She's grateful to have been dismissed. But even more grateful when the invitations keep coming.

CHAPTER 15

"MR. SCHENCK NEVER so much as lays a finger on my wrist, or tries to," Marilyn tells Whitey Snyder as she sits in his makeup chair, getting ready for another night at the mansion in Holmby Hills. "He's interested in me because I am a good table ornament and because I am what he calls an 'off-beat' personality."

Marilyn, you have an electric quality, Schenck has told her. *You sparkle and bubble like a fountain.*

"What's it like, being in a fancy place like that?" Snyder asks.

"The food is very good," Marilyn laughs, but she knows her friend won't be satisfied with that answer.

"I like sitting around the fireplace with Mr. Schenck and hearing him talk about love and sex. He is full of wisdom on these subjects, like some great explorer."

Snyder believes Marilyn.

Sid Skolsky doesn't.

In the car, he gives her a stern lecture. The rumor mill is churning with gossip that she's one of Joe Schenck's girls.

"I'm not one of his girls," she replies. "I *am* his girl."

Come February 1947, against all the odds, Fox renews Marilyn's contract.

This time it's going to be different, she feels. This time when she runs her red fingernail down the Friday call list, she will see her name.

For someone who hasn't set foot on a sound stage since her screen test, who has yet to be cast and cut, her confidence is bold. But she does start getting some tiny parts.

The Shocking Miss Pilgrim stars Betty Grable. Marilyn plays a telephone operator. It's not really a part—only a single shot—but anyone who's looking will see her.

As Marilyn writes to her half sister, Berniece, "For heaven's sake, don't blink or you'll miss me!"

She's next booked for a two-day shoot in *Scudda Hoo! Scudda Hay!* The rural romantic comedy follows half brothers who argue about how best to raise mules as they compete for the affections of the same woman.

Marilyn's first scene is two seconds of her saying "Hi" to 20th Century-Fox star June Haver and eight-year-old newcomer Natalie Wood. Most of her second scene gets cut—only a background shot of her helping to paddle a canoe remains. Marilyn's name doesn't make the credits.

She is cast again, in *Dangerous Years,* as a waitress named Eve. This time, she gets a few lines of sharp dialogue and a chance to show some comic timing in how she holds a tray and executes a half turn with a flick of her long blond hair. When the credits roll at the film's premiere in December 1947, the name Marilyn Monroe does appear, fourteenth of sixteen credited actors.

Maybe the parties, the highballs, and the gin rummy are worth it? Maybe she *can* play the Hollywood game.

Marilyn entertains Whitey Snyder with tales of her run-ins with predatory men.

"In Hollywood, we have to work overtime to outwit the wolves," she says. "That's because wolves of all varieties come from far and near to snare the Little Red Riding Hoods of the movies."

It seems that every night a man is giving her a line, trying to get her into bed.

Take last night, for instance.

"I've always gone for blondes with brown eyes," Marilyn mimics a man who claimed he couldn't stop thinking about her and why. *"I fall quick when I meet one. That's why I can't wait to see you again, so I'll be right over."*

"You don't even have brown eyes!" Whitey laughs, as he curls Marilyn's lashes.

Fortunately, her protector, Joe Schenck, is not a demanding guy. He's kind to her, buys her expensive clothes. She chooses a new black dress for an evening at his mansion.

Tonight, Schenck is seated at the head of the long table poolside. On either side of him Marilyn spots two dangerous characters, men who clearly have serious business to discuss.

Handsome Johnny Roselli—the Hollywood point person for the Mob's Chicago Outfit—is on parole after being convicted of racketeering and extortion during his wartime service in the US Army.

Pasquale "Pat" DiCicco is an actor, talent agent, producer, and part-time mobster, who famously married railroad heiress Gloria Vanderbilt. The bride was only seventeen years old and rumors of abuse quickly spread. "He could be in a room full of people and have everybody laughing. He was just funny. He was also scary. And I was very scared of him when I married him," said Vanderbilt of DiCicco, whom she divorced only four years after their 1941 society wedding.

Marilyn turns toward the pool. Splashing in the water are girls she's never seen before, each one more beautiful than the next.

"I was hoping I'd see you here coming tonight."

Marilyn turns around to see her modeling friend June.

"Can you believe all these girls?" June asks through a tight smile.

"They're all amazing," Marilyn says. "Where did they find them all?"

"The brothels downtown," June says bluntly, then lowers her voice to a whisper. "Sorry. That sounds meaner than I meant it. But I need your help." She takes hold of Marilyn's arm and squeezes it intensely. "I'm having a therapeutic abortion."

"A therapeutic—?" Marilyn repeats, certain she's misunderstood.

"Consequences of late nights." She looks around knowingly. "I need two hundred dollars by Monday."

Marilyn unclips her purse. "I have a hundred."

A week's wages. She has her rent to pay and a flat tire on her car, and she has nothing to eat at home. But Marilyn knows what it is like to go through life without kindness. June needs kindness now.

"You're an angel," says June, taking the money.

"Good luck."

Over at the poolside table, Schenck and DiCicco are so intent on their conversation that neither of them looks up as Marilyn approaches.

"Can I fix anyone a drink? A highball?"

"No," declares DiCicco, his face twisting as he shares the fate of the man Marilyn met on her first night at the mansion, the one who invited her to Las Vegas on the day after Christmas. "Bugsy Siegel is dead. He was sitting in his own house, minding his own business, reading the *LA Times,* when they shot him."

"I told him not to get involved with the Flamingo," Schenck says.

"They thought he'd skimmed the money," DiCicco says, rubbing his forehead in disbelief. "The million-dollar building overspend! They thought he'd stolen it. Lined his pockets, given it to his girlfriend. Imagine bushwhacking one of this country's finest hitmen from behind a hedge? There's nothing fair about that."

"They shot the crap out of Bacchus too," adds Schenck. "That big white marble statue of the god of wine he kept on the grand piano. It's riddled with bullets."

"So is Bugsy, as it turns out."

Both men shake their heads slowly. Johnny Roselli does the same.

"It's a shame for Bugsy." DiCicco sniffs, then snaps his fingers. "Hey, Marilyn, be a doll and fix us all a drink."

CHAPTER 16

YOU'RE HOT IN THIS TOWN, until you're not. Hollywood is a brutal place where an actor's world can fall apart in an instant.

"Come in," Harry Lipton says. The agent at the National Concert and Artists Corporation opens the door to Marilyn, whose complexion is glowing with a light suntan.

It's hot, unbearably hot. Lipton's tie is too tight, his shirt ringed with sweat beneath the arms. He's been pacing around his office, rehearsing the bad news he's about to break.

"Sorry I'm late," she says, launching into an explanation. "My silly car is broken down and I came on the bus. The buses are terrible in this town."

She has barely sat down and crossed her legs before Lipton blurts, "Fox isn't renewing your contract."

Marilyn looks at him, silently blinking her huge blue eyes. The news is not sinking in.

"But...but. I have just done three films in a row. Small parts, true, but I'm on my way. Are you sure? That can't be right."

"They have said no."

"Mr. Zanuck said that? I heard he calls me 'Straw-Head.' Maybe he doesn't like blondes. What if I changed my hair? Dyed it a different color?"

Lipton holds his breath, digging his fingernails into his palms. He watches as his client's beautiful face begins to crumple. It's a marvel how quickly she pulls herself together, shaking her head, setting her jaw, and sucking in her cheeks.

"It's a case of supply and demand," she states. "And I'm a contract player who hasn't fulfilled their demand."

Her hand doesn't waver as she signs the notice of termination dated July 26, 1947. The name Marilyn Monroe, with bold flourishes on both M's, appears beneath the signature of the assistant secretary of the 20th Century-Fox Film Corporation.

One year, nearly to the day, has passed since Marilyn signed her first contract. On August 31, 1947, she receives her final paycheck. After deductions, it amounts to $104.13. Hardly enough to make rent and her car payment.

Her childhood fears return. She knows poverty. She knows how it suffocates lives and dreams. Mostly dreams.

"How are things going at the studio?" Joe Schenck asks Marilyn.

"I lost my job there last week."

"Keep going," he says.

"I will," she promises.

What a fool she's been, allowing herself to think that she was something special. Marilyn draws her curtains, gets into bed, and stays there for a week, mourning the end of "Marilyn Monroe," before she's even been truly born.

It's Sid Skolsky who finds her, face gaunt and tearstained, hair uncombed, in a twist of unwashed bedsheets. He brings her out into the sunshine and treats her to a meal at Schwab's.

"Joe Schenck told me to keep going," she says, sitting at the counter sipping an ice-cold Coca-Cola. "It's not so easy."

"Schenck is right," Skolsky says. "You do what everyone does in this town. You put on a brave face and you pretend. You've got guts and determination, beauty, and smarts. All you're missing is craft. Come with me—"

He leaps off his high stool and grabs her hand. Together, they walk out of the drugstore and into the back parking lot.

"There." He points to a long, low warehouse of a building.

"What?" She squints.

"It's the Actors Lab, where some of the best actors in the world teach. Lee Strasberg? D'you know him? It's the Hollywood home of the Group Theatre. From New York."

"New York?" Marilyn repeats. That far, far away town, where actors and directors spend hours talking? "I heard they all wear black clothes and eyeglasses in New York."

"And they're all Communists!" Skolsky is joking, though fears of pitting the Democratic United States against a Communist Soviet Union is a serious and growing global concern.

"They're for the people, aren't they? The Communists? I think I might be for the people too," she says.

"Don't say that out loud!" he warns, only half teasing. He looks over at her. "It's where the cool kids go. The theater people."

"You know, it's shocking but I've never seen a play," Marilyn admits. "I am not sure I could read one either."

"It's no different from reading a book."

"But all those parts. They'll muddle my brain."

"We both know that's not true."

Hmm. Maybe it's time to graduate from the acting classes on the Fox lot.

Dressed in "actors' blacks," Marilyn crawls along a wooden floor pretending to be a cat. She curls up in a corner, lies on her side, and starts to lick the back of her hand. She purrs.

She's learning new terms, like "motivation" and "sense memory" and "animal improv." The Group Theatre techniques are based on the theatrical teachings of Konstantin Stanislavski, the Russian actor and director who founded the Moscow Art Theatre and is considered the father of Method Acting—which involves much self-analysis and reflection.

Marilyn has never been surrounded by so many talented actors. They take their art seriously, drawing from knowledge learned from books. They study plays by Chekhov and Ibsen. They analyze the philosophy of Engels and Marx. They've read the Romantic poems of Keats. Ashamed that she left school at fifteen, Marilyn hides at the back of the class, listening, learning, and keeping so quiet it's as if she blends in with the gray walls.

When Marilyn relates her studies to Skolsky, her voice is animated, her energy contagious.

"I don't want them to know I have been in the movies, but what a difference. Film actors might have one line, one scene, for the whole day. No knowledge required. Just wait for them to do the lighting and line up the shot. These guys learn *whole* plays."

"What did F. Scott Fitzgerald say? That movies are a place where many people sit around for a very long time, doing absolutely nothing."

"Well, Fitzgerald is right! Whoever *he* is. At the Actors Lab, they're always complaining that movie actors get paid *so* much more than theater folk. And they are always talking about the poor. The 'disenfranchised poor.' I don't want to tell them how poor I was. Or, actually... how poor I am!"

Marilyn gives Joe Schenck a call, tells him about her studies. She's kept her word. She's kept going.

Schenck says he'll reach out to Zanuck. They're pals. The studio bosses are all pals. And there are plenty of studios. Has she tried Columbia? He's got friends over there, too. Harry Cohn's always looking for new talent.

"Marilyn's hot," insists Schenck's pal Johnny Roselli, as he lines up his swing on the golf course. "Really hot. The full package."

"Sure," shrugs Harry Cohn. "Send her my way and let's see if we can use her."

In March 1948, Cohn signs Marilyn to Columbia. The six-month contract pays $125 a week.

CHAPTER 17

COLUMBIA PICTURES ACTING COACH Natasha Lytess works out of a bungalow office next to the Three Stooges sound stage. Marilyn arrives twenty-five minutes late to their first meeting, wearing a curve-clinging dress that's cut so low it reveals her bra.

"That is a trollop's outfit," declares Lytess, in lightly accented English. Lytess is German but posed as Russian to be more employable as an actress in the United States. Given her Jewish background, she'd fled her native Germany before the Nazis took power.

Despite her own stalled career, which she attributes to the vulgarity of Hollywood and its poorly made films, Lytess's tutoring ability is unsurpassed. Tall, slim, in her late thirties, with short, cropped hair, she burns with a humorless intensity and an insistence that acting is important work to be taken seriously.

Three walls of her office are lined with wooden bookshelves groaning under the weight of intellectually rigorous novels, plays, and other great works of literature. It is as if a slice of European intelligentsia has been transported to California.

While Marilyn appreciates culture and sophistication, she possesses neither.

Natasha Lytess takes a quick inventory of her new pupil. She is unimpressed. The girl knows nothing about the physical components of acting. She barely moves her lips when she mumbles her words, she has no concept of diaphragmatic breathing, and she has no idea about pace or diction. How did she ever land a contract at Columbia Pictures?

The drama coach recommends daily sessions. At first, Marilyn merely listens to Lytess tell her life story, her flight from Germany to America and the hardships that culminated with her and her young daughter Barbara's destitution following the death of Barbara's father. Marilyn nods in sympathy for a life she can understand. Poverty. Destitution. Misery. No father. No husband.

Lytess has Marilyn repeat elocution exercises — "I did not want to pet the dear, soft cat" — making sure to enunciate the *t*'s and the *d*'s. Marilyn's diction becomes clipped and precise and perhaps a little contrived. And, despite her initial doubts, Lytess begins to adore her.

"I want to re-create you," explains Lytess. "I shall mold you into the great actress that I suspect you can be. But to do so, you must totally submit to me. Do you understand?"

Marilyn nods in agreement.

She suspects there might be another agenda at play when Lytess takes hold of her shoulders and looks into her big blue eyes.

"I want to love you, Marilyn," she whispers.

"You don't have to love me, Natasha," she says with a smile. "You just have to work with me."

On March 14, 1948, Marilyn is surprised by the depth of her grief for Aunt Ana, who has succumbed to her heart ailments at the age of sixty-eight. After the funeral, Marilyn sits in Natasha Lytess's office on the lot, her bare feet tucked up under her, weeping into tissues.

"I lay in Aunt Ana's bed the day after she died, you know," says Marilyn. "Just for a couple of hours. Then I went to West-wood Memorial Park, where men were digging a grave. Not hers. Someone else's. And there was a ladder into it. They're quite deep, you know. So, I asked if I could climb down and lie there, and they said yes. I went down and I lay on the ground, in the earth, looking up at the sky. The ground is cold under your back, but it's quite a view."

Marilyn sighs. "I'm left with no one to take my hopes and troubles to. She was the one human being who let me know what love is. She looked after me like one of her own."

"There will be others," replies Lytess. "Many, many others..."

"She's the first person in the world I ever really loved, and she loved me. She was a wonderful human being. She never once hurt me. She couldn't. She was all kindness and all love."

Marilyn plucks another tissue from the box and dabs the tears from her eyes.

Lytess speaks up. "There is some good news."

"Oh?"

"They're casting for a new musical—*Ladies of the Chorus*."

"I've taken singing lessons," Marilyn says.

"Good." Lytess smiles briefly. "I have put you up for the starring role of Peggy Martin, a young chorus girl in a burlesque show. We start rehearsing for the audition tomorrow."

CHAPTER 18

FRED "FREDDY" KARGER is a composer and arranger for the Columbia music department.

Marilyn seeks out his office on the studio back lot. Clutching sheet music for *Ladies of the Chorus* to her chest, she makes her pitch: "I am hoping you can teach me to sing."

"I'll teach you whatever you want," he replies, taking the sheet music from her and placing it on a stand in the middle of the room.

The charming Karger has a Hollywood pedigree. His father, Max Karger, is a co-founder of MGM Pictures along with Samuel Goldwyn and Louis B. Mayer. His mother, Ann Conley, starred in the Ann & Effie Conley Sisters vaudeville act.

The thirty-two-year-old vocal coach casts his bright green eyes on his new pupil and assesses her voice. A little reedy and untrained, but he can help with that. *Ladies of the Chorus* is a low-budget romantic musical, and he teaches her two songs for the film, "Anyone Can Tell I Love You," and "Every Baby Needs a Da Da Daddy."

They rehearse until the light fades. To read the music more clearly, Karger reaches for a pair of glasses.

Marilyn is intrigued by the sight. *I don't know why, but I have always been attracted to men who wear glasses. Now, when he puts them on, I feel suddenly overwhelmed.*

She decides that Karger, who is divorced with a young son, will be her first true love. He's tender at times but can be critical in his demands.

"You cry too easily," he says. "That's because your mind isn't developed. Compared to your breasts, its embryonic."

Later, Marilyn looks up the word in the dictionary. She lies awake for hours, puzzling over Karger's feelings toward her. *He can't love me or he wouldn't be so conscious of my faults. How can he love me if I'm such a goof to him?*

Too emotional and exhausted to rehearse, Marilyn cancels their next session.

Karger drives to her apartment. He knocks and knocks.

"Won't you come in?" Marilyn says when she finally comes to the door. There's no hiding that she has been lying in bed, crippled with hunger pangs.

Karger has her pack her few things. He invites her to live in his parents' house, where he and his son have been living since the collapse of his marriage, a place where sisters, nieces, and nephews run up and down the stairs of the large, boisterous home and the family shares meals around a long kitchen table.

The shoot for *Ladies of the Chorus* begins on April 22, 1948, and wraps two weeks later on May 3. The musical's low budget requires the cast and crew to work quickly.

"In a movie you act in bits and pieces," Marilyn tells Freddy

Karger's mother, Ann Conley, over coffee. "You say two lines, and then 'cut.' They relight, set up the camera in another place—and you act two more lines. You walk five feet, and they say 'cut.' The minute you get going good in your characterization, they cut."

This is her first singing role, but thanks to voice work she's done, Marilyn's two numbers are favorably received. "One of the bright spots is Miss Monroe's singing," the *Motion Picture Herald* praises her performance. "She is pretty and, with her pleasing voice and style, she shows promise." *Variety* singles out "the nifty warbling of Marilyn Monroe" and says that "Miss Monroe presents a nice personality in her portrayal of the burlesque singer."

In June, Marilyn's application for a sought-after place in the Hollywood Studio Club is accepted. She moves into Room 307 of the Italian Renaissance Revival–style residence that houses one hundred young women who pay $10 to $15 per week for a room and two meals per day while they seek careers in show business. Men may visit Studio Club residents, but only on the first floor.

With strong advance notices on *Ladies of the Chorus* buoying her, Marilyn turns her attention to a new question: What will be her next picture? She hopes to have an answer in her meeting with Max Arnow, Columbia's casting director.

Everyone in Hollywood knows the story of Columbia Pictures' biggest star, teenage dancer Margarita Carmen Cansino, who, as Rita Hayworth, won a seven-year contract from the studio chief known as "King Cohn" or "White Fang."

How Harry Cohn cast her in *Gilda*, opening the film with the onscreen credit "Columbia Pictures Corporation presents Rita Hayworth as Gilda." The April 1946 film noir infuriated censors with a so-called strip tease in which Hayworth, dressed in a black evening gown and a pair of long, black gloves, removed them one by one from her shapely arms.

On June 30, in advance of the "Able" test on the Bikini Atoll in the Marshall Islands, Hayworth's husband Orson Welles announced on the ABC radio network that the atomic bomb "will be decorated with a photograph of a sizeable likeness of the young lady named Rita Hayworth."

At the height of her fame, Cohn christened Hayworth his "Love Goddess," even as she famously resisted his advances.

"I fought Cohn — and I won," Hayworth says. "I was trained to do this. Fred Astaire knew I was a dancer, he knew what all those dumb-dumbs at Columbia didn't know. I was not picked up in a corner drug store like Lana. And O.K., so I happened to be 'pretty.'"

Marilyn is thinking only of her career as she waits to meet the casting director. In her personal life, she's hopelessly devoted to Freddy Karger.

The office door swings open and, instead of the affable Mr. Arnow, in walks the "White Fang," Harry Cohn. "Follow me," the president of Columbia Pictures says, walking toward a connecting door.

"I've been told to wait here for Mr. Arnow," Marilyn replies, not moving from the chair.

"To hell with Arnow. He'll know where you are!"

"I'd rather wait here for Mr. Arnow, if that's all right with you." She clutches the office chair in a white-knuckled grip.

"Miss Monroe." His heavy face looms close. "I run this place. No one here says no to the boss."

"Of course, Mr. Cohn," she says, following him into a space with panoramic views over the lot.

"I hear you're a model," he says. "Show me."

She turns slowly in her nipped-in jacket and tight skirt.

"Good." He nods. "You look smaller than you do on screen. But then you ladies always do. Now sit." He indicates a padded armchair, then leans over his huge leather-topped desk and flicks a switch. "Hold all my calls," he orders an unseen receptionist.

Marilyn's heart stops. Her mouth is smiling. But inside, she is terrified.

"Now," he continues, opening the top drawer of his desk. He pulls out a large photograph of an impressive-looking yacht. "Do you like boats?" He uses his fat hands to smooth down a photograph of a yacht. "You're invited on board my yacht." He walks behind her and gives her shoulders a painful squeeze.

"I'd love to join you and your wife, Mr. Cohn. What a delightful invitation."

"My what?"

"Your wife."

"Leave my wife out of this!" His cheeks puff as he hisses, "The boat leaves in an hour and we're staying overnight."

Marilyn doesn't move. She sits with her back straight, staring ahead, her bottom lip quivering.

"This is a one-off invitation, Miss Monroe," he barks. "Refuse me at your peril."

CHAPTER 19

ON SEPTEMBER 9, 1948, Marilyn Monroe's contract with Columbia expires. It is not renewed.

Harry Cohn is a brute—a powerful brute who has cut her professional pride deeply and pushed her to the brink of failure.

But there was something that would not let me go back to the world of Norma Jeane. It wasn't ambition or a wish to be rich and famous. I didn't feel any pent-up talent in me. I didn't even feel that I had looks or any sort of attractiveness. But there was a thing in me, a craziness that wouldn't let up. It kept speaking to me. Telling me. To keep going.

Marilyn has long hoped that Freddy Karger might propose. He blames his indecision on the welfare of his son.

"It would be all right for me," Karger says of their potentially marrying, "but I keep thinking of my son. If we were married and anything should happen to me—such as my dropping dead—it would be very bad for him."

"Why?"

"It wouldn't be right for him to be brought up by a woman like you," he said. "It would be unfair to him."

In return for Marilyn's unconditional love, Karger commits only to paying her dental bill.

Now that her teeth are bleached and straightened, it's time to smile and say good-bye. Marilyn gives Freddy Karger an extravagant Christmas gift—a $500 wristwatch engraved *12/25/48*.

"Why didn't you have it engraved 'From Marilyn to Freddy with love,' or something?" Karger asks. He's very touched by the present.

"Because you'll leave me someday," she tells him, "and you'll have some other girl to love. And you wouldn't be able to use my present if my name was on it. This way you can always use it, as if it were something you'd bought yourself."

Karger is emotional over the gift but does nothing to dissuade Marilyn. She cries herself to sleep that night, knowing leaving him is the right decision.

Still, she'll think of him every time she makes a watch payment—for the next two years.

On December 31, 1948, Marilyn and Natasha Lytess spend New Year's Eve as guests of Sam Spiegel, a producer as famous for being unaffiliated with any studio as he is for hosting lavish parties in a borrowed house in Beverly Hills.

Anything might happen in the company of the man who in 1946 partnered with Orson Welles to make the Oscar-nominated postwar thriller *The Stranger*, as his friend Johnny Hyde, vice president of the William Morris Agency, soon

discovers. Hyde, barely five feet tall but one of the most powerful men in Hollywood, is instantly smitten by Marilyn
when they meet at the New Year's Eve party.

He's sure she'll be his next great success story. Born in
Russia to circus acrobats, Hyde is slight of figure, frail in
appearance, and chasing a receding hairline, but the fifty-
three-year-old agent has experience steering the careers of
major stars like Lana Turner, Rita Hayworth, and Bob Hope.

"You're going to be a great movie star," Hyde tells Marilyn.
"I know. Many years ago, I discovered a girl like you and
brought her to Metro — Lana Turner. You're better. You'll go
farther. You've got more."

"Then why can't I get a job?" Marilyn asks. "Just to make
enough money to eat on."

"It's hard for a star to get an eating job," says Hyde. "A star
is only good as a star. You don't fit into anything less."

Johnny Hyde is a man in love. He's also a whirlwind. Marilyn matches his energy as they lunch at Romanoff's, dance at
Ciro's, party at the Mocambo and the Troc. She sits next to
him, not uttering a word beyond "Yes, Johnny" or "No,
Johnny." Occasionally, she calls him "Daddy." Most especially
when she wants something.

He leaves his wife and his four sons and rents a house on
718 North Palm Drive, Beverly Hills, and puts Marilyn up at
the Beverly Carlton Hotel to distract the press and studio gos-
sipmongers.

Smart and well-read, he buys Marilyn enough volumes to
start a personal library, from the Russian greats — Dostoyevsky,
Turgenev, Tolstoy — to Marcel Proust and Thomas Wolfe to

Konstantin Stanislavski's *An Actor Prepares*. She studies, underlining each page, knowing that he will test her afterward.

"Johnny Hyde wants to be my agent!" Marilyn announces to Natasha Lytess. "He's buying me out of my contract with Harry Lipton. He told me so last weekend in Palm Springs." He knows that she doesn't reciprocate his feelings, but it doesn't dissuade him. "I don't think it's wrong to let him love me the way he does. I do feel sorry for him, but I swear I am never going to lie to him."

Johnny knows that I don't tell lies. He knows I'm not planning to fool him. "The truth is, I've never fooled anyone," Marilyn says. It's hardly her fault if "men sometimes fool themselves."

On March 2, 1949, Marilyn signs a contract appointing the William Morris Agency as her sole and exclusive representative in film, television, and radio.

CHAPTER 20

MY CHIEF PROBLEM next to eating, stockings, and rent is my automobile. In addition to being behind on her rent at the Hollywood Studio Club, Marilyn's behind on her car payments, and now her car's been repossessed. She's feeling desperate.

Two months before, she'd been in a minor car accident on Sunset Boulevard. Nothing too damaging, a taillight or something, but it left her late for an audition and in need of a ride. Tom Kelley, who worked as a former MGM and *Town & Country* photographer before opening his own studio, witnessed the incident and kindly gave Marilyn five bucks for a cab — plus his business card and an open invitation to visit his photography studio in Hollywood anytime.

Now, Marilyn digs out Kelley's card and takes him up on the offer. He books her for a Pabst beer ad. Soon she is posing in a two-piece bathing suit, tossing a beach ball overhead and smiling at the camera. She earns herself a quick $20.

Marilyn likes Kelley and his wife, Natalie, so she's happy to get a call from the photographer not long after. He's got a new job for her, if she's interested. Another client of his, the John Baumgarth calendar company in Chicago, has seen and loved her beer ad photos.

"This is a little different from other jobs," he warns her. "These pictures are for a calendar, and they will have to be in the nude."

"You mean completely nude?" Marilyn's surprised but not shocked. She knows it's not the kind of thing "nice girls" do, but nudity doesn't really bother her. *It's the most commonplace thing in the world,* she thinks.

"You're ideal for the job not only because you have a fine shape but you're unknown. Nobody'll recognize you," Natalie Kelley assures Marilyn.

"It'll just be a picture of a beautiful nobody," her husband agrees. "But there's fifty dollars in it for you, if you want to do it."

"For fifty dollars, I am ready to jump off a roof!" Marilyn says.

On May 27, 1949, "Mona" Monroe signs a model release, then poses nude on a red velvet drape, first seated in profile — back arched, legs in an S-curve, knees lifted, feet tucked just below her buttocks — then lying down on her side, while Tom Kelley snaps away from a ladder above.

"Your hair's so long, no one will know it's you," he promises.

His wife holds the stepladder, arranging and rearranging the velvet as if around a diamond brooch in a jewelry box.

The next day, Marilyn's able to get her car out of hock and writes out check number 101 from her account to the Hollywood Studio Club for $51 back rent.

*   *   *

United Artists is touting *Love Happy,* the Marx Brothers' new film, as a "New Musical Girlesque." With the brothers now in their fifties and sixties, this film—reputedly being made to pay off eldest brother Chico Marx's gambling debts, like 1946's *A Night in Casablanca*—may be their last.

Marilyn hurries to set when she hears there's a bit part open. Groucho Marx tells her, "This role calls for young lady who can walk by me in a such a manner as to arouse my elderly libido and cause smoke to issue from my ears."

The task is simple enough. Walk up and down in front of Groucho, his brother Harpo, and the producer, Lester Cowan. Marilyn is starstruck to meet the famous comedians. *It's like meeting familiar characters out of Mother Goose!* Though Groucho isn't wearing his big greasepaint mustache and Harpo isn't silent—but does have his trusty horn—they both have "the same happy, crazy look I had seen on the screen. They both smiled at me as if I were a piece of French pastry."

"Get behind me and walk like I do," Groucho instructs, then sashays in an exaggerated manner.

"We're going to try out three girls for the part," Cowan tells Groucho. Marilyn is the third girl.

The producer has the first girl walk across the room.

Very nice.

Next, the second girl walks.

Another good possibility.

"Now the third one," Cowan says. "You walk across."

Just before the audition, Marilyn had cut a quarter of an inch off the bottom of one of her heels, to give herself a better wiggle, a sharper swing of the hips, a more prominent tilt to her backside.

"Which one did you like the best?" Cowan asks the brothers after the auditions.

"You're kidding, aren't you? How could you take anyone except the last girl? The whole room revolved when she walked," Groucho Marx replies.

Marilyn gets the part.

"You're like Mae West, Theda Bara, and Bo Peep all rolled into one," Marx proclaims.

The scene is shot the very next day. She's paid $100 for one day's work, plus $25 for posing for some promotional stills at a couple of gas stations with product placement in the film.

Though Marilyn ends up appearing in *Love Happy* (which Groucho admits is a "terrible picture") for only a few minutes, when the film is released producer Cowan builds the nationwide publicity tour around her.

"All you have to do is be Marilyn Monroe," Cowan says when Marilyn hesitates, adding, "You will have a chance to see the world, and it will broaden your horizons."

He introduces her as the "Mmmm Girl." Some people can't whistle, the marketing concept goes, so when they see Marilyn, all they can do is say, "Mmmm."

The tour delivers her first taste of fame. And a new wardrobe. Cowan gives her $75, which Marilyn spends on three wool suits.

By the time the train reaches New York, the weather is unbearably hot.

"I feel like I'm wearing an oven!" Marilyn exclaims of her new suit.

"We must make capital out of what we have," the press agent says. He arranges ice cream cones in her hands like a sweet bouquet. "Marilyn Monroe, the hottest thing in pictures, cooling off," the photo caption reads.

One day's work turns into five months of touring.

CHAPTER 21

DIRECTOR JOHN HUSTON is casting for *The Asphalt Jungle,* a gritty crime drama about an aging criminal mastermind's doomed bid to pull off one last jewel heist.

Huston is fresh off a pair of 1948 Oscar-winning films for Warner Bros.—the western adventure *The Treasure of the Sierra Madre* and the crime noir *Key Largo.* This new picture is with Metro-Goldwyn-Mayer, where Marilyn's friend Lucille Ryman Carroll is head talent scout.

The director's first choice for the supporting role of Angela Phinlay is Lola Albright. But now that she's appeared alongside Kirk Douglas in 1949's boxing film *Champion,* Albright's rate is $1,500 a week, which is more than Huston is willing to pay.

Ryman Carroll lobbies Huston, who'd refused to audition Marilyn for one of his earlier films, to give her a chance at the role. The talent scout has a unique influence over the director, who's boarding twenty-three horses at the ranch Ryman Carroll and her husband, actor John Carroll, own in Grenada Hills outside Los Angeles.

Huston, the son of actor Walter Huston (whom he'd directed to a Best Supporting Actor Oscar in *The Treasure of the Sierra Madre*) and a former actor himself, is known to be particular about pairing actors with roles. "When I cast a picture," he describes the process, "I do most of my directing in finding the right person."

Known as one of "the wild men of Hollywood" for living as fast and hard as the scenes from his adrenaline-fueled pictures, Huston is a US Army veteran and devoted horseman who's already been married three times. He's also carrying significant debt—including gambling losses and an $18,000 bill at the Carrolls' ranch. Lucille Ryman Carroll has a soft spot for Marilyn, and makes a deal with the director that she's willing to accept a payment plan for the ranch bill, provided Huston agrees to audition the girl.

"Tell your agent to get in touch with Mr. Huston," the casting director instructs Marilyn. "I've already discussed you with him. It's not a big part, but you're bound to make a big hit in it."

Marilyn arrives for her first meeting with Huston dressed as she imagines the fictional Angela—a young woman kept by an older man—might be. She's wearing a low-cut, clingy red dress over a bra padded to the point of absurdity. The producer, Arthur Hornblow, laughs and asks her to remove all the tissues. She's given a script to look over.

"Do you think you can do it?" her agent Johnny Hyde asks. "You have to break up in it and cry and sob."

"I thought you thought I was a star, and I could do anything," Marilyn replies.

"You can," he assures her. "But I can't help worrying."

Drama coach Natasha Lytess rehearses Marilyn continuously for three days, returning her suitably dressed and styled.

Ryman Carroll consults with studio hairdresser Sydney Guilaroff, who creates "an original style, much shorter than the standard length at that time and structured to follow the contours of her face." The new look accentuates Marilyn's natural beauty, though she's still lacking confidence.

"I don't think I'm going to be any good," she admits to Huston when she comes in for the audition. "Would you mind if I read the part lying on the floor?"

Huston agrees, and a nervous Marilyn removes her shoes and lies on the ground. She does the scene once and then leaps up and requests to do it again.

There is something touching and appealing about Marilyn, Huston decides. He lets her run through the scene twice but assures her, "You got the part after the first reading."

Even MGM chief Louis B. Mayer is impressed. He signs off on Marilyn for the role and agrees to employ Lytess as her private coach ahead of the fall 1949 shoot.

Mayer isn't spending freely these days. Headlines like JUDY GARLAND LEAVES PICTURE; COSTS SOAR ran in mid-May after MGM halted the musical *Annie Get Your Gun* and suspended Garland—eight months after the star exited *The Barkleys of Broadway* following a nervous breakdown. Mayer had put Garland under the care of two studio doctors, but she was too ill and addled to perform, costing MGM millions.

On the set of *Asphalt Jungle*, Marilyn knows there's no margin for error. After every take, she glances across to where Lytess is standing on the far reaches of the set, seeking her coach's approval.

Shuttling between Johnny Hyde's guest house in Beverly Hills, the Beverly Carlton Hotel, and Natasha Lytess's apartment in Los Angeles, Marilyn is feeling the strain of displacement mirrored in the shooting script.

One evening, when it's time to run lines, Lytess knocks repeatedly on Marilyn's door—but gets no response, though she knows her student is there. When Marilyn finally answers, her eyes are wide with fear.

There's a gang of men stalking me, a terrified Marilyn tells her. *I can hear their voices, mocking and goading.*

At first Lytess thinks that Marilyn is projecting, getting into character for the suspenseful scene they're about to rehearse. In an unnamed Midwestern city, Marilyn's character, Angela, is ensconced in a hideaway by the corrupt lawyer who controls her. But Marilyn keeps pausing, sitting in rigid silence to listen for voices that only she can hear.

The drama coach has been waiting for an excuse to complain about the pressure she feels MGM is applying. Marilyn needs to be nurtured and looked after, not exploited and used. Lytess marches into Johnny Hyde's office at the William Morris Agency.

"She's hearing voices!" Lytess declares, glaring across the agent's desk.

Hyde barely reacts, conceding only, "We need to help her."

MGM calls in the doctors, the same ones Judy Garland complained would "give us pep pills, then they'd take us to the studio hospital and knock us cold with sleeping pills...That's the way we got mixed up." Anything to get the scenes in the can.

A medicated Marilyn finishes the shoot.

MGM executives turn out in force to preview *Asphalt Jungle*. Spontaneous wolf whistling and generous applause erupt whenever "Angela" walks into the frame. In the darkness of the screening room, Marilyn sits beside Johnny Hyde, holding his hand as he beams with the pride of vindication. He was right all along.

On May 12, 1950, *Asphalt Jungle* opens in theaters.

"There's a beautiful blonde, too, name of Marilyn Monroe," *Photoplay* magazine proclaims, who "makes the most of her footage." Along with critical acclaim comes an outpouring of popular enthusiasm. The studio receives sacks of letters from fans inquiring about the pretty blonde.

Life magazine photographer Ed Clark gets an inside tip on Fox's new "hot tomato" and brings Marilyn to Los Angeles's Griffith Park, where she poses under the shade of the trees, reading scripts.

Not everyone is as impressed. When Clark sends a few rolls of film to his editors at *Life*, they wire back, "Who the hell is Marilyn Monroe?"

CHAPTER 22

JOHNNY HYDE BELIEVES in medical miracles. He also has a fear of wasting time. Since his heart attack in 1948, he's been popping nitroglycerin tablets to keep his angina at bay. But his health is fading. He is weak, out of breath, and in considerable pain.

Working from his bedroom, he continues to push Marilyn's career as if she's his only client. He's left all the others in the lurch, relying on his fuming colleagues at the William Morris Agency to pick up the slack. But lovelorn Johnny is obsessively determined to make her a star. Even if it is the last thing he does.

Director Joseph L. Mankiewicz is doing *All About Eve* at 20th Century-Fox, a drama starring Bette Davis about the cycle of aging actors and the fledgling talent pushing to take their place. Hyde wants Marilyn to audition for one of the supporting roles. "It's not a big part but it will establish you at 20th," he tells her.

"But they don't like me there," Marilyn protests. It was only three years ago that studio boss Darryl Zanuck declined to renew her contract, calling her unphotogenic.

"They will," says Hyde. "This is it, honey. You're in. Everybody is crazy about your work."

Sometimes party chatter offers a more honest assessment than even the least flattering mirror.

"There goes the chinless wonder." Those are the words Marilyn overhears as she passes by a cluster of well-dressed Hollywood partygoers.

Whitey Snyder checked her makeup before she left the studio lot, but even his best work can't hide a flaw in her bone structure.

Marilyn makes an appointment with Dr. Michael Gurdin. His UCLA medical practice caters to Hollywood stars. Gurdin's receptionist keeps a list of aliases to ensure discretion for those booking appointments.

She's seen by Gurdin's associate John Pangman, who diagnoses "a mild flatness of the chin" to be treated with a cartilage graft.

"No, Marilyn is not available for a screen test," she has Johnny Hyde say to dodge the request. "She's taken a fall on her chin."

When the scar beneath her chin has healed, she resumes auditions and takes that screen test.

"Honey, you should have cut your chin two years ago," the director says.

Her nose seems a little different, too, especially around the tip.

"Marilyn looks more beautiful than ever" is what she over-hears at the next party.

Which are kinder, the insults or the compliments? It's impossible to know for sure.

Marilyn auditions for *All About Eve,* and Joe Mankiewicz casts her in the supporting role of Miss Claudia Casswell, theater critic Addison DeWitt's party date. When Miss Casswell sees the fur coat belonging to the Broadway star played by Bette Davis, Marilyn delivers the scene-stealing line, "Now there's something a girl could make sacrifices for."

Johnny Hyde is thrilled.

He was so happy for me, Marilyn thinks. *No man had ever looked on me with such kindness. He not only knew me; he knew Norma Jeane, too. He knew all the pain, and all the desperate things in me. Nobody has ever loved me like that. I just wished in all my heart I could love him back.*

Hyde proposes to Marilyn, but she declines. "I'm rich," he wheedles. "I have almost a million dollars. If you marry me, you'll inherit it when I die."

She won't think about him dying, won't consider it, even as she recognizes that he shares many of Aunt Ana's symptoms. "I'll not leave you. I'll never betray you," she promises. "But I can't marry you."

Hyde continues to propose — often — but she does not, will not, accept.

She's a romantic. She'll marry only for love.

Though she telephones him often as his health declines, entertaining him with funny stories, she rarely visits his bedside, leaving Johnny to fret about her whereabouts and her companions. There is something about the ailing man, the airlessness of his bedroom, and his increasing neediness that puts her off.

For Marilyn's twenty-fourth birthday on June 1, Joe Schenck, the 20th Century-Fox production chief with whom she's often seen around town, gives her a Chihuahua she names Josepha. She's besotted with her new pet.

Maybe with its namesake, too, Johnny Hyde fears. Incessantly, he calls over to 1309 North Harper Avenue, the apartment Marilyn and her dog currently share with Natasha Lytess and her young daughter, Barbara.

"Where is Marilyn, Natasha?" Hyde begs of her acting coach. "I have been waiting. Never, in all my life, have I come across such cruelty or such selfishness."

Hyde grows increasingly jealous. He cancels a photo shoot between Marilyn and her fellow 20th Century-Fox studio contract player Dale Robertson, to fend off impressions that she's dating the handsome actor.

Marilyn's next seen in six small scenes in *The Fireball,* starring Mickey Rooney as a roller-skating champion, and in an uncredited role as the fashion model Dusky Ledoux in *Right Cross,* a boxing drama starring June Allyson, Dick Powell, and Ricardo Montalban. Both films are released the first week of October 1950, right before *All About Eve* hits screens to great accolades.

She signs a new three-year contract with the William Morris Agency on December 5. A few weeks before Christmas, Johnny Hyde's feeling well enough to travel to Palm Springs for the holiday season. He suggests to Natasha Lytess and

Marilyn that they go visit Tijuana, Mexico, and sends them south with enough money to treat themselves to some Christmas shopping.

But on December 18, 1950, fifty-five-year-old Hyde suffers a series of catastrophic heart attacks. "Marilyn! Marilyn!" are reportedly the last words on his lips in Cedars of Lebanon Hospital in East Hollywood.

Marilyn hurries to his deathbed when she hears the news, legs shaking, eyes dark with heartache. She stands over his corpse and slowly pulls back the white sheet, remembering what he used to tell her: *All she had to do was lean over and hug his cold body and he would resurrect like Jesus to see her one last time.*

"I did love you, Johnny," she whispers. "Please know that I did."

In the following days, Marilyn can't stop crying. Devoid of her rock, her friend, her mentor, the one person who would move heaven and earth for her, she feels alone in the world.

She has so few friends. Reporters Sid Skolsky and Bob Slatzer. Talent scout Lucille Ryman Carroll. Acting coach Natasha Lytess. Whitey Snyder, the makeup artist. She seems to carry almost no one with her through life. Now Johnny Hyde is dead, and she is eaten up by grief and guilt over not having rushed over in his last few days when he telephoned, begging her to come to the hospital.

"Be sure that Marilyn is treated as one of the family," Hyde had instructed his secretary as he lay dying.

Instead, Hyde's family not only repossesses all of the clothing and jewelry he'd gifted his beloved, but bars her from attending his funeral at Forest Lawn Memorial Park in the Hollywood Hills.

Yet the grieving Marilyn is defiant. Heavily veiled and dressed in a new black suit purchased for the occasion, she and Natasha Lytess sneak into the funeral service. Marilyn simply sits, weeps, waits. When the mourners finally disperse, she contemplates the altar for another hour, then waits alone at the grave until dusk, when a security guard asks her to leave. In her final moments, she bends down and plucks a white rose from one of the bouquets on his grave.

She presses this rose flat into the pages of a Bible.

On Christmas Eve, like some ghoulish practical joke, Hyde's pre-ordered Christmas presents are delivered all over town.

Marilyn is lying with her dog Josepha in the apartment on North Harper Avenue when a huge red box with a giant bow arrives.

"Every Star should have one of these" the message attached reads, signed, "All my love as ever, Johnny."

Inside is a beautiful stole of the softest mink. Marilyn once again bursts into tears and clutches the fur to her face.

Natasha and Barbara Lytess come home with a bag of groceries. It's Marilyn's turn to cook dinner, but the kitchen is empty.

She can't be asleep, can she? She does keep odd hours, but Lytess blames those wretched sleeping pills she's been taking, lined up in bottles in the bedroom.

Lytess calls for her. There's only silence.

Propped up on the table is a note. "I leave my car and my stole to Natasha."

Another note is taped to Marilyn's bedroom door. "Barbara, do NOT enter."

What the hell has she done?

Lytess bursts in to find the curtains closed and clothes piled all over the room. On the bed is Marilyn, her arms above her head, her curls on the pillow, her face swollen.

Marilyn!

Lytess shouts in her ear and shakes her friend's warm, limp body. There are greenish capsules half-dissolved in her mouth, and more down to the back of the throat. Marilyn's lips are blue and her face is waxy, but she is still alive.

"Barbara!" Lytess yells to her daughter from the bedroom. "Call an ambulance!"

CHAPTER 23

WHY WOULD I want to kill myself? Johnny has given me so much to live for!

Marilyn explains away the earlier "mishap." Natasha Lytess overreacted, she insists. She'd simply overdone it on some sleeping pills Sid Skolsky had bought her at Schwab's. She hadn't drunk enough water to wash them down and they'd crystallized in her mouth, turning the corners green.

In January 1951, she's back at the Fox lot to film the screwball comedy *As Young as You Feel* by New York playwright Paddy Chayefsky.

Marilyn had once modeled for the studio's 1948 publicity piece "How to Exercise." Now she dedicates herself to a regimen of calisthenics, weight lifting, and jogging, an unusual pursuit that draws puzzled glances from passersby. In February, a photographer snaps Marilyn in a park in Los Angeles, hefting a lightly weighted barbell overhead.

She may be stronger physically, but her emotions remain fragile as she embarks on the final role Hyde had negotiated for her. She's out of sync with the role of Harriet, a secretary who colludes with the sixty-five-year-old president of Acme Printing in his scheme to avoid forced retirement.

Despite living almost opposite the lot, Marilyn often over-sleeps and misses her call times. Her behavior frustrates direc-tor Harmon Jones, who finds her "a ridiculous person" and sends runners and assistant directors to hammer on her door. When she finally wakes, her face is puffy from crying and doesn't look good on film.

Jones introduces Marilyn to his friend and fellow director Elia Kazan. "I took her to dinner because she seemed like such a touching pathetic waif. She sobbed all thru dinner," Kazan writes. "She was like all Charlie Chaplin's heroines in one."

You can't help but be touched, Kazan thinks. *She's talented, funny, vulnerable, helpless in awful pain, with no hope, and some worth and not a liar, not vicious, not catty, and with a history of orphanism that's killing to hear.*

Kazan's interest in Marilyn is more carnal than merely pro-tective. He affectionately calls her "Darling" and visits her on set, bringing with him his playwright friend Arthur Miller, a mutual pal of *As Young as You Feel* screenwriter Chayefsky.

Miller's drama *All My Sons* won him an award for Best Author of a Play at the inaugural Tony Awards in 1947, as well as a New York Drama Critics' Circle Award for Best American Play. Kazan, who directed *All My Sons* and won the Best Director Tony for the play, then went on to direct Gregory Peck in the film *Gentleman's Agreement,* winner of the 1948 Oscar for Best Director and Best Picture. He and Miller next returned to Broadway in 1949 for *Death of a Salesman,* which garnered even more awards: six Tonys, including Best Director, Best

Author, and Best Play; the Drama Critics' Circle Award for Best Play; and the Pulitzer Prize in Drama. It's a coveted playwright's "triple crown" for the then thirty-three-year-old Arthur Miller, and a smash hit on stage, earning $2 million.

"I tell ya, kid, art pays," an ecstatic Miller wrote to Kazan.

Now, on the set of *As Young as You Feel,* Miller is transfixed by "the saddest girl he ever saw." Backlit by a white spotlight and positioned in profile, she is wearing a black lace veil and dabbing her eyes. Marilyn is still in mourning for Johnny Hyde. It's barely been a month since the death of "the kindest man in the world."

Kazan makes introductions. Marilyn extends a soft white hand toward the tall, bespectacled Miller. He later remarks that the touch sent electricity coursing through his body. Marilyn, however, carries on with her scene, apparently failing to notice him at all.

Columbia Pictures will release its film adaptation of *Death of a Salesman* in December 1951, so Miller is in town for meetings. He and Kazan pitch studio head Harry Cohn *The Hook,* Miller's new screenplay about union corruption on the Brooklyn waterfront. It's not easy following up the massive success of *Death of a Salesman,* however.

Cohn shows Miller's screenplay to the FBI. If Miller would simply change his gangster villains into Communists, Cohn insists, the script would be viable.

Miller refuses.

Cohn fires off a telegram. "The minute we try to make the script pro-American, you pull out."

The Hook is not picked up.

The "Red Scare" campaign, led by the House Un-American Activities Committee and Joseph McCarthy, the right-wing senator from Wisconsin, is intensifying the hunt for a perceived domestic Communist threat, insisting that Hollywood is teeming with Trots, Marxists, and Commies.

Elia Kazan and Arthur Miller are both staying at the Coldwater Canyon home of agent Charles Feldman of Famous Artists Corporation while they're in Los Angeles. Feldman's a producer on Kazan's latest directorial project, *A Streetcar Named Desire.*

Marilyn's often at the house, visiting Kazan and driving Miller to distraction.

Feldman throws a party in Miller's honor. Marilyn sits beside Miller on a sofa, drinking champagne while he tickles the arches of her feet. By the time Kazan arrives, late, "the lovely light of desire in their eyes" is unmistakable.

"It was like running into a tree. You know, like a cool drink when you've had a fever," Marilyn says of Miller. That he *doesn't* make a pass at her only heightens the attraction.

Miller's been married since 1940 to Mary Grace Slattery, who works as a proofreader at *Harper's* magazine and with whom he has two children. He hasn't broken his vows. Yet.

But the playwright keeps extending the length of his visit—until he runs out of excuses and must return to New York.

The sight of her was something like pain, and I knew that I must flee or walk into a doom beyond all knowing. With all her radiance, she was surrounded by darkness that perplexed me is Miller's impression of Marilyn. *I was retreating to the safety of morals, to be sure, but not necessarily truthfulness.*

At the airport, he embraces Marilyn and gives her a good-bye kiss on the cheek. They promise to write.

Flying home, her scent still on my hands, I knew my innocence was technical merely, and the secret that I could lose myself in sensuality entered me like a radiating force.

Marilyn frames a photo of Arthur Miller and keeps it by her bedside.

CHAPTER 24

MARILYN MONROE IS BACKSTAGE at the 23rd Academy Awards in a sequined bouffant gown. Tonight, March 29, 1951, *All About Eve* is up for a record fourteen Oscars.

"The Oscars are something people yearn for, fight for, and cry for, and there is never an end to the competition until the tributes are finally won," proclaims host Fred Astaire. As a nod to her supporting role in the film, Marilyn has been chosen to present the award for Best Sound Recording.

The picture has already won a statuette for Best Costume Design, but Marilyn is in tears over what's happened to her dress: A large rip has appeared down the side of the strapless dress of layered tulle that she's chosen from the Fox wardrobe department. Luckily, a seamstress rushes to repair it, and when Marilyn goes on stage to announce another of *All About Eve*'s eventual six Oscar wins, the audience of eighteen hundred in the Pantages Theatre is unaware of the near calamity.

Less than two weeks later, Marilyn wins a prize she's coveted more than any other—a full contract with 20th Century-Fox. Her weekly salary will start at $500 and rise in annual increments for a period of seven years. On April 11, 1951, she signs the document. It's Johnny Hyde's final gift to the woman he loved.

Darryl Zanuck walks through the Fox lot on a sunny afternoon in mid-June. Folded under his arm is today's *New York Times*. "Marilyn Monroe is superb as the secretary" in *As Young as You Feel,* the film critic praises.

The man in charge is confused and irritated at the same time. Is he the only person who doesn't see it? The only one who finds her delivery annoying and her acting stiff?

Sid Skolsky's latest column describes Marilyn's feat of silencing a film crew simply by appearing on set in a bathing suit. Another report touts the blonde as "one of the brightest up-and-coming actresses."

Zanuck passes the mailroom just as a delivery boy hefts a huge brown sack over his shoulder.

"That's a lot of mail," he jokes.

"It's been like this for weeks," puffs the boy, throwing the sack down on the floor. "And they're all for Marilyn Monroe."

"All of them?"

"She gets over three thousand letters a week. More than everyone else combined."

Zanuck invites Marilyn to the Fox Publicity and Sales party at the Café de Paris, where the studio's most important executives toast June Haver, Betty Grable, and Gregory Peck.

Marilyn arrives late. Whether by design, or nerves, or both, she seems determined to put on a show. Her black strapless gown is in high contrast with her skin, a luminous shade of marble white that perfectly matches her ever-more lightened hair.

She pauses at the door, pursing her scarlet lips. Holding the room. Fox president Spyros Skouras breaks the spell. He rises from the table in his tuxedo and offers her the seat next to his.

The next day, Zanuck orders that Marilyn Monroe be given "star" treatment with the full weight of the Fox publicity team behind her. He casts her in the suspense thriller *Don't Bother to Knock*. It is her first leading dramatic role. Her name will appear above the title.

In August, as the Korean War rages on, the US military news organization *Stars and Stripes* names Marilyn "Miss Cheesecake of the Year." At a party at the Farmers Market in Hollywood, she poses in a white strapless swimsuit, a chef's toque, and a sheer white apron over a giant cheesecake, pretending to cut through the layers with a military-style saber. It's a morale-boosting role, but hardly a serious one.

She begins taking acting lessons from Michael Chekhov. The famous playwright's nephew studied with Stanislavski at the Moscow Art Theatre and has spent the last ten to fifteen years teaching thespian greats—the likes of John Gielgud and Max Reinhardt. He's a gentle, patient soul, the antithesis of Natasha Lytess.

Marilyn has moved out of Lytess's apartment and into the Beverly Carlton Hotel. But the two haven't parted ways. Marilyn helps her Fox acting coach with the down payment on a new home in West Hollywood by giving her $1,000 she gets from selling the mink stole from Johnny Hyde. Marilyn insisted, even though the studio pays both women $500 a week. Add in the $250 Marilyn pays Lytess for private lessons, and the star is earning less than the coach. Marilyn, whose new contract stipulates annual pay raises upon renewal—$750 weekly in year two, $1,250 in year three, and so on—always insists that she doesn't mind. "I just want to be wonderful!" she says. "I don't care about money at all."

But she does care about her parts. Their questionable quality is beginning to depress her. She complains to Michael Chekhov, "I want to be an artist, not an erotic freak. I don't want to be sold to the public as a celluloid aphrodisiac. It was all right for the first few years. But now, it's different."

"But Marilyn," he replies, with his soft Russian accent. "You're a young woman who gives off sex vibrations, no matter what you are doing or thinking. Unfortunately, your studio bosses are only interested in your sex vibrations."

Chekhov and Marilyn work on reducing the "vibrations" in her performance. She imagines herself growing larger or smaller, reducing the importance of the physical body in the performance.

"Our bodies can either be our best friends or worst enemies," Chekhov explains. "You must try to consider your body as an instrument for expressing creative ideas. You must strive for complete harmony between body and psychology."

Yet the small walk-on, walk-off "erotic vibration" parts persist. In October 1951, the polka-dot bikini Marilyn wears in *Love Nest* gets reviewed—"hardly enough room for the polka dots"—with more precision than her performance does.

Consolation comes from the newfound financial stability her contract provides. She generously pays Natasha Lytess's dental bill. She also hires a private investigator to track down her father, Stan Gifford, whom she hasn't spoken with since he hung up on her back in 1944.

Lytess is set against her student repeating this extreme act of self-sabotage. But Marilyn is adamant. She's never stopped looking at her father's photograph, the smiling one where he looks just like Clark Gable.

"Maybe he'll be excited that his daughter is a movie star?"

"You could be hurt by this."

"After all this time, he is not going to be the same person who walked out on my mother."

"What if he has moved on? What if he has forgotten about you?"

"He would never do that."

As Lytess stares at Marilyn's determined face, she sees the forgotten child screaming "Look at me!" and deciding that the only way to get her father's attention was to achieve stardom, fame, and adulation. Yet he's still nowhere to be seen.

They set out for Hemet, California, a San Jacinto Valley town eighty-seven miles south of Los Angeles. Along the way, Lytess persuades Marilyn to pull in at a gas station.

"Most people hate surprises," she says. "Much better to call ahead."

She deposits a dime in the gas station telephone booth and telephones her father.

A woman answers. "Hello, this is Mrs. Gifford. Who is calling?"

"I am Gladys Baker's daughter...a little girl from a long time ago. I'm Marilyn. Marilyn Monroe. He is sure to know who I am."

There's a pause, the sound of a hand covering the receiver and then a lengthy silence. Marilyn glances over at Natasha, who is sitting in the car, staring through the open window. Marilyn's hand grips the receiver. Her knees are bent, she's hunched forward with the pain of waiting. She has waited for twenty-five years.

"Hello?" comes the voice through the telephone. "He doesn't want to speak to you." Then, after a pause, "Do you have a pencil?"

Marilyn lurches forward with hope and scrambles in her small white purse. "Yes, yes I do!"

"He suggests you speak with his lawyer in Los Angeles if you have a complaint. I'll give you his number..."

Marilyn hangs up. Her shoulders slump. He doesn't love her. He doesn't want to know her. She sobs. Big heaving sobs, her shoulders shaking. And then she breathes in deeply, holds her head high until she's back inside the car.

In the driver's seat, she clutches the steering wheel with both hands as she cries and cries. There is nothing Natasha Lytess can do or say to comfort her. Marilyn starts the car and doesn't speak a word on the drive back to Hollywood.

In her room at the Beverly Carlton Hotel, Marilyn takes a handful of pills and goes straight to sleep.

CHAPTER 25

ON A STAR-STUDDED EVENING at Santa Monica's Club Del Mar, Marilyn poses for *Life* magazine with Mitzi Gaynor, Tony Curtis, and John Derek. It's January 1952 and the Hollywood Foreign Press Association is honoring her with a "Henrietta" award statuette.

In a velvet gown with a plunging bustier, bare shoulders covered by a fur stole, twenty-five-year-old Marilyn crosses the room to receive the award for Best Young Box Office Personality.

It's a glamorous, champagne-soaked evening. But in the light of day, Marilyn demands more.

"I want to expand my horizons," she tells Grace McKee.

And her self-esteem: *There was no hiding from it anymore. I was terribly dumb. I didn't know anything about painting, music, books, history, geography. I didn't know anything about sports or politics.*

The Westwood campus of UCLA is less than three miles from the Fox lot. Marilyn decides to enroll in an extension course.

On February 12, 1952, a photographer from *Movies Day* is on hand to snap Marilyn—the magazine's "Most Exciting Woman of the Year"—studying in the library, laughing with fellow students in the cafeteria, and holding a stuffed brown bear, the university's "Bruin" mascot.

In her literature class, she slips into the back, wearing a scarf, sweater, and jeans. No one recognizes her, or pays her much interest or attention, but Marilyn is in awe of the worlds her professors reveal to her. She reads Freud, Proust, Turgenev. "I read them till I got dizzy," she says. She learns how to digest books and break down stories—and she learns about herself. She possesses a mind that is quick, smart, and voracious for knowledge.

Next month, she'll be on set for a master class in comedy from Howard Hawks, director of *Bringing Up Baby* and *His Girl Friday.*

Darryl Zanuck had complained to Hawks that he didn't know what to do with Marilyn Monroe or her baffling popularity.

Hawks is pretty sure he sees the problem. Marilyn's not a dramatist; she's a persona. "She's as phony as a three-dollar bill, and you're trying to make her real," the director told the studio chief. "She belongs in an outrageous comedy or in a musical." Now Hawks is making good on his theory. He casts Marilyn in his newest screwball comedy, *Monkey Business,* as Lois Laurel, secretary to the head of a chemical company who directs a research scientist played by leading man Cary Grant to create an elixir of youth.

Zanuck soon finds another reason to be irritated with Marilyn.

Aline Mosby of United Press calls up the studio. "I've got a hot tip," she says, "that the anonymous nude model in that 'Golden Dreams' calendar all over town is actually 20th Century-Fox starlet Marilyn Monroe."

The hand-wringing executives at the studio immediately deny the story.

Marilyn is also initially concerned but quickly changes her mind. Why lie? She's not embarrassed. It amuses her to spot the 1952 calendar popping up in local barbershops and garages. She's proud that it's so popular.

In March, Marilyn gives Mosby an exclusive interview and dares to tell the truth. "I was told I should deny I'd posed . . . but I'd rather be honest about it," she tells the reporter. Her voice is soft but serious, words flowing in a breathless rush. "Besides, I'm not ashamed of it. I've done nothing wrong."

The truth is that she posed for photographer Tom Kelley because she needed the money. "I was in debt," she admits. "I always supported myself. No one else ever supported me in my life. I had no family. And I had no place to go."

Honest work to pay the bills, now that's a situation the public can relate to—far more than Fox's strategy of deception. Instead of adding fuel to the scandal, Marilyn's decision to publicly admit the photos nips it in the bud. *The public was not only touched by this proof of my honest poverty a short time ago, but people also liked the calendar—by the millions.*

"I've gotten a lot of fan letters on it. The men like the picture and want copies. The women, well. One gossip columnist said I autographed the pictures and handed them out and said, 'Art for art's sake.' I never said that." She grins a little. "Why, I only gave two away."

Cary Grant, Marilyn's *Monkey Business* co-star, comes to her defense as well. And he is willing to make the art comparison. "There wouldn't be any great art if girls hadn't posed in the nude," he reminds reporters.

"We're all sexual creatures," Marilyn says. "Thank God."

The calendar sells out. Fan mail surges.

MGM is pitching the musical *Singin' in the Rain* ahead of its April release, but journalists demand, "We don't want to interview Debbie Reynolds. We want to talk to the girl with the big tits."

Marilyn will take what she can get. She has over-the-title billing in RKO Studio's *Clash by Night,* and she would rather talk about her role in the romantic film noir than her physical measurements. It's her largest part yet, with fourth billing behind lead Barbara Stanwyck and co-stars Robert Ryan and Paul Douglas. But she makes the most of this increase in attention. It's what she's hoped, prayed, and waited for.

Besides, all the publicity surrounding the nude calendar significantly heightens the public's interest in *Clash by Night.* Some folks gossip that it might've even been *Clash* director Fritz Lang who first dropped the hint in Aline Mosby's ear.

Stanwyck is supportive. Marilyn is "just a carefree kid," in the film star's opinion.

"There was a sort of magic about her which we all recognized at once," Stanwyck says of the up-and-coming actress.

Reviewers are beginning to agree.

"Marilyn Monroe, the calendar girl...proves she can also act and can hold her own with top performers," says the *Los Angeles Examiner* of *Clash by Night*. The *New York World Telegram and Sun* raves, "This girl has a refreshing exuberance, an abundance of girlish high spirits. She is a forceful actress, too, when crisis comes along. She has definitely stamped herself as a gifted new star, worthy of all that fantastic press.... Her role is not very big, but she makes it dominant."

"I'm on calendars, but never on *Time*," Marilyn jokes to reporters, at once sending up both the weekly news magazine and her reputation for perpetual lateness. But now she *is* on *Time*—as well as on the cover of *Life,* which notes that "Every so often, more in hope than conviction, Hollywood announces the advent of a sensational new glamor girl... today the most respected studio seers, in a crescendo of talk unparalleled since the debut of Rita Hayworth, are saying that the genuine article is here at last: a sturdy blonde named Marilyn Monroe."

Success came to me in a rush. It surprised my employers much more than it did me, Marilyn thinks, as she smiles for the cameras that now seem to follow her everywhere she goes. *I knew what I had known all those years ago when I was thirteen walking along the sea edge in a bathing suit for the first time. I knew I belonged to the public and to the world, not because I was talented or even beautiful, but because I had never belonged to anything or anyone else. The public was the only family, the only Prince Charming, and the only home I had ever dreamed of.*

CHAPTER 26

A FEW DAYS BEFORE a 1951 Major League Baseball charity exhibition game against the minor league "Hollywood Stars," Marilyn's press agent Dave March sent her to take publicity shots with members of the Chicago White Sox at their training camp in Pasadena. She wore heels, a short-sleeved sweater, and a tiny pair of white shorts, posing with players and twirling a bat.

"How come I never get to pose with beautiful girls like that?" Joe DiMaggio jokes with Sox player Gus Zernial after seeing the photos. The "Yankee Clipper" wants the name of the person who set up the photo shoot, then contacts press agent March to set up a new assignment: arrange a dinner date.

It takes a while. Marilyn's not interested.

"Don't you know who he is?" her friend Sid Skolsky pressures her.

She really doesn't. She only knows he's some sort of athlete. "He's a football or a baseball player," she guesses.

"DiMaggio is one of the greatest names that was ever in baseball. He's still the idol of millions of fans!" she's told.

She remains unmoved. "I don't care to meet him."

"Why not?"

"I don't like the way athletes dress, for one thing," she says. "I don't like men in loud clothes, with checked suits and big muscles and pink ties."

After much persuasion, she finally agrees to a group dinner on March 8, at Villa Nova, an Italian restaurant on Sunset Boulevard.

It's a small but popular spot, not too far from the studio soundstages, and is owned by former actor Allen Dale with backing from Charlie Chaplin and director Vincente Minelli.

Marilyn's late.

"She is always late," March laughs nervously, leaping from his seat when he spots a flash of platinum blond by the door.

"It's not really me who's late," Marilyn says. "It's the others who are in such a hurry."

Joe DiMaggio smiles in appreciation of her humor, revealing a mouth full of crooked teeth. With his lanky frame and sharp-featured face, DiMaggio is not a conventionally good-looking man. He's "a reserved gentleman in a gray suit, with a gray tie and a sprinkle of gray in his hair," far from the loud and flashy jock Marilyn expected. *If I hadn't been told he was some sort of ball player, I would have guessed he was either a steel magnate or a congressman.*

Though they sit next to one another at dinner, DiMaggio doesn't say much, doesn't meet her gaze. As a naturally shy person herself, Marilyn recognizes that by being quiet and enigmatic, he is beating her at her own game. *You learn to be silent and smiling like that from having millions of people look at you with love and excitement while you stand alone getting ready to do something,* she thinks.

What's most surprising to her is the effect he's having on all the men at the table.

"The other men talked and threw their personalities around. Mr. DiMaggio just sat there," she says later. "Yet somehow he was the most exciting man at the table. The excitement was in his eyes. They were sharp and alert.

"Then I became aware of something odd. The men at the table weren't showing off for me or telling their stories for my attention. It was Mr. DiMaggio they were wooing. This was a novelty. No woman had ever put me so much in the shade before."

This is a fascinating phenomenon, but as dinner winds down, Marilyn makes her excuses. She has an early call time on set.

DiMaggio asks for a lift back to Ivar Avenue, where he's staying at the Hollywood Knickerbocker. As Marilyn slows her car near the hotel, she realizes with a pang of regret that her first date with Joe DiMaggio may also be her last.

Until the New York Yankee, who boasted a career batting average of .325, hitting 361 home runs against just 369 strike-outs, steps up.

"I don't feel like turning in," he says. "Would you mind driving around a little while?"

"It's a lovely night for a drive," Marilyn agrees. For the next three hours, they drive and slowly begin to get to know one another.

"I saw your picture," DiMaggio tells her.

"Which movie was it?"

"It wasn't a movie," he says. "It was a photograph of you on the sports page."

She knows the one he means. "I imagine you must have had your picture taken doing publicity stunts like that a thousand times," Marilyn says.

"Not quite," DiMaggio replies. "The best I ever got was Ethel Barrymore or General MacArthur. You're prettier."

Marilyn practically blushes. "I'm sorry I don't know anything about baseball," she says.

"That's all right," DiMaggio replies. "I don't know much about movies."

He opens up to Marilyn about his life. Asks her in a deep and genuine way about hers. Marilyn recognizes in him a kindred spirit.

Both come from humble origins, Joe the eighth of nine children of an Italian immigrant fisherman who learned to play baseball on the sandlot playgrounds of San Francisco. Both pursued dreams of fame and fortune, though as she's stepping into the limelight, he's receding into its shadow. Six months ago, at age thirty-six, "Joe D." turned down an offer of a $100,000 annual salary—the largest paycheck in sports—ending thirteen seasons as the New York Yankees' superstar center fielder through ten American League pennants and nine World Series wins.

The famous ballplayer mentions that he doesn't mind going on first dates, but often must enlist his good friend George

Solotaire to "pry loose" women who attach themselves too tightly.

"I'll try not to make him too much trouble when he starts prying me loose," Marilyn promises.

"I don't think I will have need for Mr. Solotaire's services this trip" is DiMaggio's response.

What began as a blind date blossoms into a bicoastal romance. She can't stop thinking about him. *I was surprised to be so crazy about Joe. I expected a flashy New York sports type, and instead I met this reserved guy who didn't make a pass at me. I had dinner with him almost every night for two weeks. He treated me like something special. Joe is a very decent man, and he makes other people feel decent, too.*

He visits her on set in Hollywood. She nicknames him "Slugger" and travels to New York, where she accompanies him to Toots Shor's, a restaurant and unofficial men's club a ten-minute walk from DiMaggio's suite at the Hotel Elysée in New York City.

Although a steady stream of gossip links Marilyn to Fox contract player Nico Minardos, who's making his first, uncredited film appearance in *Monkey Business,* and also to studio president Spyros Skouras, it's her new relationship with DiMaggio that she tips to Sid Skolsky, who writes: "Joe DiMaggio is looking over Marilyn Monroe's curves and is batting fine."

"It just happens I like Joe," Marilyn tells her friend, "so much better than I like most actors."

Actors are often wonderful and charming people, she thinks, but as an actress, *to love an actor is something like incest. It's like loving a brother with the same face and manners as your own.*

"We talked a lot about baseball, believe it or not," Marilyn tells *Photoplay* magazine. "Joe explained it to me."

And he introduces her to his friend George Solotaire, who's impressed that "she's a real down-to-earth girl. She has plenty of heart. She has not gone Hollywood."

CHAPTER 27

AS THE *MONKEY BUSINESS* shoot wraps, Marilyn is struck down by appendicitis, bent double with abdominal pain and a fever brought on by infection.

On April 28, instead of visiting Marilyn on the Fox lot, Joe DiMaggio finds her in a grand Art Deco building near the Paramount lot—the Fountain Avenue branch of Cedars of Lebanon Hospital.

Marilyn is scheduled for an appendectomy but is suddenly struck by a terrible thought while prepping for surgery. What if her "routine procedure" turns out to be a "Mississippi appendectomy"? She's heard rumors of unauthorized hyster-ectomies given to unsuspecting young women.

In the operating room, the surgeon pulls back the gown on an unconscious Marilyn and makes an unexpected discovery: she's scotch-taped a message to her abdomen.

Dear Dr. Rabwin,

Cut as little as possible. I know it seems vain, but that doesn't really enter into it. The fact that I am a woman is important and means much to me.

Save please (can't ask enough) what you can — I'm in your hands. You have children and you must know what that means — please Dr. Rabwin — I know you somehow will!

Thank you — thank you — thank you — For God's sake Dear Doctor no ovaries removed — please, again, do whatever you can to prevent large scars. Thanking you with all my heart,

Marilyn Monroe

Recovering in her hospital room, Marilyn is surrounded by bouquets of flowers and "Get Well Soon" cards. DiMaggio sends a dozen roses that stand in a vase by her bedside.

The studio sets up a photo shoot to show fans that their favorite star is on the mend.

Whitey Snyder arrives to do her hair and makeup. He sets her famous blond curls, applies her favorite red lipstick, and adds a bloom of health to her complexion.

Just before the photographers arrive to snap photos of her reading the get-well cards — especially the one from DiMaggio — Marilyn plants a kiss on Snyder's cheek.

"Thank you for making me look like myself again," she smiles. "Promise you'll do this for my funeral."

"Your funeral!" he laughs. "I'll be dead myself by then!"

"Promise," she insists.

"I promise," he replies. "Sure, bring the body back while it is still warm and I'll do it."

"With your pinky," she adds, extending her own as they shake little fingers.

A few days later, Whitey Snyder receives a golden Tiffany money clip engraved "Whitey Dear: / While I'm still warm / Marilyn."

While Marilyn lies in the hospital recovering, questions about her past are coming to light.

There's boundless curiosity about the 20th Century-Fox star, now receiving over five thousand fan letters a week. On the heels of the nude photo revelation, Marilyn recently gave an interview to a reporter from ladies' magazine *Redbook* about her childhood as an orphan, titled "So Far to Go Alone," which it's slated to publish in its June edition. But what if the endearing little-girl-lost story of the orphan who made good isn't airtight?

MARILYN MONROE CONFESSES MOTHER ALIVE, LIVING HERE runs the headline to Erskine Johnson's May 3, 1952, story in the *Hollywood Reporter*. A photograph shows Homestead Lodge, a nursing home outside Pasadena where her mother, Gladys Monroe Baker (now Gladys Eley), is working a low-wage job.

This latest blow is a harder recovery than either the nude photo scandal or the appendectomy. Marilyn is immediately branded a liar. An eager young hustler. The most focused, most determined, most ambitious, and most pushy starlet out there.

Maybe in those first few years I didn't do anything to deserve other people's trust, Marilyn frets. *I don't know much about these things. I just tried not to hurt anybody, and to help myself.*

As annoyed as he is that *Redbook* magazine will be now on press with a discredited story of an orphaned Marilyn, Fox's lead press agent, the hard-nosed former newsman Harry Brand, is still doing his best to guard a far more explosive secret: that Marilyn was born illegitimate.

In full damage-control mode, Marilyn writes an apology to *Redbook,* taking the position that as a child she'd been unaware her mother was alive. "I frankly did not feel wrong in withholding from you the fact that my mother is still alive… since we have never known each other intimately and have never enjoyed the normal relationship of mother and daughter."

The anger toward Marilyn subsides, replaced by a flow of letters from people claiming to be her mother.

Not long after the *Hollywood Reporter's* scoop runs, Gladys writes Marilyn herself.

Please dear child, I'd like to receive a letter from you. Things are very annoying around here and I'd like to move away as soon as possible. I'd like to have my child's love instead of hatred.

With love, Mother

Marilyn doesn't reply.

I just want to forget about all the unhappiness, all the misery she had in her life and I had in mine, she thinks. *I can't forget it, but I'd like to try. When I am Marilyn Monroe and don't think about Norma Jeane, then sometimes it works.*

CHAPTER 28

"EVERY INCH AN ACTRESS!" declares the trailer for *Don't Bother to Knock*. "The screen has never shown this kind of woman before...The most talked about actress of 1952 rockets to stardom!"

Though filmed at the end of December 1951, the movie opens at the Globe Theater in New York City on July 18, 1952. Marilyn plays Nell Forbes, a grieving young woman whose uncle puts her up for a babysitting job in the New York City hotel where he works. A case of mistaken identity over a man Nell's convinced is her dead beau plunges her into a psychosis that endangers the baby she's been hired to care for. With depth and intensity drawn from her own family history with mental illness, Marilyn delivers a convincing performance of sanity destroyed by war.

Her costar Richard Widmark wasn't convinced they'd get there. "Zanuck wanted to make her a dramatic actress, even though acting scared her to death. So we had a lot of trouble just getting her out of her dressing room," he recalls.

The lede of the *New York Times* review highlights the studio publicity campaign: "The story is that Marilyn Monroe is being groomed by Twentieth Century-Fox for razzle-dazzle stardom on the assumption, we are told, that she is the hottest number to hit Hollywood in years."

Her next role is in the noir film *Niagara,* the latest from *Sunset Boulevard* co-screenwriter Charles Brackett. During the two weeks Marilyn spends on location directly across from the Falls, it's a toss-up which one is the more popular sight. "Milling crowds are often around her" come news reports from set locations around the area, from the landmark Rainbow Bridge to a specially constructed six-unit motel facade.

Twentieth Century-Fox has set up headquarters on the American side, at the General Brock Hotel—where Marilyn has Room 801—and budgeted $2 million for the shoot in lavish Technicolor.

Marilyn's delighted to take on a darker role, playing Rose Loomis, a femme-fatale type vacationing in Niagara Falls with her jealous, brooding older husband, George (played by Joseph Cotten). When Rose attends a casual motel party in a fuchsia off-the-shoulder dress with a peek-a-boo midriff, George complains it's so low-cut that he can "see her kneecaps."

It's the same sort of criticism Joe DiMaggio gives. Though the world at large seems entranced by the pairing of "the greatest woman in the world and the greatest guy in the world," as DiMaggio's former Yankee teammate Jerry Coleman calls them, the couple isn't racing to the altar.

Sporting News reports: "The blond beauty denied that she and Joe were contemplating marriage—at least in the immediate future."

"Marilyn Monroe won't be able to marry Joe DiMaggio right away even if she wants to," Sheilah Graham reports in August. Her column, "Hollywood Today," runs in 180 newspapers worldwide. "Starting this week, Monroe plunges into 50 poster sittings and 40 fan-magazine layouts. Every paper and periodical in the country is clamoring for more of Marilyn."

DiMaggio wishes they wouldn't. He's of the opinion that wives stay home, take care of the house. They cook, they clean, they set the table, and they don't express opinions.

They certainly don't live their lives in front of film and news cameras.

After all, that's what had happened with his first wife, Universal Pictures' "Oomph Girl," Dorothy Arnold, whom he divorced in 1944. Though she'd been a successful actress on stage, screen, and radio, Arnold gave it all up when they'd married in 1939 and had a son, Joe Jr., in 1941. Why won't Marilyn do the same?

DiMaggio wants to give Marilyn every luxury and more, but America's favorite unmarried couple is locked in conflict about their real-life roles.

"We'll buy a house in San Francisco," he says, "and just live a simpler life."

"At the expense of my career?" Marilyn counters. "Absolutely not."

He storms out one October night when she accuses him of "a lot of name-calling."

Marilyn wrestles with the differences between them. *Joe is always cool and practical. When I get excited over some magazine giving me a big picture spread, he grins and sneers a little.*

"Yes, but where's the money?" he asks.

"It's the publicity," I yell back.

"Money is better," he says in the quiet way men use when they think they have won an argument.

It's an impossible choice. *I didn't want to give up my career and that's what Joe wanted me to do most of all. He wanted me to be the beautiful ex-actress, just like he was the great former ballplayer. We were to ride into the sunset together. But I wasn't ready for that kind of journey. I wasn't even thirty, for heaven's sake.*

The uneasy feeling continues when they return to New York. At Toots Shor's, the food is "nuttin' fancy," though fame is very much on the menu. Everyone looks at Frank Sinatra, Jackie Gleason, Yogi Berra, Ernest Hemingway, and Joe DiMaggio, but no one bothers them. When a woman, even Marilyn, walks into the dining room, the maître d' looks right through her.

DiMaggio's been covering the 1952 Yankees as a guest analyst for PIX television. But as graceful as he was playing center field and running the bases, his color commentary is strained and awkward.

After his very first broadcast, DiMaggio telephoned Marilyn, asking for her impressions.

He's a really shy guy, she thought at the time. *That's why I have to be so careful what I say about him.*

As he continues to miss his cues and stumble over his words in postgame interviews, Marilyn tries to help. But he's not interested in the breathing techniques she's learned from Natasha Lytess and at the Actors Lab.

On September 2, three days ahead of the release of *Monkey Business,* Fox arranges for Marilyn to appear in Atlantic City,

New Jersey, as the 1952 Miss America Pageant Grand Marshal. Wearing a polka-dot day dress, she poses with representatives of the women's armed services.

Movietone News's segment "Beauties on Parade" shows her waving from the back of an open-topped convertible. She's wearing a gown the studio provided, a black-and-white chiffon number with deep V's cut in the front and back.

"We give you Marilyn Monroe," intones the voiceover. "The brightest star in the 1952 heavens. *Good heavens!*"

"People were staring down at me all day," she says to a journalist, "but I thought they were admiring my grand marshal's badge."

For her sexy glamour, Marilyn draws frequent comparisons with the Depression-era platinum-blond Jean Harlow, who cemented her stardom in a film titled *Blonde Bombshell.* Knowing how personal tidbits delight gossip columnists, Marilyn lets drop her preference for wearing "nothing, but nothing at all—no panties, slips, girdles or bras beneath my outerwear. I like to feel unhampered."

When he sees the photos, Joe DiMaggio telephones Marilyn. He's incensed at the display organized by Fox. "Show them nothing," he demands. "And wear your own goddamn clothes."

The truth is, she doesn't have many. *Niagara* director Henry Hathaway had initially asked Marilyn to wear her own clothes during some of the filming, until it was revealed she had nothing appropriate except some casual-wear and the black suit she'd purchased for Johnny Hyde's funeral.

DiMaggio flies to Los Angeles and takes her shopping on Rodeo Drive in Beverly Hills. The shop assistant averts her eyes at the glimpse of Miss Monroe changing behind the curtains with not a stitch of underclothes. She tries a few modest frocks, only to emerge in tight slacks and even tighter tops.

Why does she need all this attention? DiMaggio fumes.

Marilyn's rented house in West Hollywood is too accessible to photographers determined to snap her comings and goings, especially when she's with Joe. They find a new address — 2393 Castilian Drive — together.

The rental home in the Outpost Estates is nestled among the canyons of the Hollywood Hills. It's also a longer drive to the Fox lot, where in November she begins shooting her second picture directed by Howard Hawks, *Gentlemen Prefer Blondes*.

Hawks's interest lies in the comedic character of the work. He has no desire to shoot the song-and-dance numbers in the film adaptation of the book-turned-silent-film-turned-hit-Broadway-musical. Marilyn begins working with vocal coach Hal Schaefer in preparation for her solo number. Schaefer, also an accomplished jazz pianist and nightclub performer, gives her a 1950 Ella Fitzgerald record, *Ella Sings Gershwin*. Marilyn listens to it over and over again as a tutorial on musical phrasing.

Choreographer Jack Cole directs the dance numbers, rehearsing Marilyn for hours in "Diamonds Are a Girl's Best Friend," which Schaefer arranges. Marilyn practices "the hell out of it" with Cole's assistant, Gwen Verdon.

Marilyn and Jane Russell play Lorelei Lee and Dorothy Shaw, fast friends and showgirls. "Marilyn and I had never danced before; we were a pair of klutzes," Russell says. "Jack was horrible to his own dancers, but with us, the two broads, he had the patience of Job. He would show us and show us and then turn us over to Gwen."

Marilyn keeps going even when Russell is too exhausted to continue.

Life magazine reports from Stage 3 on the Fox lot:

> Marilyn sings and dances with a surprising technical competence. Full-fleshed and fancy-free, she and her dark-haired girlfriend, played by Jane Russell, start the show off with a bang in tight red dresses for the song "The Little Girl From Little Rock."...In her biggest number she spurns a whole panel of penniless and prostrate admirers and gives their fallen forms the benefit of her philosophy of life: "Diamonds Are a Girl's Best Friend."

Marilyn nearly wasn't even cast. It's her $18,000 rate that convinces producers to choose her over their top choice, Betty Grable, whose rate is $150,000. Russell earns $200,000 for her work—though Marilyn quickly proves that she is a true co-star. Though she does have to plead for her right to a dressing room. "Look, after all, I am the blonde, and it is *Gentlemen Prefer Blondes!*" she argues.

But the studio claims she's not a real star. "Well, whatever I am, I am the blonde!"

On set, Marilyn tells Howard Hawks that she's thought of a new line for the script: "I can be smart when it's important, but most men don't like it." The director adds it to her final scene in *Gentlemen Prefer Blondes.*

The shoot is set to wrap in January, but first there's Fox's annual holiday party to attend. She leaves the party late, dreading another lonely Christmas.

As she opens the door to her dark house, she gets a strange, fearful feeling. But when she flicks on a light switch, she sees her holiday dreams come true.

A huge Christmas tree covered in silver baubles is arranged on a stand. Propped up against it is a large handwritten cardboard sign.

MERRY CHRISTMAS TO MARILYN

Sitting on a chair in the corner, smoking a cigarette and nursing a bourbon and soda, is Joe DiMaggio.

"Oh Joe! Oh Joe!" She collapses on the floor at his feet. Hugging his knees, she looks up, her eyes full of tears. "You said you were spending the holidays in San Francisco with your family and now you are here! What a surprise!"

"Merry Christmas, my darling." He smiles at her and gently asks, "Why are you crying?"

"It's the first time anyone ever gave me a Christmas tree."

CHAPTER 29

MARILYN HAS EVERY INTENTION of dressing in the new clothes Joe DiMaggio's bought her, but in January 1953, the costumes Dorothy Jeakins designed for her role in *Niagara* become the talk of the film's successful release. One dress in particular—the fuchsia off-the-shoulder one from the party scene—dubbed "the Rose," is a sensation, and so is Marilyn for the alluring way she wears it.

MARILYN INHERITS HARLOW'S MANTLE runs the headline in the *New York World & Telegram,* where Erskine Johnson declares in his column: "Hollywood took 14 years, three-score screen tests and a couple of million dollars to find a successor to Jean Harlow."

In February, an offer from costume designer William Travilla proves too tempting to resist. The gold lamé dress with sunburst pleats he's created for *Gentlemen Prefer Blondes* can be hers to wear at the 1953 *Photoplay* Awards.

Film censors deem the garment—its plunging bustline secured solely with V-shaped iron bars—so risqué that it may be shown only from the back. The studio decides to let her wear it anyway, strategizing that Marilyn modeling the censored gown will help promote *Gentlemen Prefer Blondes* ahead of its August 1953 release.

By design, Marilyn must be sewn into the dress. To slim down, she undergoes two sessions of colonic irrigation. Joe DiMaggio complains that the dress "looks as if it has been painted on" and walks out of the fitting, suddenly called "to San Francisco on family business," Sid Skolsky explains in his column.

As Marilyn crosses the ballroom of the Beverly Hills Hotel wearing the golden gown to accept *Photoplay*'s New Star Award, she's also subjected to a spontaneous critique.

"She looks vulgar," hisses Joan Crawford, who's currently filming the MGM musical drama *Torch Song*, about a tough, unhappy Broadway star.

Crawford's jealous is the response that ripples through the audience. The gossip columnists play the moment for all it's worth.

"With one little twist of her derrière," one writes, "Marilyn stole the show. The assembled guests broke into wild applause. Two other screen stars, Joan Crawford and Lana Turner, got only casual attention. After Marilyn every other girl appeared dull by contrast."

Another likens the motion of her buttocks to "two puppies fighting under a silk sheet."

William Travilla designs over thirty gowns for the stylish comedy *How to Marry a Millionaire*, which co-stars Marilyn

Monroe, Lauren Bacall, and Betty Grable as three models who rent a luxury Manhattan apartment in order to attract wealthy husbands. Marilyn's costumes, for once, are relatively demure. "It was the first time that Marilyn was not self-consciously the sex symbol," screenwriter Nunnally Johnson says. "The character had a measure of modesty."

Shooting on location in New York City and Idaho in March and April 1953, Fox spares no expense on the first romantic comedy ever to be filmed with the CinemaScope lens billed as "the new miracle medium." Bacall, best known for her sultry noir performances with husband Humphrey Bogart, is returning to the screen after a three-year absence. She's been cast in her first comedic role, as the trio's unofficial leader, Schatze Page. Marilyn uses her gifts of physical comedy as the nearsighted Pola Debevoise, though the part she'd originally wanted was Loco Dempsey, which is played by Grable—whose hefty salary of $150,000 is three times what Bacall is earning, and in another stratosphere from Marilyn's $750 a week rate.

For more than a decade, Betty Grable has been Fox's top star—her legs famously insured by the studio for $1 million—but it's clear that Marilyn is gaining on her popularity. Tensions are expected on set, but Grable deftly defuses them.

"Honey, I've had mine. Go get yours. It's your turn now," she tells her nervous co-star. To United Press reporter Aline Mosby, Gable declares, "Marilyn's the biggest thing that's happened to Hollywood in years. The movies were just sort of going along, and all of a sudden—zowie!—there was Marilyn. She's a shot in the arm for Hollywood!"

The two develop a close friendship. Even Lauren Bacall, initially irritated by Marilyn's constant lateness, eventually sets it aside. "I couldn't dislike Marilyn. She had no meanness in her—no bitchery," says Bacall.

She takes Marilyn under her wing and advises her not to let the studios push her around. "I'm a little rebel too. And I know that when you stand up to them, the bastards back off." Marilyn in turn tells Bacall about how conflicted she feels between what she wants for her career versus for her home life.

"She came into my dressing room one day and said that what she really wanted was to be in San Francisco with Joe DiMaggio in some spaghetti joint," Bacall says. Marilyn asks a lot of questions about her co-stars' marriages and children. "She seemed envious of that aspect of my life—wistful—hoping to have it herself one day."

Romanian-born Jean Negulesco, known for his deft touch with the genre, is directing Marilyn for the first time. "When I started work with Marilyn, I realized she was one of the most atomic personalities ever to come out of Hollywood," he tells the *Los Angeles Times*. "But I was surprised to find how hard she worked and how much she wanted to give a good performance."

Natasha Lytess takes her usual place on set, but during the shoot, she gives an interview deeply critical of Marilyn. "She is not a natural actress. She has to learn to have a free voice and free body to act. Luckily Marilyn has a wonderful instinct for the right timing. I think she will eventually be a good actress."

Lytess suggests retake after retake, annoying the other actors and infuriating Negulesco. If he once again hears "Well, that was all right, dear, but maybe we should do it again one more time," *he* is leaving the film.

The director's dislike for the drama coach nearly matches Joe DiMaggio's. "Maybe I could get through to Marilyn if I didn't have this broad to deal with," DiMaggio tells a friend. "She's going to ruin her, I'm telling you."

Lytess likes DiMaggio even less. DiMaggio is "the punishment of God in your life," she tells Marilyn.

Yet when Lytess is dismissed from the picture, Marilyn protests by complaining of bronchitis and is a no-show on set. What begins as a lone act of defiance quickly becomes a pattern.

When Marilyn doesn't get her way, the studio doesn't get her performance. If she does show up, she arrives late and deliberately forgets or botches her lines, until she gets what *she* wants. She is beginning to realize that the studio needs her more than she needs the studio.

CHAPTER 30

GRACE MCKEE LIES in bed, dying of uterine cancer.

She's arrived at Unit 3 in the Doheny Apartments seeking Marilyn's help and a place to stay. McKee is a Christian Scientist who believes that prayer is a more effective healer than any medicine. She refuses to consider a hysterectomy that might save her life, but the pain has become so severe that she's willing to accept relief.

Painkillers, sleeping pills, uppers, downers, the apartment is awash with them. Some are prescribed to McKee by doctors. Others are procured from Schwab's by Sid Skolsky, whom Joe DiMaggio calls Marilyn's "pill-pal not pen-pal." Skolsky's column has made the place a top Hollywood destination, so he's allowed anything he wants.

What everyone wants in 1950s Hollywood is pills. Just as talkies replaced the silent era, marijuana and heroin have been pushed aside by the latest offerings from the pharmaceutical industry. Benzedrine, or "bennies," keep a person slim and alert. The perfect high of Dexedrine and Dexamyl is counteracted by sleep-inducing barbiturates, Seconal and Nembutal, or "yellow jackets."

Marilyn's bathroom cabinet is full of them. When, two or three times a week, she arrives at the studio to dress for an event, she slaps a plastic bag full of pills onto her dressing room table—uppers, downers, vitamins—no one is quite sure what cocktail of drugs the mixture contains.

McKee, who's struggled with alcoholism, is astonished by how many pills Marilyn takes and how often.

"Don't worry," Marilyn replies. "I have been taking them every day for years."

Marilyn Monroe and Jane Russell are standing in white rhinestone-encrusted dresses and high heels on the forecourt of Grauman's Chinese Theatre at 6925 Hollywood Boulevard. It's June 26, 1953, and the co-stars of *Gentlemen Prefer Blondes* are promoting the 20th Century-Fox musical comedy ahead of its August release.

An enthusiastic crowd has gathered to watch as the pair—Hollywood's "First Blonde" and "First Brunette," according to newsreels—place their hands and feet in wet cement.

Continuing the tradition that Grauman's began in the 1920s, the actresses make their hand- and footprints, then sign their names—Marilyn dotting the *i* in hers with a rhinestone—and scrawl *Gentlemen Prefer Blondes* across their adjoining squares.

Marilyn recalls going to Grauman's as a child. *I used to go to Grauman's Chinese Theatre and try to fit my foot in the prints in the cement there. And I'd say 'Oh, oh, my foot's too big. I guess that's out.' . . . When I finally put my foot down into that wet cement, I sure knew what it really meant to me, anything's possible, almost.*

"It's for all time, isn't it?" Marilyn observes.

"Yes," Russell replies. "It's for all time, or as long as the cement lasts."

Then the fun begins. Marilyn cheekily suggests that Jane, for whom Howard Hughes once designed a special bra, immortalize her bust in the cement, while she imprints her buttocks, famous for her wiggle walk in *Niagara,* on the slab.

It's only a joke. They don't go through with it. Marilyn's on enough of an emotional high. *This could be her life's proudest moment.*

But when she scans the crowd, looking for familiar faces, there are none. Joe has refused to attend. Jane Russell disappears with her husband and children, leaving Marilyn entirely alone.

Even the studio has abandoned her. They didn't even book her a car. If not for the kindness of her hairdresser, Gladys Whitten, Marilyn would have no way home.

CHAPTER 31

MARILYN PACKS HER BAGS for Alberta, Canada, where she'll spend August and September shooting a Western called *River of No Return*.

Though the Canadian Rockies are as pretty as a picture postcard, it's hardly her destination of choice. And she couldn't be less interested in the action-adventure genre, even if Fox has upped the budget to include CinemaScope and Technicolor. Marilyn is cast as Kay, a dance-hall singer who joins Matt, a widowed farmer played by Robert Mitchum, in a desperate, waterborne chase after Kay's villainous fiancé steals Matt's rifle and his only horse.

The director is Otto Preminger, known for *Laura*—a star turn for Gene Tierney and a hit for Fox—and his legendary tantrums. Dubbed "Otto the Terrible" and the "Mad Prussian," Preminger has one thing in common with Marilyn: their clashes with Darryl Zanuck.

The script includes four musical numbers. "Marilyn," Preminger says, "I don't mind you shaking your derriere and your shoulders in this scene, but you have to shake your VOICE, too!"

She does, singing the title song, "River of No Return," with a melancholy that brings the crew to tears.

But when Marilyn speaks her lines, Preminger becomes enraged. He can't stand her stilted, mannered enunciation, which is not at all in keeping with her role. Preminger blames Natasha Lytess and bans the acting coach from the set, only to have Marilyn insist to Darryl Zanuck that Lytess be reinstated.

Tensions rise further when Preminger orders Marilyn to do her own stunts. Forcing "our beautiful Marilyn" onto several local rivers is branded as sadism by the press. In scene after scene she tumbles into freezing torrents, submits to hammering blasts from a firehose, and navigates a log raft.

They're on the raft hurtling through white water when conditions become dangerous. The safety ropes around the raft break, unleashing the craft toward sharp rocks. The rescue boat starts toward them.

"You're sick, you shouldn't even be out here," Marilyn says to Mitchum, who's suffering from the flu. "I don't get off until you do."

"This could be a matter of life and death," Mitchum tells her. "In another three minutes, we're going to be over those rapids and cut into forty pieces."

"I still won't leave," she says.

They somehow complete the scene and safely return to shore.

The shoot presses forward. The treacherous river sequence culminates in the log raft plunging over Bow Falls in Banff National Park.

Mitchum thinks Marilyn has "the guts of a lion," but the director unleashes a string of scathing insults. "You are the most untalented actress I have ever worked with. You have no poise, no brain and no skills," he rants, as Marilyn, who's wearing hip-wader boots to protect her costume, trips and injures her left ankle.

The headlines shout, MARILYN MONROE NEARLY DROWNS. MISS MONROE INJURES LEG IN CANADA.

Joe DiMaggio comes running. So does John Vachon, a photographer for *Look* magazine, who snaps Marilyn in a black bikini, her arms resting on crutches, lower left leg in a light cast, right foot clad in a black high-heeled shoe.

She's given a few days off to heal. When not exercising her injured leg in the swimming pool, she and DiMaggio explore the jagged peaks, turquoise lakes, and woodlands forested with pine, fir, spruce, and aspen trees.

Against the backdrop of a snow-capped mountain vista, Vachon creates the first formal portrait of the couple. Happy smiles play across their faces.

Makeup artist Whitey Snyder knows better than anyone what hard work it is to be "Marilyn Monroe." Maybe Marilyn could take a break from all that work. She could marry "DiMag and raise lots of kids," Snyder suggests.

She replies, "I might just do that."

On September 28, 1953, Marilyn receives devastating news. Grace McKee has committed suicide. The cause of death is allegedly from an overdose of barbiturates.

Another of the few remaining ties to her past is gone.

Now there's her mother, Gladys, to consider.

Marilyn turns to her business manager, Inez Melson, who Joe DiMaggio had recommended. Melson took a maternal interest in Marilyn, and in 1952, Marilyn had appointed her the legal guardian of her own mother, Gladys Baker Eley.

Shortly after the news scandal that Marilyn was *not* orphaned, Gladys had been re-institutionalized—perhaps from the stress of the publicity. Melson sees to it that Gladys is placed in Rockhaven Sanitarium, a groundbreaking facility run by women, for women. That's where she'll get the best care.

Marilyn has Melson set up a trust fund to make sure of it. Though she avoids visiting Gladys, Melson does, and provides Marilyn with regular updates on her estranged mother.

"Celebrities and the man in the street crowd Hollywood's famous boulevard to the CinemaScope premiere of *How to Marry a Millionaire*," reports Movietone News from the Wilshire Theater.

On November 4, 1953, the decorative lights blinking on the Art Deco building are no match for the flashbulbs popping around a certain celebrity quartet.

Arm in arm are Marilyn's co-star Lauren Bacall; her husband, Oscar winner Humphrey Bogart; Nunnally Johnson, the producer and screenwriter; and Marilyn Monroe, who sparkles in a strapless white lace, sequin, and crepe de Chine gown, embellished by diamond chandelier earrings and a white ermine stole. Betty Grable, who's now officially parted with the studio despite having three years left on her contract, does not attend.

In all her finery, Marilyn makes time to wrap one opera-gloved arm around a young movie fan and give the astonished boy her widest smile.

"This is just about the happiest night of my life," Marilyn tells reporters. "It's like when I was a little girl and pretended wonderful things were happening to me. Now they are. But it's funny how success makes so many people hate you. I wish it wasn't that way. It would be wonderful to enjoy success without seeing envy in the eyes of everyone around you."

Photographers hoping for a shot of Joe DiMaggio are disappointed.

"He dislikes crowds and glamour," Marilyn says, explaining away his absence from yet another Hollywood event. To Sid Skolsky, she says, "All he does is watch TV night and day."

CHAPTER 32

TWENTY-SEVEN-YEAR-OLD CHICAGO ENTREPRENEUR Hugh Hefner's pulled a fast one. The first issue of his new magazine, *Playboy*, hits newsstands in December 1953 with a picture of Marilyn on the cover.

She didn't pose for that photo. It's a shot recycled from the 1952 Miss America Pageant parade where Marilyn served as Grand Marshal. And the cover line claiming the "FIRST TIME in any magazine FULL COLOR the famous MARILYN MONROE NUDE" refers to the two shots Tom Kelley took back in 1949 for the "Golden Dreams" pinup calendar. Hefner tracks them down and buys the rights to the whole calendar. "I discovered that the Marilyn Monroe calendar—which everyone had heard about but nobody had seen—was owned by the John Baumgarth Calendar Co. out on the West Side of Chicago, very close to where I had grown up," he says. "So I drove out to Chicago and talked to John Baumgarth, and I walked out of there with the rights to the Marilyn Monroe calendar and the color separations—all for five hundred dollars."

The Marilyn photos are a big chunk of his $8,000 budget, but an amazing payoff.

"She is natural sex personified. It is there in every look and movement. That's what makes her the most natural choice in the world for our very first *Playboy Sweetheart,*" the magazine proclaims.

The fifty-cent magazine quickly sells out its 70,000-copy run. Marilyn is paid nothing.

Yet Marilyn is starting to push back when she feels advantages are being taken. Twentieth Century-Fox tells her that her next picture will be *The Girl in Pink Tights,* a remake of the 1943 Betty Grable picture *Coney Island.*

MARILYN MONROE PLAYING TEACHER IN NEW MUSICAL, Erskine Johnson announces in his column.

But she refuses to be typecast as yet another "dumb blonde," especially when she learns that co-star Frank Sinatra's salary for *The Girl in Pink Tights* is to be $5,000 per week—more than three times her $1,500 rate.

She asks to see the script.

More difficult behavior from "Straw Head," Zanuck grouses, but he agrees to the contract player's bold request and sends her the script.

The role of Jenny, a prim schoolteacher turned burlesque dancer, is poorly written, banal, and foolish. Marilyn scribbles "TRASH" across the cover in bright red ink before hurling the script across the room. She refuses to play the part.

Joe DiMaggio is relieved. The studio has been exploiting Marilyn, and not just in business matters. Shots calculated to show her legs and her bust, both at the same time, are too risqué for his taste.

The Fox executives are furious. Last month, they success-fully launched *How to Marry a Millionaire.* She's a star. She's *their* star. They made her, and they demand their pound of crystal-clad flesh. Marilyn must take the part to fulfill her contract. She is *not* bigger than the studio. No one is bigger than the studio.

Work on *The Girl in Pink Tights* is to begin immediately upon completion of the retakes needed to complete *River of No Return.* On December 9, a letter goes out by registered mail to the Famous Artists Corporation, where Charles Feldman now represents Marilyn following the end of her contract with William Morris. "You are hereby notified and instructed to report immediately to the studio," it begins, rattling off a list of her contractual obligations.

She's a no-show.

"Marilyn Monroe is a stupid girl and is being fed some stupid advice" declares the *Hollywood Reporter.* The piece head-lined 20TH STANDS PAT ON MONROE characterizes "industry opinion" as the certainty that she's "picked herself a fight that she'll have a tough time winning."

Fox dangles a relatively unknown actress named Sheree North—a blonde with measurements identical to Marilyn's— as her replacement.

Marilyn won't relent. She has Joe DiMaggio's backing. And that's enough.

She spends Christmas 1953 in San Francisco with the DiMaggio family. After giving Marilyn a Maximilian "Black Mist" mink coat, Joe proposes to her—without an engagement ring.

The gesture is neither romantic nor passionate, tender nor

amorous. She's having trouble at work. He has a practical solution.

The couple has been "talking about getting married for some months," Marilyn says. "We knew it wouldn't be an easy marriage. On the other hand, we couldn't keep on going forever as a pair of cross-country lovers. It might begin to hurt both our careers." Marriage, they decide, is "the only solution to our problem. But we had left time and place in the air."

Rumors of a Las Vegas wedding now swirl.

At the city's Hotel El Rancho, the couple schedules a ceremony for January 4, 1954—then cancels it.

The press spiral into a frenzy. Their only lead, from one of DiMaggio's four sisters, is that the couple is on "a motor trip."

That same day, Fox officially suspends Marilyn.

On January 5, the *Los Angeles Times* speculates, "It could be that she was having so much fun up north with Joe DiMaggio, the former Yankee baseball star, that she simply didn't feel like coming back to work."

CHAPTER 33

"I MET HIM two years ago on a blind date in Los Angeles," Marilyn tells reporters, "and a couple of days ago we started talking about this."

She's climbing the steps of City Hall in San Francisco, answering questions from the pack of reporters who have finally tracked down the elusive celebrity couple on their actual wedding day, January 14, 1954.

They've had a little help.

Marilyn had called Fox Studio PR head Harry Brand. Clearly, the Fox press agent couldn't resist leaking the news. Or was it Sid Skolsky? Her good friend certainly deserved the scoop. When she couldn't reach him directly, she'd also left word with competing columnists Louella Parsons and Kendis Rochlen.

"All right, fellas," DiMaggio says, "I don't want to rush you, but we've got to get on with the ceremony."

He's brought six witnesses — brother Tom, Pacific Coast

League baseball manager Frank "Lefty" O'Doul, and business partner Reno Barsocchini, along with their wives—into Judge Charles S. Peery's City Hall chambers. Five hundred other people have also pushed their way inside the building.

"That's the problem with spontaneous weddings," Barsocchini grumbles as he stubs out his cigarette. "Nothing runs smoothly."

Marilyn clutches a bouquet of three fragile orchids as she stands in a demure brown suit with a white ermine collar, waiting for the chief clerk to find a typewriter.

"Okay, let's get this marriage going," declares DiMaggio, rubbing his hands together.

The clerk opens the window to let in some air, only to distract the judge with the excited chattering of the crowd below. Judge Peery hushes them just as Marilyn's sweet, breathy voice promises to "love, honor, and cherish" — "obey" being no longer fashionable in 1954—the baseball hero who's become *her* hero. She smiles as DiMaggio slips a family heirloom ring onto her finger. There's been no time to buy a new one.

They pose for a kiss in front of the judge's law books, then sign the register. Though DiMaggio gives his correct age of thirty-nine, Marilyn suddenly loses two years by stating that she's twenty-five.

Crowds milling in the corridors are blocking the exits. The couple rushes toward the real estate department. It's a dead end. Deploying a few sharp elbows, Joe's friends finally clear a path toward the elevator car.

At street level, an explosion of photographers' flashbulbs and reporters' questions awaits.

"Marilyn? Have you married your millionaire?"

"I have certainly married a brilliant baseballer and my sweetheart," she coos.

"Hey, Joe! What are you and Marilyn going to do next?"

When we got together in the bedroom, DiMaggio thinks, *it was like the gods were fighting; there were thunderclouds and lightning above us.* But that's private.

"Are you going to have children?"

"We expect to have one," replies DiMaggio.

"I'd like to have six," says Marilyn, who has a loving relationship with DiMaggio's young son Joey—in many ways, the twelve-year-old boy is closer to his new stepmother than his distant father.

"We've got to get going," Joe interrupts. "We've got to put a lot of miles behind us."

One last question. "Where are you going on your honeymoon?"

"North, south, west and east" is all Joe will say.

First, they go to church.

As a backdrop for their wedding photos, they've chosen the steps of Saints Peter and Paul Church in DiMaggio's native North Beach. It's a far cry from 1939, when twenty thousand fans turned out at the San Francisco cathedral, site of DiMaggio's first wedding.

Not only has the couple, both previously married and divorced, been denied a wedding in the Catholic Church, but DiMaggio's technically been excommunicated for marrying a second time. If he's bothered by the move, he shows no sign of it.

The press celebrates the "Romance of the Century" on front pages nationwide. MARILYN WEDS JOE IN FRISCO trumpets the

New York Daily News, captioning the front-page wedding photo DIMAGGIO SIGNS WITH A NEW MANAGER.

The *Los Angeles Herald & Express* gets clever, pairing the famous couple's "uniforms" — Marilyn's calendar girl "birthday suit" with DiMaggio's "baseball suit."

If only they had a better hideout than his dark blue convertible Cadillac. They drive south along US Highway 101 to the California central coast town of Paso Robles and pay $6.50 to check into the Clifton Motel for their wedding night.

"Oh, Joe," says Marilyn as they walk slowly to their bedroom. "Look at that." She still carries her wedding bouquet, now wilted. "They're all dead and broken." She turns to look at him, slipping her hand into his. "Promise me something."

"Anything."

"If I die before you, will you put fresh flowers on my grave, every week after I am gone? I would hate to lie there on my own, all cold and forgotten."

"I promise."

CHAPTER 34

FIFTEEN HOURS LATER, the newlyweds emerge.

They climb back into the Cadillac and continue driving south on US 101, stopping around 2 p.m. for lunch at the Motel Inn in San Luis Obispo.

A newsman from the local *Telegram-Tribune* is finishing his meal when the couple takes a corner table.

"You're kind of lost, aren't you?" he asks them. "Nobody seems to know where you are between here and San Francisco."

"No," DiMaggio says, "but it won't take them long to catch up."

The newsman calls in the chance celebrity sighting to his editor, who sends a photographer over to the Motel Inn.

The cameraman takes a sympathetic approach. "I would like to shoot your picture but I know you're on your honeymoon. You name it."

"My wife doesn't have any makeup. I'd really rather not,"

DiMaggio says, rejecting the photographer's idea to shoot Marilyn with her back to the camera.

"We've had so much of this," the new husband pleads. "I'll appreciate it very much if you don't shoot us at all."

Remembering the Yankee great as being generous and decent with the press, the photographer lowers his camera.

Two hundred miles to the south, 20th Century-Fox has issued a fresh round of stern correspondence with its star actress.

"You are hereby instructed to report…on January 25, 1954… for the purposes of rendering your services in connection with our motion picture tentatively entitled Pink Tights, in respect to which you have heretofore been assigned to portray the role of Jenny."

Mrs. Joe DiMaggio, now sporting a new platinum eternity band set with thirty-six baguette-cut diamonds, has other plans. As she told reporters outside San Francisco's City Hall yesterday, she's an actress who's "looking forward to being a housewife too."

At San Francisco International Airport, the B-377 Strato-cruiser, Pan American's "flying hotel," is preparing for its January 29 flight to Tokyo.

On the passenger list are Joe DiMaggio, Marilyn Monroe, and baseball ambassador Lefty O'Doul. Marilyn's never traveled as far as Japan, but DiMaggio has, in 1950 and 1951, as a member of Larry O'Doul's American exhibition team, the All-Stars. The baseball pros are embarking on a three-week junket for the Japanese professional baseball league, which will double as a honeymoon trip for Joe and Marilyn.

Marilyn arrives with a splint on her thumb. *What's happened to her hand?* Reporters' concerned whispers swell into pointed questions that Marilyn is finally forced to answer.

"I bumped it," she says, gingerly holding up her bandaged hand as she wraps her black fur coat more tightly around her. "I have a witness. Joe was there. He heard it crack."

"Joltin' Joe" doesn't know his own strength, she tells herself. He didn't mean to push her away as she came to hug him, interrupting a conversation with his friend George Solotaire, but the force had been powerful enough to break her thumb.

By the time the Stratocruiser touches down for a fueling stop in Honolulu a few hours later, thousands of fans on the tarmac are all screaming Marilyn's name.

"How are you, Marilyn?"

"Do you like Hawaii, Marilyn?"

"Are you happy to be here, Marilyn?"

"Are you pregnant, Marilyn?"

"Are you going to have a baby?"

The questions come thick and fast. The flashbulbs are blinding. She shields her eyes and smiles.

"What's next for you, Marilyn?"

"What are your plans?"

Though World War II tensions were not long past, DiMaggio had previously arrived in Tokyo every inch the living legend.

"That half a million Japanese turned out in Tokyo to shout 'banzai' for Joe DiMaggio and Lefty O'Doul," the *New York*

Times reported in 1951, "keeps up our hope for some eventual international understanding." A military band welcomed the baseball players with "The Stars and Stripes Forever."

By February 1, 1954, the tune has changed. It's Marilyn Monroe, Hollywood's sexy songstress, who's captivating global imagination.

On the descent into Tokyo, Major General Charles W. Christenberry poses an important question. "How would you like to entertain the soldiers in Korea?" American troops have been stationed in Seoul as part of a UN occupation force. Though the Korean War ended in July of 1953, the boys still stationed there could do with a morale boost.

"I'd like to," DiMaggio is quick to answer, "but I don't think I'll have time on this trip." He'd also missed the chance in 1951, when a delegation of O'Doul's All-Stars had visited troops serving at the Kumsong front, then an active war zone.

"I wasn't asking you, Mr. DiMaggio," Christenberry says. "My inquiry was directed at your wife."

Marilyn doesn't hesitate. "I'd love to do it." She pauses then and says, "What do you think, Joe?"

"Go ahead if you want," DiMaggio grins. "It's your honeymoon."

Cary Grant, Marilyn's co-star in *Monkey Business,* had written encouraging her to visit the soldiers if she had an opportunity. He and his wife Betsy had recently done so, and "in practically every ward Betsy and I visited you were, I am delighted to tell you, a happy and prevalent topic of conversation. 'Monkey Business' had just been shown over here and my principal claim to fame, and their interest, seemed to be in the fact that I had made a picture with you; it helped our conversation at each bedside immeasurably."

It's arranged that Marilyn will go to Korea for four days next week. First, she and her new husband visit Tokyo. But though her official Department of Defense ID is issued under the name "Mrs. Norma Jeane DiMaggio," it rankles her new husband that the press refers to him as "Mr. Marilyn Monroe."

In an open convertible thronged with adoring fans, the ten-mile drive from Tokyo's Haneda Airport to the Imperial Hotel takes six hours.

Hundreds of police link arms to stop the crowd surging forward with shouts of "Marilyn!" and "Mon-Chan!" (the Japanese word for "sweet little girl"). Some fall into the hotel fishpond, others jam its revolving door, and someone smashes a plate-glass window.

It's after 10 p.m., but the crowd refuses to disperse until Marilyn appears on the couple's hotel room balcony. She waves self-consciously, fighting the feeling that she was "a dictator."

At the promotional press conference for the baseball tour, the sports legend is once again overshadowed in favor of the white-hot film star.

"Marilyn! Marilyn!" reporters begin. "Is it true you don't wear underwear?"

"I'm planning to buy a kimono tomorrow," she says with a slight grimace.

"Marilyn! Do you sleep naked?"

"No comment," she replies.

"What kind of fur are you wearing right now?"

"Fox," she smiles. "And not the Twentieth Century kind."

Joe DiMaggio is the only person in the room not laughing at the disrespectful questions. Reporters have no questions for him. All the photographers have their lenses trained on Marilyn. Her new nickname, "Honorable Buttocks-Swinging Madam," makes the front pages, but not Joe's picture.

The attention is so intense that for the first week in Japan, they rarely leave the Imperial Hotel.

"No shopping, Marilyn," DiMaggio warns. "The crowds will kill us."

She accepts a Mikimoto "pearl necklace with a diamond clasp" from Emperor Hirohito and Empress Kojun, but when she does venture out to shop for a kimono, photographers angle their cameras up her skirt. Gossips speculate that it must be too cold in Japan for even the "Honorable Buttocks-Swinging Madam" to go without underclothes.

Luis Miranda is serving on a Korean army base when a helicopter touches down and out steps Marilyn Monroe. The dreary winter atmosphere changes in an instant when Monroe poses for a photo with him.

"To me she has a good personality," Miranda observes of the "happy lady" who "didn't mention anything about her private life — she was attending the troops."

From February 16 to 19, Marilyn tours Korea by plane and helicopter, performing ten shows and entertaining more than one hundred thousand soldiers and thirteen thousand marines. *Stars and Stripes* reports that fans wait for seven hours to claim front-row seats.

"Gosh, I've never seen so many men in my life," Marilyn says when she takes the stage, having changed out of her fur-collared flight jacket and combat boots into a sparkly purple cocktail dress and gold stiletto heels in the makeshift changing room draped with military canvas.

She's decided to sing "Diamonds Are a Girl's Best Friend," "Bye Bye Baby," and the Gershwin song "Do It Again."

One of the generals had questioned her choice of material. "It's too suggestive to sing to soldiers. You'll have to do a classy song instead."

"But 'Do It Again' is a classy song," Marilyn insisted. "It's a George Gershwin song!"

There was no use arguing about it, she realized. *I'd been up against this sort of thing before. People have a habit of looking at me as if I was some kind of a mirror instead of a person. They didn't see me, they saw their own lewd thoughts. Then they white-masked themselves by calling me the lewd one.*

"If I change the phrase 'do it again' to 'kiss me again,' will that be all right?"

The compromise is allowed. But she is warned, "Try not to put any suggestive meaning into it."

Many among the crowds are huddled in blankets, but they give her a warm welcome, their deafening applause punctuated by wolf whistles. In the biting cold, Marilyn sings and dances and blows kisses to the boys as she dances in high heels. The exhausted troops don't know what has hit them.

As they wave and cheer and shout her name at the top of their lungs, Marilyn glows with confidence. There's no critical acting coach, no demanding studio head, no grumpy husband. Just Marilyn. And just Marilyn, it turns out, is enough.

It has started snowing. But I felt as warm as if I were standing in a bright sun, she thinks. *I have always been frightened by an audience, any audience. My stomach pounds, my head gets dizzy, and I am sure that my voice has left me. But standing in the snowfall facing these yelling soldiers, I felt for the first time in my life no fear of anything. I felt only happy.*

"The sky kept lighting up from the constant flashing of bulbs as cameras clicked," writes one journalist at her show for the 7th Division, to the point that "the Reds probably thought the 7th Infantry Division was on night maneuvers."

Marilyn impresses her handlers with how open and easygoing she is. "She was unspoiled to the nth degree," says First Lieutenant George H. Waple III. "She gave us the feeling she really wanted to be there," says Ted Cieszynski, a photographer for the public information office of the Army Corps of Engineers. "She took her time, speaking with each of us about our families and our hometowns and our civilian jobs. It was bitter cold, but she was in no hurry to leave. Marilyn was a great entertainer. She made thousands of GIs feel she really cared."

Even after she spots a copy of her infamous "Golden Dreams" calendar, Marilyn's only response is "I'm very pleased to have my picture hanging in a place of honor."

Her visits are recorded and played on newsreels all over the world. The beautiful star, surrounded by our boys. "I'd say the highlight of my life has been playing for the soldiers," Marilyn says. "I stood out on an open stage and it was cold and snowy, but I swear it didn't feel a thing except good."

This is what I've always wanted, I guess. I never really felt like a star. Not really, not in my heart. I felt like one in Korea. It was so wonderful to look down and see all those young fellows smiling up at me. It made me feel wanted.

Just before climbing aboard a helicopter after her last performance, for the 45th Division, she waves and blows kisses to the audience. "This is my greatest experience with any kind of audience," she declares. "It's been the best thing that ever happened to me. I'll never forget my honeymoon—with the 45th Division."

She returns to the Imperial Hotel in Tokyo—and a cold welcome from her husband.

"Joe," she says, as she lies in bed, shivering with a chill that feels like the beginnings of the flu. "I can't tell you how wonderful it was. Have you heard such cheering? Tens of thousands." She smiles. "Have you ever heard such cheering, Joe?"

"Yes, I have," he replies curtly. "Seventy-five thousand at a time. Just miss the ball once and you'll see they can boo as loud as they cheer."

The bittersweet honeymoon ends on February 24, when the couple returns to Los Angeles and a rented house in Beverly Hills.

On March 7, at her first public appearance since marrying Joe, Marilyn arrives at the Beverly Hills Hotel on the arm of another man. Alan Ladd and Marilyn are the Gold Medal couple for the evening, as *Photoplay* magazine honors them as most popular actor and actress of the year.

Wearing a new platinum-blond hairstyle and a daringly low-cut white satin sheath with an ermine stole, Marilyn is a sensation.

MARILYN MONROE MOST POPULAR STAR, Movietone headlines its newsreel.

Joe DiMaggio, cast in the role of jealous husband, plays the part with feeling.

"It's no fun being married to an electric light," he complains.

CHAPTER 35

"MARILYN MONROE, RITA HAYWORTH, and Lana Turner all fired me on the same day," Charles Feldman jokes every chance he gets.

But with *The Girl in Pink Tights* shelved and the latest dustup with Fox archived in Hollywood's past, Feldman has found a new project.

Adapting the Broadway hit *The Seven Year Itch* for film is generating so much enthusiasm, Feldman tells Marilyn, that it's considered "a plum by every studio in the business."

Feldman's pitch to Darryl Zanuck is that he will produce, Billy Wilder will direct, and Marilyn will star for 20th Century-Fox.

On May 17, 1954, Feldman sends a letter addressed to Mr. and Mrs. Joe DiMaggio in Beverly Hills, California, updating them on the status of the negotiations.

Wilder, who won Oscars for directing and co-writing the screenplay for *The Lost Weekend,* lobbies Zanuck that Marilyn "is an absolute must for this story...nothing would make up for her personality."

Fox agrees to cast Marilyn in *The Seven Year Itch*. There's one catch—Marilyn must also join the ensemble cast of the Irving Berlin musical revue *There's No Business Like Show Business*.

It's a beautiful summer evening, the perfect occasion for Charles Feldman to put on one of the dinner parties he so enjoys hosting. Though Feldman and his MGM-starlet-wife Jean Howard divorced in 1947, they continue to host gatherings at their Coldwater Canyon house.

Tonight's guests are three newlywed couples. Marilyn and Joe DiMaggio live nearby at 508 North Palm Drive. British actor Peter Lawford and Patricia Kennedy Lawford, who married in April, have invited their houseguests, Pat's brother Jack Kennedy, a first-term US senator from Massachusetts, and his chic wife of less than a year, Jacqueline Bouvier Kennedy.

Jackie Kennedy dazzles in a cocktail dress with a triple strand of pearls around her neck. But they're nothing compared to the Mikimoto pearls with a diamond clasp that Marilyn was gifted by Japanese emperor Hirohito. When Marilyn arrives late, as usual, the commotion interrupts the conversation over hors d'oeuvres, screwdrivers, and champagne.

With her white dress and halo of white-blond hair, she glows like a comet hurtling across the cosmos. Jack Kennedy can't take his eyes off her.

"Senator," she coos, giving him her hand, which he holds for a little too long.

"Miss Monroe," he replies. "I believe we've met before."

"Mrs. DiMaggio," corrects Joe, standing protectively close to his wife.

Over an elegant multicourse dinner, Kennedy stares at Marilyn with an intensity that it's impossible for DiMaggio and Feldman to ignore, much less the new Mrs. Kennedy. The senator asks Marilyn about her film career and compliments the patriotism she showed in entertaining American troops in Korea.

"What a very brave woman you are, performing in front of so many men," he declares, refilling her champagne flute.

DiMaggio has had enough. "Let's go," he hisses in Marilyn's ear. "We're leaving."

"That would be rude. Anyway, I don't want to." She juts her chin out at him.

"I don't care what you want," he says.

He snatches her stole and they're out the door without saying good-bye to the others.

Marilyn later calls her old friend Bob Slatzer in Ohio and tells him about the dinner party with Jack Kennedy.

"I may be flattering myself," she says, "but he couldn't take his eyes off me."

Could it be that she felt something more?

CHAPTER 36

ON STAGE 9 at the Fox lot, the summer 1954 production of *There's No Business Like Show Business* is running late and over budget.

Marilyn plays Vicky Parker, a hatcheck girl whose aspirations for a career on the stage ignite when she meets Tim Donahue and convinces him to break away from his family vaudeville act, the Five Donahues, so that the couple can perform a show on their own.

Fox is spending big on this first romantic comedy to be filmed in both CinemaScope and DeLuxe color, with a screenplay by Phoebe and Henry Ephron, costumes by William Travilla, and Ethel Merman, Donald O'Connor, and Mitzi Gaynor among the accomplished cast.

But Marilyn may have contracted influenza, or possibly even pneumonia, while performing outdoors in Korea, and is now fighting bronchitis. She arrives to set late, so sluggish from the effects of sleeping pills that she can barely remember her lines.

Travilla, who's worked with Marilyn on numerous pictures,

declares his designs "an act of love" for her. Yet even Travilla's dazzling array of jewels and furs, exquisitely tailored day dresses and spangled showgirl garb, can't disguise Marilyn's mounting anxiety. After every take, she looks to the wings, where only the black-clad Natasha Lytess seems capable of coaxing a performance from the ailing star.

Walter Lang, an accomplished director of musical motion pictures, sets up a sequence that requires three pages of the script to be filmed in a single take. Hair and makeup and wardrobe have been preparing since 4 a.m. Hundreds of extras are on standby, a jazz band poised to play.

Marilyn has one line, which she fluffs. Repeatedly.

To break the mounting tension, Lang announces they'll wrap the scene without her.

Shaking with tears of humiliation, Marilyn takes refuge in her dressing room.

Travilla rushes after her, discovering Marilyn sitting in front of the mirror, crying at her own reflection.

"Don't worry," he says. "It happens to the best of us."

"Oh, Billy!" she howls, tears flowing down her pale cheeks. "I'm losing a piece of my mind each day. My brains are leaving me. I think I'm going crazy, and I don't want to be seen this way. If I go crazy, please take me away and hide me. I don't want to be locked up like my mother."

"You're talking yourself into the idea of being mad. Don't be crazy!" he laughs.

"I am crazy!"

Her lack of sleep is taking its toll. After Joe DiMaggio goes to sleep, she calls friends, hoping someone, anyone, will pick up at one or two o'clock in the morning.

It's often Natasha Lytess on the other end of the line, but one night Marilyn reaches Brad Dexter, a fellow cast member from *Asphalt Jungle*. "I'm extremely unhappy," she tells him. "I married Joe with love. I thought I was going to have a good life. I thought we were going to have a decent marriage. I thought we were going to have a relationship as a husband and as a wife. And all the things that are entailed in a good marriage. And I've discovered that the man is absolutely obsessed with jealousy and possessiveness...He doesn't want to know about my business. He doesn't want to know about my work as an actress. He doesn't want me to associate with any of my friends. He wants to cut me off completely from my whole world of motion pictures, friends, and creative people that I know."

The arguments with DiMaggio are becoming angrier, more physically intense, as his dream of making her a dutiful housewife dies by the day.

Even DiMaggio's good friend George Solotaire can see that his pal fundamentally misunderstands his new bride. "Like, here's this young, beautiful woman on the verge of becoming one of the most successful and famous actresses in the world, and she's going to give it all up to make lasagna for Joe and spend her days changing diapers?"

On set, Whitey Snyder hovers over her, covering up bruises on her arms and shoulders, though never on her face.

Fox executives are only interested in the PR opportunities the superstar marriage affords. "We haven't lost a star, we've gained a center fielder," one said after Marilyn's City Hall wedding, and the studio is holding that line.

Except the center fielder loathes the star's playbook. He complains that "she brings out the worst in him," that "she's spoiled and self-centered," and he's fed up with "coddling her" and listening to her "woe-is-me stories."

One afternoon in Marilyn's dressing room, Lytess confronts DiMaggio. Their mutual dislike has only intensified since the wedding. But when the acting coach suggests that divorce might be the best option, DiMaggio shouts in her face, "Hell if I'm letting her go."

He's never enjoyed watching Marilyn perform for the camera, but on August 27, the studio convinces him to attend the production of "Heat Wave," one of the dance numbers in *There's No Business Like Show Business*.

"We're having a heat wave" — Marilyn sings Irving Berlin's lyrics as male dancers carry her onto the stage in a litter festooned with flowers and bird cages. "The temperature's rising, it isn't surprising."

She is dressed in a black bikini embellished with sequins, along with a black-and-white palm print flamenco skirt slit up the front to reveal tiers of pink ruffles on the inside. She also wears a floppy white straw hat bedecked with flowers. It's costume designer Billy Travilla's nod to Spain, but DiMaggio cares nothing for artistic authenticity.

When, between takes, Marilyn rushes over to embrace him, he recoils with revulsion, his rejection so complete that she is unable to continue. She's lost the music and the lyrics and the dance beat. While she takes a break in the makeup chair, he storms off set.

In another stage on the Fox lot, the production of *Désirée* is wrapping ahead of its November release. Marlon Brando, who's generating Oscar buzz for his star turn in this summer's *On the Waterfront,* is playing Napoleon.

Marilyn doesn't know Brando well, but when he sees a bruise on her arm, he asks, "What's happened? That looks painful."

She laughs and runs her hands through her hair. "Can you believe I bit myself in my sleep?"

"No, I can't," he replies, shaking his head. "I'm afraid I don't believe that at all."

On September 1, 1954, *The Seven Year Itch* begins filming in New York City.

Darryl Zanuck has authorized a two-month shoot and is pleased with the initial rushes. He telegrams Marilyn's agent, Charles Feldman, who's also producing the film: "Monroe was particularly outstanding. Keep up the tempo of the dialogue...I'm really impressed by everything I saw."

Working with Tom Ewell, who's reprising his Broadway role of Richard Sherman, and Marilyn as "The Girl," director and screenwriter Billy Wilder amplifies the sexual energy of this screwball comedy about a bookish married man who becomes infatuated by his beautiful upstairs neighbor.

In the predawn hours of September 15, the movie crew gathers at the corner of 52nd Street and Lexington Avenue to film a scene described in the script as the "flying-skirt sequence."

To create excitement for the movie, word has gone out to hundreds of press and public to come witness the scene being shot.

Joe DiMaggio doesn't plan to be among them. He'd rather go for a couple of drinks at the hotel bar with his friend George Solotaire while Marilyn works. "It would make her nervous, and it would make me nervous, too," he tells reporter Walter Winchell.

"Oh, come on, Joe. You have to be there. It might make some copy for me," the newsman wheedles.

The scene they walk into is mayhem. The two co-stars are meant to be walking out of a movie theater during a heat wave, but the crowd's raucous enthusiasm keeps drowning out the actors' lines.

"Ooh, can you feel the breeze from the subway?" Marilyn's character asks Ewell. "Isn't it delicious?"

"Sort of cools the ankles, doesn't it?" Ewell answers, while visibly admiring her legs.

They're standing on a subway grate. Air is forced from below to simulate a passing train, blowing the skirt of Marilyn's white halter-neck dress up over her knees, over her thighs, over her hips, even over her head.

Billy Wilder intends the scene as a sight gag, and Marilyn plays it to comedic perfection.

The action is captured by the film cameras and by Sam Shaw, Fox's special still photographer on set. Shaw, who previously met Marilyn on the Fox lot — on the set of the 1952 Fox film *Viva Zapata!* starring Marlon Brando and directed by Elia Kazan — makes a daring pitch to the studio. *Promote the film using stills of Marilyn in her levitating skirt.*

Marilyn, who typically wears no underclothing, tonight dons two pairs of white underpants beneath her billowing skirt. But even that's not enough to protect her modesty in the glare of the set lights and the flashbulbs, which reveal more than she intends — and more than her husband can stand.

DiMaggio is incandescent with rage. "What the hell is going on here?" he demands as the crowd chants "More!" and "Higher!"

He barrels off the set and back to the hotel bar.

That night at the St. Regis, he erupts. The argument is so intense and prolonged that the shouting, the screaming, and the thudding of thrown objects is overheard by cast and crew also staying at the hotel.

Marilyn turns up on set the following morning, hurting and humiliated. Her back and shoulders are covered with bruises that the hair and makeup department work to cover up.

"Exposing my legs and thighs, even my crotch — he said that was the last straw," Marilyn says. His behavior is the last straw for her as well.

Marilyn tells her hairdresser Sydney Guilaroff that when DiMaggio first got rough with her, she'd told him, "Don't ever do that again. I was abused as a child, and I'm not going to stand for it."

So that night at the St. Regis, she informs Guilaroff, "Joe slapped me around the hotel room until I screamed, 'That's it!' You know, Sydney, the first time a man beats you up, it makes you angry. When it happens a second time, you'd have to be crazy to stay. So I left him."

CHAPTER 37

FOX PRESS AGENT Harry Brand is the first to know.

Marilyn calls Brand in tears, saying that her marriage of less than nine months is over. Within minutes, a press release citing "conflicting demands of their careers" goes out to the newspapers and the all-powerful gossip columnists.

On October 4, 1954, United Press reports: "Marilyn Monroe revealed today that she will file suit to divorce baseball great Joe DiMaggio tomorrow, and her attorney reluctantly agreed: 'Joe has struck out.'"

Her charge is "mental cruelty."

When the couple wed on January 14, Louella Parsons had made a stern prediction. "They must resign themselves to the fact that it can't ever be a completely normal union," Parsons wrote in her influential column. "Marilyn will remain in show business and Joe will not be able to take it."

Marilyn denied the claim, saying, "It's not like I'm giving up my career. I'm simply starting a new one."

"There is no other man," Sid Skolsky reports in his column.

DiMaggio isn't convinced. He's going to have her investigated.

"Shock waves swept round the world," the *New York Mirror* emotes. MARILYN TELLS JOE: YOU'RE OUT AT HOME the *Chicago Sun-Times* cries.

Now what? To find out, nearly a hundred reporters descend on the front lawn of 508 North Palm Drive.

Marilyn's lawyer, Jerry Giesler, spins an unlikely domestic scene. His client is sick "with a virus" and her soon-to-be-ex is at her bedside, having "brewed a pot of soup for his ailing wife."

Two days later, Giesler orchestrates what the Associated Press describes as "an exit worthy of an Academy Award." Joe emerges first, bags packed. With a terse announcement that he's heading "home" to San Francisco, he drives away in his dark blue Cadillac.

Then it's Marilyn, walking between Giesler and Harry Brand. "Miss Monroe has nothing to say to you this morning," Giesler dismisses the press, thinking, *The girl is only twenty-eight years old. How much longer can she endure this life?*

At least until tomorrow, when Marilyn is due back on set to continue principal photography for *The Seven Year Itch*. After all DiMaggio's outrage, the flying-skirt footage from New York is unusable. It will have to be reshot on the Fox lot, away from noisy crowds.

"The show must go on," the Fox press office insists.

"Why?" asks a reporter. "Why now?"

"We're fifty thousand dollars and three days behind production on the picture already."

CHAPTER 38

DARRYL ZANUCK AND Charles Feldman exchange rapid-fire set memos.

On October 22, 1954, Feldman lobbies for his client. For context, he compares Marilyn's recent work on *The Seven Year Itch* with what he experienced on *A Streetcar Named Desire,* the 1951 picture he produced for Warner Bros.

"There have been tough days—immediately after the divorce proceedings, the 18-takes have only happened on rare occasions with the girl... for the last two weeks this girl has worked as hard as anyone I have known in my life. Incidentally I don't know how Kazan worked with you but I can tell you that on STREETCAR, it was a daily occurrence for us to have 25 to 30 takes with Brando and Vivien Leigh. This has not been happening on ITCH."

Still, the Fox studio head finds fault. Production costs are mounting. Director Billy Wilder needs to film scenes more quickly. Marilyn needs to stop rehearsing on the studio's time.

*   *   *

On October 27, Marilyn enters the Santa Monica Superior Court and delivers harrowing testimony before a packed gallery and Judge Orlando Rhodes, who is presiding over her appeal for a divorce from Joe DiMaggio.

She's lived every line she speaks, frequently breaking down in tears as she chronicles her heartbreak, the long stretches where her husband refused to talk to her, his relentlessly critical attitude, his refusal to allow visits from her friends.

"I hoped to have out of my marriage love, warmth, affection and understanding," she tells the judge, "but the relationship was one of coldness and indifference."

A corroborating witness is Inez Melson, the business manager whom Marilyn has entrusted with sensitive personal matters, including her mother's care.

"Don't bother me," Melson recalls Joe DiMaggio saying when Marilyn tried to shower him with affection.

After fifteen minutes of testimony, Judge Rhodes grants the divorce.

Marilyn is powerless to restrain her sobs as she exits the proceedings into a barrage of press. The cameras capture her funereal black suit with its glamorous plunging neckline and open collar—and her flowing tears.

"I'm sorry. I can't say anything. I'm so sorry," she pleads to reporters clamoring for her comment.

The divorce headlines have Joe DiMaggio commiserating with his pal Frank Sinatra, who is going through a second divorce of his own. Sinatra's second wife—Ava Gardner, an actress known for her green eyes, auburn hair, and femme fatale roles—had filed for divorce in June.

The Italian American icons have been close since wartime, when DiMaggio's Sicilian immigrant parents were declared enemy aliens out of fear for Italy's role in the Axis alliance.

On November 5, 1954, a week after the divorce is granted, Sinatra and DiMaggio meet for dinner at the Villa Capri in Hollywood.

When DiMaggio spots actor Brad Dexter, he pleads with Marilyn's co-star from *Asphalt Jungle* to speak with her on his behalf.

Dexter places the call immediately, from the restaurant kitchen, and tells Marilyn who he's with and why he's calling. "Joe realizes that he's made a terrible mistake in how he's handled himself in his marriage with you. And he'd like very, very much to be able to pick up again and get together with you and maybe you could reconstitute your marriage."

Marilyn listens quietly, then says, "Brad, I don't want to talk to him. I absolutely don't want to have any communication with him at all. I've had it and this is it."

Dexter hangs up, then delivers the bad news. "Joe, she does not want to talk to you or have anything to do with you."

Devastated, DiMaggio returns to the dining room. Not long after, an urgent call comes for him. It's not from Marilyn, but it is about her.

Barney Ruditsky—a private investigator DiMaggio had hired to tail Marilyn in search of evidence in the divorce case—is still on the job. The legendary Prohibition-era former NYPD detective has impressed both Sinatra and DiMaggio with his Hollywood résumé: consultant on crime and police pictures; undercover debt collector for the late Bugsy Siegel; co-owner of Sherry's Restaurant, where "big names of gangland" congregate on the Sunset Strip.

Ruditsky alerts DiMaggio that he's spotted Marilyn entering an apartment house on Kilkea Drive and Waring Avenue. Could she be with Hal Schaefer, her confidant and vocal coach on *Gentlemen Prefer Blondes*? There have been rumors that the two have become close after working together again on *There's No Business Like Show Business.*

DiMaggio and Sinatra down their drinks and mount a search party.

As it happens, Marilyn and Schaefer *are* together. Half-dressed, Marilyn feels some warning "vibrations" compelling her to look outside. She and Schaefer spot a half dozen men approaching, DiMaggio and Sinatra among them.

They scramble out the back way to terrifying sounds of a forceful break-in and a woman's screams.

Ruditsky had zeroed in on the right address but the wrong apartment. The woman discovered in bed—alone—is Mrs. Florence Kotz Ross.

The *Los Angeles Times* reports: "Mrs. Ross was fast asleep about 11 p.m. when five or six men suddenly battered down the back door to her apartment, tearing it from its hinges and leaving glass strewn on the floor...A bright flash of light was shone in her eyes and she was confronted with a number of men, some of whom seemed to be carrying an instrument which at first sight she believed to be an ax."

Once she recovers from her fright, Ross threatens to sue.

For Marilyn, the incident is all of a piece with her mounting frustrations. She's fed up with the lot of them. Joe. The studio. Everyone.

Marilyn has become accustomed to the barbed tongues of film critics, but the way they single her out of the ensemble cast for *There's No Business Like Show Business* feels like a stinging rebuke. Her "wriggling and squirming... are embarrassing to behold," says the *New York Times*. With a wink and a nudge, *Time* magazine wagers that she "bumps and grinds as expressively as the law will allow."

Marilyn makes a decision. "Now I want to be an artist. I want to be a real actress."

She tells Fox that she wants to expand into dramatic roles, maybe an adaptation of a Dostoyevsky novel like *The Brothers Karamazov*. Instead, they've commissioned Nunnally Johnson, producer and screenwriter of *How to Marry a Millionaire*, to direct her in his latest screenplay, *How to Be Very, Very Popular*.

What Fox sees as a "high-class screenplay" Marilyn dismisses as yet another "sex role." She's under contract until 1958, but terms are dangled. If she takes the new part, the studio will pay her a $100,000 bonus for her work on *The Seven Year Itch*. If she doesn't, they'll suspend her. Again.

Nothing is resolved. Still, the Fox wardrobe department outfits her in a strapless, backless gown of red ruched chiffon to wear to Romanoff's on November 6, where Charles Feldman and Billy Wilder are throwing the *Seven Year Itch* wrap party.

Marilyn's car runs out of gas on her way to Rodeo Drive, so when she arrives late, she's surprised to find eighty of Hollywood's most famous names among the attendees of the formal dinner in her honor.

She's even more astonished when Clark Gable appears before her and asks her to dance. Meeting the "King of Hollywood" is like a dream. The eyes, the debonair mustache. Just like the photograph of her father.

The Seven Year Itch set photographer Sam Shaw captures the moment as they float around the room.

Marilyn dances with her co-star, Tom Ewell, her agent and producer, Charles Feldman, and even studio head Darryl Zanuck—and has a second dance with Gable.

Humphrey Bogart tops up her champagne flute.

"I feel like Cinderella," Marilyn says.

With the great and the good here to applaud her, she has at last been accepted into the highest echelons of Hollywood.

The spell breaks at 1 a.m., when Feldman sees her home.

A few days later, Gable sends Marilyn an enormous floral arrangement, stem after stem of red roses.

CHAPTER 39

FOR CHRISTMAS 1954, Marilyn gives herself a new identity. "Zelda Zonk" wears a black wig and dark glasses. And she has a one-way ticket to New York City.

It's not until the plane is airborne that she removes her Ray-Ban Wayfarers and shakes her blond curls free from the wig that's kept them under wraps.

She's successfully evaded the press all the way to the airport—unlike last month, at Cedars of Lebanon Hospital, where she had been in-patient for a week after undergoing surgery for endometriosis. Though a nurse had tried to help her sneak out a back exit, hundreds of reporters and photographers were there to snap photos of her looking pale and ill, and covering herself in a long mink coat.

On board the last flight out of Los Angeles, she's sleepless with nervousness and excitement. From her window seat, she stares out at the dark sky, trying not to bite her nails any shorter than they already are. At age nineteen, she'd set her sights on a career in Hollywood. Nine years later, she's fleeing its corrupt dream factory.

There is no one to keep her here any longer. Her marriage to Joe DiMaggio is over. The studio system is suffocating her. Aunt Ana is dead. So is Grace McKee. Her mother's weekly letters contain a string of impossible demands. That Gladys be released from the sanitarium. That Marilyn return to God and to the Christian Science faith.

The last time she reinvented herself, Norma Jeane became Marilyn Monroe.

This sad bitter child who grew up too fast is hardly ever out of my heart, she thinks. *With success all around me, I can still feel her frightened eyes looking out of mine. She keeps saying, "I never lived. I was never loved."*

MARILYN HAS LEFT HOLLYWOOD, newspaper headlines venture, then ask, "Where's Marilyn?" Darryl Zanuck can't answer that question. Neither can Charles Feldman or Sid Skolsky.

Marilyn tells almost no one of the secret project she's hatched with fashion photographer Milton Greene, drawing up the papers with a New York lawyer. She's creating her own production company, Marilyn Monroe Productions, Inc. She'll be president, and Greene will be vice president.

She met Greene a little over a year ago, when he was assigned to photograph her for a September 1953 *Look* magazine cover story. Marilyn had greeted the youthful-looking thirty-one-year-old, "Why you're just a boy!"

"And you're just a girl!" Greene answered right back.

Their fast friendship led to an intimate creative partnership. Two months ago, in October 1954, Marilyn posed in Greene's

New York photography studio for the "Ballerina Sitting" series, barefoot in a white tulle and satin gown.

Now Greene and his wife, Amy, pick Marilyn up from New York's Idlewild Airport and drive her into an unfamiliar landscape. She presses her face against the windowpane, staring at the snow-covered fields and the bare, frosted trees of Fairfield County, Connecticut, where the Greenes live in an eighteenth-century farmhouse in rural Weston.

She spends the holidays in their rambling bohemian farmhouse, helping trim the Christmas tree and meeting the Greenes' artistic friends. Among their sharp crowd are dancer Gene Kelly, star of films like *Singin' in the Rain* and most recently *Brigadoon;* composer Leonard Bernstein and his actress wife, Felicia; and novelist and screenwriter Truman Capote, whom Marilyn previously met on the set of *The Asphalt Jungle.* She listens to them gossip about unfamiliar ideas and people, then steals away to the Greenes' library to educate herself.

Amy Greene—a former model for Saks Fifth Avenue—helps Marilyn create a New York look, enlisting her friend the designer Anne Klein.

"Come get what you want," Klein says of her new capsule collection of black dresses in slip and sheath cuts.

Marilyn still insists on bleaching her own hair, but she begins wearing clothes with more forgiving lines and much less makeup, forgoing her signature red lipstick. Before stepping out, she dons one of Klein's simple black slip dresses and a tight black cap that covers her curls.

Back in Los Angeles, the lawyers are still arguing. It's like *The Girl in Pink Tights* all over again. Marilyn is in breach of

her contract. She can't just walk out and abandon her obligations. There's a script and a film to be made.

The plans for Marilyn Monroe Productions, Inc., are finalized on December 31, 1954. With characteristic misspellings,
she writes out her resolutions for 1955:

> *Must have the disipline to do the following—*
> *z—go to class—my own always—without fail*
> *x—go as often as possible to observe Strassberg's other*
>   *private classes*
> *g—never miss actor's studio sessions*
> *v—work whenever possible—on class assignments—*
>   *and always keep working on the acting exercises*
> *u—start attending Clurman lectures—also Lee Strass-*
>   *berg's directors lectures at theater wing—enquire*
>   *about both*
> *l—keep looking around me—only much more so—*
>   *observing—but not only myself but others and*
>   *everything—take things (it) for what they (it's) are*
>   *worth*
> *y—must make strong effort to work on current problems*
>   *and phobias that out of my past has arisen—making*
>   *much much much more more more more more effort*
>   *in my analisis. And be there always on time—no*
>   *excuses for being ever late.*
> *w—if possible—take at least one class at university—in*
>   *literature—*
> *o—follow RCA thing through.*
> *p—try to find someone to take dancing from—body*
>   *work (creative)*

t — take care of my instrument — personally & bodily
(exercise) try to enjoy myself when I can — I'll be
miserable enough as it is.

She takes up residence at the Gladstone Hotel on Park Avenue in New York. On January 7, Marilyn calls a momentous press conference. She's announcing her new role: as president of her very own company.

"I feel wonderful! I'm incorporated!" she declares. Sipping a glass of sherry, Marilyn signals her newfound self-worth. Single. Free. In control.

"I am going to do some pictures and TV and things," she says. "I want to expand, to get into other fields, to broaden my scope...People have scope, you know, they really do."

What kind of scope is she thinking?

"Strong dramatic parts," she states. "Like Grushenka, in *The Brothers Karamazov*...I don't know how to spell it. I only hope I can act in it."

Three times a week, Marilyn studies craft at the Actors Studio.

In 1947, her friend Elia Kazan and others affiliated with Konstantin Stanislavski's Group Theatre had founded a new artistic home here in New York. Membership to the Actors Studio is granted only by audition, but Artistic Director Lee Strasberg bends the rules and permits Marilyn to observe.

He does insist that she undergo psychoanalysis. Key to Method acting, known simply as the Method, is an actor's using her own emotions. Milton Greene recommends his own

Upper East Side analyst, Dr. Margaret Hohenberg. Marilyn begins attending five sessions a week, hoping to unblock what she's holding inside herself via Freudian techniques.

Of the intensive therapy, Strasberg says, "Do this and you'll feel something."

Marilyn's association with the Actors Studio brings it nearly as much attention as two films from last March that featured Studio members like Sidney Poitier and Elia Kazan. In *Blackboard Jungle,* Poitier plays a rebellious teen whose life is changed by his teacher. And founder Kazan's adaptation of John Steinbeck's bestselling novel *East of Eden* features a performance by newcomer James Dean that's already drawing comparisons to Studio mainstay Marlon Brando.

Kazan recently directed Brando in *On the Waterfront,* for which he's garnered a Best Actor Academy Award nomination. That ceremony will take place in Los Angeles on March 30, but first he'll be attending the *East of Eden* world premiere at New York's Astor Theatre on March 9.

When word gets out that Brando and Marilyn will serve as celebrity ushers, the event instantly sells out. Ticket sales are to benefit the not-for-profit Actors Studio and its new venue — a former church building on West 44th Street. Marilyn's fans snap up tickets for three times their face value. Unfortunately for Lee Strasberg, the take won't include scalpers' profits.

She arrives at the theater in full Hollywood regalia — an off-the-shoulder gown in biscuit-colored brocade, opera gloves, and a white ermine wrap.

One of the ticket holders is Arthur Miller. The longing that kindled back in 1951 has quickly ignited into a passionate love affair. A daring, secret one. They check into hotels as "Mr. and Mrs. A Miller," noting the expense as "for meeting held at suite with De Laurentis and MCA officials from time to time."

The playwright attends the *East of Eden* premiere with his sister, not his wife. *I no longer knew what I wanted,* Miller's told himself, *certainly not the end of my marriage, but the thought of putting Marilyn out of my life was unbearable.*

After the premiere, Miller is followed going to Marilyn's hotel. Gossip columnist Walter Winchell breaks the story — "America's best-known blonde moving picture star is now dating the darling of the pro-left Intelligentsia" — all but spelling out Winchell's allegiances to FBI Director J. Edgar Hoover and anti-Communism crusading senator Joseph McCarthy.

Hoover first started a file on Miller in 1944, closely timed to the opening of Miller's first Broadway play, *The Man Who Had All the Luck.* The bureau deemed his entire résumé suspicious. His years in the mid-1930s as a student-journalist-turned-playwright at the University of Michigan. His support of the 1938 American Relief Ship for Spain to supply anti-fascist rebels during the Spanish Civil War. His exemption from World War II service due to a knee injury sustained playing high school football. His opposition to nuclear weapons and affiliation with the American Labor Party, which the FBI deemed "a communist front."

The couple takes to meeting in remote corners of New York City. With Marilyn dressed plainly, they bicycle in Coney Island, walk in Battery Park, or attend poetry readings hosted by Norman and Hedda Rosten.

In an interview with NBC, Marilyn reveals only that she's

"fallen in love with Brooklyn," that she enjoys "almost every-thing" about the borough. "I just like walking around," she says. "The people and the streets and the atmosphere, I just like it."

Author Truman Capote, who at age seventeen had a job at *The New Yorker* magazine and who published his first novel, *Other Voices, Other Rooms,* at twenty-three in 1948, quickly sweeps his friend Marilyn into his New York social circle. On March 24, the pair is photographed dancing at the El Morocco club. Marilyn, in the black slip dress that's become her signa-ture New York attire, throws off her high heels so that she doesn't tower over her diminutive partner.

Capote introduces her to seventy-seven-year-old Constance Collier, famed acting coach to Katharine Hepburn, Vivien Leigh, and Audrey Hepburn. Marilyn becomes Collier's new-est pupil, one she affectionately calls "my special problem."

Their sessions are nothing short of astonishing. "I suppose people would chuckle at the notion, but really, she could be the most exquisite Ophelia," Collier tells Capote. "What she has—this presence, this luminosity, this flickering intelligence—could never surface on the stage. It's so fragile and subtle, it can only be caught by the camera. It's like a hummingbird in flight: only a camera can freeze the poetry of it. But anyone who thinks this girl is simply another Harlow or harlot or whatever is mad."

Collier recognizes that Marilyn's gifts are fragile, and so is she.

"Somehow I don't think she'll make old bones," the acting coach confides. "Absurd of me to say, but somehow I feel she'll go young. I hope, I really pray, that she survives long enough to free the strange, lovely talent that's wandering through her like a jailed spirit."

On April 25, it's Constance Collier who dies unexpectedly of a sudden heart attack.

The funeral service for Collier is held on April 28 at the Universal Funeral Home at Lexington Avenue and 52nd Street, just down the street from the Waldorf Astoria.

Marilyn covers her hair in a black chiffon scarf, her face in large black sunglasses, her legs in black silk stockings, and her famous figure in a loose-fitting black dress. Even to Capote, she's barely recognizable. The friends steal into the chapel's back row.

"I hate funerals," Marilyn tells Capote afterward, as they wait for the crowd to clear. "I'm glad I won't have to go to my own. Only, I don't want a funeral—just my ashes cast on waves by one of my kids, if I ever have any. I wouldn't have come today except that Miss Collier cared about me, about my welfare, and she was just like a granny, a tough old granny, but she taught me a lot. She taught me how to breathe."

CHAPTER 40

EMERGING FROM AN advance screening of *The Seven Year Itch*, Fox's Darryl Zanuck has never felt such optimism. He jots a memo and dates it May 19, 1955. "This is great house count and projection room was really in roar most of the time. There was no doubt at all but what this picture is packed with is entertainment. Tommy Ewell does a terrific job. Marilyn Monroe looks better than ever and plays her role most convincingly. Direction wonderful. It should be smash box office. Impatient for New York Opening date."

But ambitious promotional plans are derailed as film censors and advertising partners begin to weigh in. Some are pushing for the flying-skirt scene to be cut entirely.

Telegrams fly between producer Zanuck and producer Charles Feldman. "They're replacing a big cutout of Marilyn outside Loew's Theatre in Times Square. It was showing Marilyn with her skirts blowing above her waist. Not good taste...Some papers refuse to accept the wind blowing ad because of Kefauver investigation and pressure groups...this is a very delicate situation."

The Seven Year Itch premieres on June 1, 1955, Marilyn's twenty-ninth birthday. She is radiant in a white dress and a white stole—and on the arm of Joe DiMaggio.

Despite their divorce, she has not cut him out of her life entirely.

When he's in New York, he takes her to his favorite Italian restaurant in the Village, and to celebrity clubhouse Toots Shor's. He writes her letters, all addressed to Mrs. Joe DiMaggio. "Dear Baby," he wrote last October as the end of their marriage loomed. "I love you and want to be with you. There is nothing I would like better than to restore your confidence in me." Marilyn keeps the letter, reading and rereading the postscript scribbled in pencil. "Please forgive me, my perfect girl. I love you."

"No, we're not getting back together," she tells reporters at the premiere, smiling through bright red lips. "We're just good friends. Very good friends."

Innuendo delights the press, but not the censors.

Director Billy Wilder telegrams the Catholic Legion of Decency: "I do not have the reputation of ever being connected with pictures of lascivious character. Obviously, the picture deals with a man's temptations but they are very human and utterly harmless."

The film is a phenomenal success.

"Miss Monroe brings a special personality and a certain physical something or other to the film," says the *New York Times* in its review.

*   *   *

Marilyn appears at an even more important premiere on September 29, 1955, when she attends the Broadway opening of Arthur Miller's newest play, *A View from the Bridge,* a one-act drama written in verse and based on stories from his Red Hook neighborhood in Brooklyn—and on his own internal conflicts.

Also at the Coronet Theatre premiere are his parents, Isidore and Augusta Miller. Miller introduces them to Marilyn, though he keeps from them the nature of their relationship—as he's still married to Mary Slattery, his wife of nearly sixteen years and the mother of his two children, eleven-year-old Jane and eight-year-old Robert.

Miller is a man utterly obsessed but not fully happy, either with his personal life or with the production.

How to get up on the stage and describe to the actors the sensation of being swept away, of inviting the will's oblivion and dreading it?

Marilyn has become Fox's most bankable star. Her last five films have grossed a spectacular $50 million. Yet her contractual rate remains $1,500 per week. Milton Greene, her business partner in Marilyn Monroe Productions, is determined to right the imbalance.

How is it possible, Greene argues to the Fox legal team, that director Billy Wilder has been paid $500,000 and producer Charles Feldman $318,000, while the film's star is paid a fraction of her worth?

The once-mighty studio system proves no match for Marilyn's unimpeachable demands.

She's offered a new, seven-year contract. During that time, she'll owe Fox four A-level pictures and be paid a salary of $400,000 for each. From director to story to cinematographer, she'll have total creative control—and freedom to make her own films through Marilyn Monroe Productions. The contractual bonuses are mammoth.

The breakthrough deal is the first of its type. As a Hollywood businesswoman, she is truly a pioneer.

Zanuck concedes defeat.

Straw Head has won.

On December 20, 1955, Marilyn purchases a black Ford Thunderbird with a V8 engine and a convertible top. She registers the car to Marilyn Monroe Productions, Inc.

Eleven days later, on New Year's Eve, she signs her new contract with 20th Century-Fox. It's one year to the day since she finalized the plans for the company that bears her name.

In January 1956, the Los Angeles *Mirror News* reports: "Marilyn Monroe, victorious in her year-long sit-down strike against 20th Century-Fox, will return to the studio next month with a reported $8,000,000.00 deal. Veterans of the movie scene said it was one of the greatest single triumphs ever won by an actress."

Over the past year, Marilyn's realized many, so many, of the resolutions she made upon arriving in New York. But old demons won't be outrun. In his diary, Truman Capote records his sense of impending tragedy. "Saw Marilyn M. and Arthur

Miller the other night, both looking suffused with a sexual glow. They plan to get married, but I can't help feeling this little episode is called 'Death of a Playwright.'"

Marilyn calls Miller "Arturo" and he calls her "Sugar Feeny" after his cat. The lightness is a reprieve from their shared burdens of fame. In Marilyn, Miller sees "a poet on a street corner trying to recite to a crowd pulling at her clothes."

Capote makes the stark assessment that "1955 was a year of growth and discovery for Marilyn. It was also the time when she started swallowing too many pills and drinking too much champagne." He also knows a secret in the workings of Marilyn Monroe Productions. Its president and vice president are being over-prescribed by Milton Greene's doctor brother. "Tons of pills," Milton's wife Amy Greene admits. "Anything we wanted, uppers, downers, it was all available."

Sleeping pills at 3 a.m., then Dexamyl to puncture the soporific bubble on the way to a 9 a.m. meeting. And maybe stronger drugs too.

Marilyn is a frequent presence in the apartment at 135 Central Park West where Actors Studio Artistic Director Lee Strasberg lives with his second wife, Paula, also an instructor at the Studio, and their teenage children, Susan and Johnny. The place is filled with Strasberg's extravagant collections of classical music recordings, theater books—and celebrity guests.

Though Marilyn trusts Paula, it's seventeen-year-old Susan Strasberg in whom she often confides. "I always felt I was a nobody," Marilyn tells her. "And the only way for me to be somebody was to—well, be somebody else, which is probably why I wanted to act."

Marilyn had been in the audience at the Cort Theatre a few

months earlier, on October 5, 1955, when the teenager made her Broadway debut in the title role of *The Diary of Anne Frank*. That the *New York Times* praised Susan as having "the soul of an actress" astonished her father. "I just don't know how she picked it all up. She's never had any formal training."

Marilyn and Susan Strasberg are friends as close as sisters, often sharing a room and vying for Lee Strasberg's attention.

"My dad treated Marilyn Monroe more like his daughter than me," says Susan. "He constantly validated her. With her Pop was vulnerable, paternal, permissive. With me he was impersonal, critical, forbidding."

Like many of the men in her life, Marilyn calls Lee Strasberg "Daddy."

The first film in Marilyn's new contract with Fox will be *Bus Stop*.

Marilyn is set to play the role of Cherie, a Phoenix café singer kidnapped by the rodeo cowboy who loves her more than he should.

Last year, she met with columnist Hedda Hopper at the Waldorf Towers on Park Avenue, where Marilyn sublet Suite 2728 from British American comedienne and Broadway star Leonora Corbett for an eye-watering $1,000 per week.

"I heard Darryl Zanuck bought *Bus Stop* for you," Hopper said at the time.

Bus Stop, William Inge's new play—after *Come Back, Little Sheba* and the Pulitzer Prize–winning *Picnic*—is a hit at the Music Box Theatre on Broadway.

"I hope it's true," Marilyn replied, "but I've heard nothing about it from the company. All I'm asking for is good stories from good directors because I have to learn."

Bus Stop fits the bill, as does Marilyn's choice of director, Joshua Logan, who directed *Picnic* on Broadway and adapted it into a 1955 Oscar-winning film. Logan also credits his studies in Moscow with Konstantin Stanislavski for his Pulitzer Prize–winning achievement as co-author, co-producer, and co-director of the 1949 stage musical *South Pacific*.

It's the challenge she wants.

"I never had a chance to learn anything in Hollywood. They worked me too fast. They rushed me from one picture into another," she says. "It's no challenge to do the same thing over and over. I want to keep growing as a person and as an actress, and in Hollywood they never ask me my opinion. They just tell me what time to show up for work. In leaving Hollywood and coming to New York, I feel I can be more myself. After all, if I can't be myself, what's the good of being anything at all?"

On February 7, 1956, Marilyn welcomes visitors at her new apartment on 2 Sutton Place. Sir Laurence Olivier, the Oscar-winning actor widely regarded as the best in the world, enters with both his agent and popular and prolific British playwright Terence Rattigan.

Marilyn has decided that her next project after *Bus Stop* will be *The Prince and the Showgirl*. The movie is a film adaptation of Rattigan's play *The Sleeping Prince: An Occasional Fairy Tale*, which opened in London in 1953, the year of Queen Elizabeth II's coronation. Olivier will reprise his starring role as a prince regent who attempts to seduce an American showgirl—played on stage by his wife, Vivien Leigh, who won an Oscar in 1940 as Scarlett O'Hara in *Gone with the Wind.*

It's the first acquisition for Marilyn Monroe Productions. "Last week there was persuasive evidence that Marilyn Monroe is a shrewd businesswoman," *Time* magazine reports, "apparent when Marilyn Monroe Productions bought a property to serve as a starring vehicle for its president, M. Monroe." Milton Greene and Olivier will both be producers, and Warner Bros. will distribute.

The now forty-eight-year-old Olivier, who will also direct the picture, is looking to revive his somewhat stodgy reputation by starring in the film adaptation alongside the sexy Hollywood starlet. Marilyn is hoping that the association with the highly respected legend of stage and screen will confer more respectability upon her.

"Monroe and Olivier," says *Bus Stop* director Joshua Logan, "that's the best combination since black and white."

Although Marilyn keeps her guests waiting for an hour and a half, Olivier is instantly smitten with his future leading lady.

One thing was clear to me: I was going to fall most shatteringly in love with Marilyn. She was adorable, so witty, and more physically attractive than anyone I could imagine.

He sends her a floral arrangement and a note:

"Marilyn, It has been so lovely meeting you, knowing you and now knowing that such exciting things and such fun are ahead. Love and Thank You, Larry."

The co-stars make their first public appearance together on February 9, posing cheek-to-cheek in the neo-Renaissance Terrace Room at the Plaza Hotel, with its arched openings, floral motifs, and crystal chandeliers that replicate those in the Palace at Versailles.

Much fanfare greets the announcement of their new project. The film will also be Olivier's non-Shakespearean directorial debut.

"What do you think of Marilyn as an actress?" reporters ask him.

"She is a brilliant comedienne, and therefore an extremely good actress," Sir Laurence says. "She has the cunning gift of being able to suggest one minute that she is the naughtiest little thing, and the next minute that she is beautifully dumb and innocent."

As if on cue, the strap of Marilyn's black slip dress suddenly snaps. It's not unusual for her seams to pop, since she insists on tailoring all her clothing skin tight. Amid an explosion of blinding flashbulbs, she deftly prevents her bosom from spilling out.

"Sir Laurence has always been my idol," Marilyn says.

When he returns to London, he sends her a note. "I am terribly excited at our prospects. You were so angelic in New York. Thank you for all your sweetness. I think with great joy of our future meeting. Ever, Larry."

CHAPTER 41

MARILYN'S PLANE LANDS at Los Angeles International. She's dressed in a smart black suit for the airport press conference.

"How do you feel about coming back to Hollywood?" a reporter asks. "Is it a happy time?"

"Yes, it's a very happy time," she says. "I'm happy to be back. It is my hometown."

Others have questions about what Marilyn's accomplished in New York.

"You said you wanted to grow. Do you feel you've grown?"

"Well, I hardly know how to answer that, since they misinterpret that, meaning, in inches or something."

At that, Marilyn laughs along with the press corps.

It takes two hours to make her way through the throng of photographers, fans, and autograph hunters and on to 595 North Beverly Glen Boulevard. For $950 a month, Milton and Amy Greene have rented the nine-room house near the Fox lot, where the outdoor scenes of *Bus Stop* will be filmed.

Marilyn's longtime acting coach Natasha Lytess telephones right away. She's been dismissed by the studio. Surely that's an error. Isn't she needed to work on the new picture with Marilyn?

What Lytess doesn't know is that she's been replaced. Paula Strasberg is Marilyn's new coach, and already has the final screenplay for *Bus Stop* bound in a blue cover and dated February 27, 1956. She's circled every mention of Marilyn's character, Cherie, in red ink and marked up the dialogue with her notes.

Marilyn Monroe Productions lawyer Irving Stein informs Lytess that her contract with Marilyn, and therefore Fox, is terminated. "All legal means necessary" will be taken to prevent her from contacting Marilyn in any way.

Stein is a tough lawyer, but his client is the one requesting this treatment. The exact reasoning behind Marilyn's decision to abruptly end the association with her former mentor is opaque, but rumors about Lytess cooperating with an exposé of their professional and personal relationship surely don't help.

"My only protection in the world is Marilyn Monroe," a dismayed Lytess tells friends. "I created this girl—I fought for her—I was always the heavy on set...I am her private property, she knows that. Her faith and security are mine."

The drama coach can't accept that this is Marilyn's doing. Ignoring Stein's stern warnings, Lytess shows up at the Greenes' house on North Beverly Glen Boulevard, only to have the door slammed in her face and to be threatened with a restraining order. As she staggers back onto the street, in tears, she sees a movement inside the house. She is shocked to see Marilyn between the curtains in an upstairs window, her face impassive as she draws the curtains closed.

Though Natasha Lytess continues to reach out, especially "when she's broke," Marilyn never replies.

In March, filming begins on *Bus Stop*. Now it's Paula Strasberg to whom Marilyn defers on every take. Consistent with the philosophy of the Actors Studio, her technique is pure Method. If a scene calls for Marilyn to cry, Strasberg instructs her to reflect on a moment in her own life that brought her to tears.

There are plenty. Marilyn also draws from a deep well of fear. Fox's biggest box-office draw is still terrified of making mistakes. She's haunted by the feeling she described in a recent interview: *Hollywood will never forgive me — not for leaving, not for fighting the system — but for winning.*

Bus Stop is Broadway veteran Don Murray's first film.

She's such a big star, Murray observes of his co-star Marilyn Monroe, but he's surprised to see that she behaves like an insecure actress. *She has done so many films, and yet, she is so frightened to act in front of the camera.*

She stays in her dressing room until ten or eleven o'clock every morning, when she's finally ready to perform. Even after hours of rehearsal with Paula Strasberg, Marilyn struggles through take after take, barely able to remember her lines.

All too often, Josh Logan appeals to the cast to help move Marilyn's scenes forward.

"Persuade her, humor her," the director pleads with the cast after Marilyn jumbles her line twenty-seven times.

"Outside of saying her own line, what the hell do you want me to do?" demands one of the supporting actresses, who nevertheless steels her nerves to approach Marilyn and grip her by the shoulders.

"Look, either we get it right this time or I'm walking out of the picture," the actress says.

A startled Marilyn perfectly executes her line.

When Murray and Marilyn play a love scene, her body breaks out in a red rash. Makeup artists rush on set with creams and brushes and work to cover up the evidence of her nervousness.

Logan patiently films her scenes in fragments. When the script calls for Marilyn's character, Cherie, to fight for Murray's character, Bo Decker, she amazes the director with the fiery intensity of her performance.

"It just wells up from some deep place," Logan says. "She's a natural."

On a good day.

Despite her issues, Marilyn takes her part seriously. She rehearses with Strasberg until all hours and listens to director Logan, striving to create a character that meets her increasingly exacting standards.

Logan is impressed. "I was beginning to feel that she had always been brilliant. No one seemed to have listened to her before," he says of Marilyn, lamenting, "I nearly missed one of the high spots of my directing life because I had fallen for the popular Hollywood prejudice about Marilyn Monroe."

* * *

Time magazine chooses Marilyn for a prestigious cover profile, assigning Hollywood reporter Ezra Goodman to travel with her as *Bus Stop* continues filming on location in Phoenix, Arizona, and Ketchum, Idaho.

Though the six-week project is an in-depth undertaking informed by more than one hundred interviews by Los Angeles bureau staffers, journalist Walter Winchell dismisses it entirely. He writes in his column: "I can't imagine them digging up anything people haven't read before."

On the chartered flight to Idaho's Sun Valley, Marilyn immediately proves Winchell wrong by demonstrating that, even in close quarters, she's a master of disguise.

A person wearing dark glasses and a straw hat in the style of a Venetian gondolier, gray and black menswear pieces, and a floor-length mink coat steps through the cabin in high heels and takes a seat.

When she shows her face, without a trace of makeup, Ezra Goodman is astonished to discover that it's Marilyn. And that she's watching him.

"You look like a writer," she says later, during a sit-down interview in her dressing room.

"I'm not sure that's a compliment," the *Time* reporter hedges.

But Marilyn is decisive. "Writers, when you're talking to them, look like they're listening to you."

On another flight from Los Angeles to Arizona, where she'll be filming rodeo scenes for the film, Marilyn is seated alongside English journalist Donald Zec of the *Daily Mirror*.

When a meal is served, Marilyn pushes it aside, saying, "I have to watch my figure."

"You eat, Marilyn, I'll watch your figure," Zec quips suggestively, earning himself a teasing slap on the arm.

Zec has known Marilyn since *Niagara* in 1953, long enough to be allowed a few liberties.

Things soon take a serious turn.

Alarm bells sound as one of the plane's engines fails. Through the window, they can see dark clouds of smoke billowing out. Despite assurances from the pilots, things look dire—bad enough, Zec says, that he and Marilyn "discussed the unthinkable. I soothed her with the thought that if we crashed her name would be on every news bulletin and front page in the western world."

He asks Marilyn how she'd like to be remembered, and she thinks on it for a while.

"Then she scribbled a note: 'Here Lies Marilyn Monroe, 38-23-36,'" Zec relates.

He's unsure whether to consider her self-penned epitaph clever, sad—or both. Marilyn often wavers between the two. Zec's asked her on more than one occasion if she's happy.

Marilyn's reply is always the same: a shrug and a dismissive "Who's happy?"

Director Josh Logan agrees, saying of his leading lady, "I doubt if she had two consecutive days' happiness in her entire life."

"Broadway's biggest becomes Marilyn's best," teases 20th Century-Fox in its trailer for *Bus Stop.*

Ahead of the film's premiere, the cast gathers for a preview.

Cast members Bill Murray, Hope Lange, Arthur O'Connell, and Eileen Heckart aren't sure what to expect. As Broadway veterans, they're all used to running their lines straight through, but that wasn't what happened on the set of *Bus Stop*.

"We would see all these little pieces, and we thought the film was going to be a disaster," Murray says.

Daily rushes never captured a complete scene with Marilyn.

As the preview rolls, they're amazed and astonished. "All of a sudden we realized what the magic of films was, with the editing and cutting it all together; she was magnificent!"

Critics agree. The *New York Times* praises Murray as "a wondrous new actor" who "sets up a mighty force to be curbed by Miss Monroe. And the fact that she fitfully but firmly summons the will and the strength to humble him—to make him say 'please,' which is the point of the whole thing—attests to her new acting skill."

Miller writes Marilyn a letter as one creative force acknowledging another. "The whole *Bus Stop* reception is a personal triumph for you of a magnitude which I don't think you yet realize. You have done what you set out to do. You are an actress and an artist."

CHAPTER 42

KETCHUM, IDAHO, IS 538 MILES from Reno, Nevada. That's where Arthur Miller spends six weeks at the Pyramid Lake Ranch, awaiting the finalization of his divorce.

On weekdays, Miller observes "misfit" cowboys wrangle wild horses. These authentic scenes from Western life spark the idea for a story. Miller makes notes — until the phone rings at the ranch house with a daily call from a "Mrs. Leslie" for a "Mr. Leslie." Then he rushes from his isolated desert cabin to talk to her for hours.

"I don't want this anymore, Papa, I can't fight them alone, I want to live with you in the country and be a good wife," "Mrs. Leslie" tells him.

On weekends, Miller crosses the state border to Idaho or California for clandestine meetings with Marilyn in Reno. His FBI surveillance detail is never far behind.

Though questions about the couple's future are unavoidable, Miller agrees to sit with Goodman for *Time*'s cover story on Marilyn, with a cover portrait from illustrator Boris

Chaliapin, Marilyn's name drawn on a piece of motion picture film.

"I can't afford to get married for a long time," Miller tells the magazine's reporter. "Where will I get the money to support two families? My play *A View from the Bridge* just closed on Broadway. I got thirty-five thousand dollars, and that will have to last me for two years until I can write another one."

June 2. Miller writes to Marilyn from the Pyramid Ranch, as *Bus Stop* is wrapping: "It is ten to eight here...the radio is play-ing 'Let's Fall in Love,' in a corny Dorsey brothers arrangement, and I have just walked over to my wall and kissed your lips that kiss the glass. How in love I am!...I adore you...I love your every lunacy. Only love me. I will make you so happy you will not really believe it is possible. I want to be your lover and your husband and the papa of your new family and our home."

"We're so congenial," Marilyn tells her *Gentlemen Prefer Blondes* co-star Jane Russell. "This is the first time I've been really in love. Arthur is a serious man, but he has a wonderful sense of humor. We laugh and joke a lot. I'm mad about him."

June 11. Reunited in New York, the newly divorced Miller and Marilyn make plans for their life together. First, they'll travel to London, where *The Prince and the Showgirl* begins filming in August and where *A View from the Bridge* will have its West End opening in October.

Before then, Miller is subpoenaed to appear before the House Un-American Activities Committee, or HUAC, on June 21.

It's not his first run-in with them.

In 1952, celebrated director Elia Kazan had been called to testify before HUAC. Kazan, himself once a member of the Communist Party, named seventeen others, reasoning that he was doing no harm by calling out those who'd already been blacklisted.

Miller is one of many on Broadway and in Hollywood who vehemently disagree with Kazan's choice, to the point that when Miller sees his former friend and collaborator on the street, he turns away, refusing to acknowledge him.

Miller writes *The Crucible,* in which the Salem witch trials of 1692 act as an allegory for Senator Joseph McCarthy's dangerous and circumstantial anti-Communist crusades. The drama opens on Broadway in January 1953 and wins four Tony Awards, including Best Play and Best Author of a Play. But in March 1954, Miller is blocked from attending a premiere of *The Crucible* in Brussels, Belgium, when the US State Department denies his passport renewal due to suspicions that he supports Communism.

The issue returns when Miller applies again for a renewal, now amplified by Marilyn's celebrity aura, and he is hauled into court.

"The next stop is trouble," Walter Winchell writes in his column. "The House Un-American Activities Committee subpoena will check into his entire inner circle, which also happens to be the inner circle of Marilyn Monroe — and all of them are former Communist sympathizers."

Months earlier, Winchell — a stalwart friend to Joe DiMaggio — had likewise stoked these rumors, declaring on his radio show, "America's best known blonde moving picture star is now the darling of the left-wing intelligentsia, several of whom are listed as red fronters."

Fellow columnist Vincent X. Flaherty speculates that Marilyn's fame risks making Communism appealing to young Americans. Since "teenage boys and girls worship Marilyn," Flaherty argues, if "Marilyn marries a man who was connected with communism, they can't help but start thinking that communism can't be so bad after all!"

June 21. Representative Francis Eugene Walter, chairman of the House Un-American Activities Committee, presides as Richard Arens, HUAC counsel and former aide to Senator McCarthy, questions Arthur Miller in Washington, DC.

The committee lays out a lengthy timeline dating back sixteen years, specifying Miller's attendance at a Marxist study group in 1940 and a gathering of Communist Party writers in 1947, fewer than a dozen meetings in total.

"The record reflects that this witness has identified these meetings as the meetings of the Communist writers," Arens says. "In the jurisdiction of this committee he has been requested to tell this committee who were in attendance at these meetings."

Doing so, Miller knows, can mean careers ended and livelihoods lost. Blinking behind his glasses, Miller does what Elia Kazan would not. He defies Congress.

"I could not use the name of another person and bring trouble on him. These were writers, poets, as far as I could see, and the life of a writer, despite what it sometimes seems, is pretty tough. I wouldn't make it any tougher for anybody. I ask you not to ask me that question."

Miller confers with his lawyer before continuing, "I will tell you anything about myself, as I have."

During a break in the testimony, reporters cajole Miller into revealing more information about his personal life than he intended.

"Mr. Miller, why did you file an application for a passport?" he's asked.

"I wanted to go to England."

"For what reason?"

"I want to be with the woman who is going to be my wife."

"Marilyn Monroe?"

"That's correct."

He's been busy, the playwright says, far too busy to set a wedding date with Marilyn, who's leaving in three weeks on July 13 to shoot *The Prince and the Showgirl*.

"I hope to settle it all right soon," he says, adding, "When she goes to London, she will go as Mrs. Miller."

"Have you heard?" an emotional Marilyn telephones poet Norman Rosten. "He told the whole world he was marrying Marilyn Monroe. Me!"

The press immediately descend upon Marilyn's apartment building in New York following Miller's slip, dozens of reporters crowding in her face.

Marilyn is delighted but flustered, and not entirely prepared for a press conference. She smiles widely and touches her face as the questions come thick and fast.

"How long ago did you decide to get married? Was there talk about it before the formal engagement?"

Marilyn dips her head and smiles. "Well, um...a little, maybe."

"Miss Monroe, do you think your marriage plans are going to change your career any?"

She lifts up both hands. "Well, ah, I don't think so, I mean, Mr. Miller is a playwright and I think he would like me to be a good actress too, as much as I would like to be."

"When are you planning to have some children?" one of the female reporters asks.

Marilyn pauses a moment, then says, "Well, I'm not married yet, dear!" The crowd laughs appreciatively.

"Miss Monroe, this is rather a personal question, but is there anything in particular about Mr. Miller that attracted you?"

"Have you seen him?"

The crowd laughs again, unsure what to make of her answer. He's the intellectual; *she's* meant to be the beauty.

Marilyn couldn't be more serious. *I am so concerned about protecting Arthur,* she writes in her journal. *I love him — and he is the only person — human being I have ever known that I could love not only as a man to which I am attracted to practically out of my senses — but he is the only person — as another human being that I trust as much as myself.*

* * *

Miller is granted his passport. Overnight the playwright is transformed from a leftie Communist Red to the harried lover of Hollywood's most glamorous star.

It's the last week of June and the press demand details about the upcoming wedding. They continue to surround Marilyn's New York apartment, effectively imprisoning her until Miller collects her in his ancient station wagon and drives her at speed to his colonial house on Tophet Road in Roxbury, Connecticut.

Almost a decade earlier, in 1947, Miller purchased forty-four acres in Litchfield County. An accomplished carpenter, he built a writing studio on the hillock behind the house, crafted a desk from an old door, and began to write. The first act of *Death of a Salesman* emerged during a single day, and Miller finished the play in the days and weeks that followed—later creating *The Crucible* in this same space.

This quiet, contemplative location suits the solitary work of a writer. Or a person contemplating faith.

Miller is Jewish, though since his 1925 bar mitzvah, he's preferred a secular life. Despite no pressure from him, Marilyn wants to convert to Judaism before they marry. She's never had any formal religious education, and she feels no attachment to the Protestantism she was born into.

Beyond attending synagogue at the High Holidays, the Millers aren't especially observant, though they're close to Rabbi Robert Goldburg. The rabbi travels from New Haven to Roxbury to guide Marilyn through an expedited course of study. Studying Jewish texts and practicing the rituals brings her great comfort and fulfillment.

And solidarity. Marilyn had once told Lee and Paula

Strasberg's daughter Susan that she could "identify with the Jews" because "Everyone's always out to get them, no matter what they do. Like me."

"This is the girl I'm going to marry," Miller tells his parents, Isidore and Augusta. He'd been nervous about getting their blessing, and greatly relieved when they gave it to him. "It is not that I would hesitate to marry you if they disapproved," he'd written to Marilyn. "Truly, sweetheart, that was not it. It was that somewhere inside me I wanted their love to flow toward both of us because it would give me strength, and you too. It is not that they are my judges, but the first sources of my identity and my love."

Marilyn pours out her longing for family in the kitchen of their home on East Third Street, near Avenue M, in Brooklyn. "For the first time in my life," Marilyn tells them, "I have somebody I can call Father and Mother."

The Millers have three children: oldest son Kermit, then Arthur, then youngest child and only daughter Joan, an actress who uses the name "Joan Copeland" professionally. As an early member of the Actors Studio, Copeland's known Marilyn via the New York theater scene for quite some time.

"She didn't think of herself as a fully qualified actress. She felt out of her depth at the Actors Studio, though she shouldn't have," Copeland says. Marilyn would shyly nod and smile at Copeland when they crossed paths, and eventually "would search me out at the Studio and we'd have lunch, talk about scenes."

"She wanted to be part of our family," Copeland says. "My mother made it comfortable for her, and my dad did. I did. So now she was in heaven because she had a nice boyfriend, she had a father, and a girlfriend. So it made her feel like an ordinary person. A real person who has a family...She loved being in the family, and the idea of having a family was sacred to her."

Hundreds of press descend upon Miller's Connecticut property in the days after the news of the engagement breaks. A wedding between "America's foremost foremosts," as one columnist dubs them, is major news. Reporters are looking for quotes and details to fill their columns and double-page spreads. In the summer heat, they're knocking on doors, hoping for water, food, cups of coffee.

The Roxbury paper runs a brief announcement: LOCAL RESIDENT WILL MARRY MISS MONROE OF HOLLYWOOD, noting, ROXBURY ONLY SPOT IN WORLD TO GREET NEWS CALMLY.

But Miller is a private man who wants to be left alone. He puts off answering their questions by promising a press conference at the end of the week.

On Friday, June 29, 1956, some five hundred reporters surround Miller's colonial house, smoking cigarettes while they wait for a joyous announcement.

Their vigil is interrupted by tragedy.

Around one o'clock in the afternoon, brakes screech, glass shatters, and metal smashes. The assembled reporters collectively hold their breath and turn to look up the narrow lane toward the source of the terrible sound.

Careering around the corner comes the old station wagon with Arthur Miller and his cousin, Morton Miller, at the wheel.

The car comes to a hard stop. Out bolts Marilyn. Her face is tearstained, and there's blood on her shirt. She runs into the house, Miller following closely behind her.

Cousin Morty tearfully relates that there's been a car crash. The driver of a press car in pursuit of the soon-to-be Mr. and Mrs. Miller lost control on the unfamiliar road and has smashed head-first into a tree. Its passenger, Mara Scherbatoff, the New York bureau chief of *Paris Match,* has fatally severed an artery in her neck.

The poor woman. How did that happen? We've just come from getting our marriage license. It's a bad omen for our future. Marilyn's thoughts run together as she paces the kitchen. *Now television cameras are being set up on the lawn.*

There's no avoiding the promised press conference now. But Miller still refuses to answer any questions.

Inside the house, Marilyn takes her friend and business partner Milton Greene aside and begs his advice.

"Arthur wants me to marry him," she says. "Now—tonight. Tell me if I'm making a mistake. What do you think?"

Greene is stunned that after all the couple's fervent declarations of love, Marilyn doesn't know her own heart.

"Marilyn, you must do what you think best," Greene tells her.

They concoct a secret plan. Once the crowd dissipates, the couple drives across the Connecticut state line to New York. There, at the Westchester County Courthouse in White Plains, Judge Seymour Robinowitz cuts short his own anniversary celebration to perform a four-minute civil ceremony at 7:21 in the evening before two witnesses, Morty Miller and his wife.

Other attendees include Milton Greene and Samuel Slavitt, Miller's lawyer. On the marriage certificate, Marilyn records her true age, thirty. Miller is forty, nearly forty-one.

The *New York Times* later reports that "Miss Monroe wore a sweater and a skirt and no hat. Mr. Miller wore a blue suit and a white shirt but no tie."

They have successfully evaded the press.

But in all the haste, there's been no time to buy a ring. Just as in Marilyn's marriage to Joe DiMaggio, her groom borrows a family ring to slip on his bride's finger, a 22k gold family heirloom from 1876.

Two days later, Rabbi Goldburg signs the certificate of Marilyn's conversion to the Jewish faith. A Jewish ceremony is planned for later in the afternoon, at the French-country-style home of Miller's entertainment agent, Kay Brown.

Arthur Miller has a vision for their wedding. "I have been thinking crazy thoughts. For instance, a wedding with maybe fifty people. Maybe in Roxbury, maybe somewhere else in a big house. And Bob and Jane there. And just a little bit of ceremony," he writes. "I want the kids to see us married, and to feel the seriousness and honorableness of our marriage...I want this for their sakes as much as for my own pride and my joy; so that they will see their Grandma and Grandpa full of happiness."

His vision is largely realized.

Marilyn trades the simple pencil skirt, shirt, and gloves she wore to the courthouse for an empire-waist tea-length muslin chiffon gown with ruched sleeves by designers Norman Norell and John Moore, along with a short chin-length veil Amy Greene has soaked in coffee to more closely match the dress's beige color. Hedda Rosten is the maid of honor, and Marilyn's acting guru, Lee Strasberg, gives the bride away.

The couple is married by Rabbi Goldburg in the home's living room, in front of around twenty-five friends and family, including Miller's parents; his children; his brother, sister, cousin, and their spouses; the Strasbergs; the Greenes; the Rostens; and a handful of others. Kermit Miller and Lee Strasberg witness the couple's traditional Jewish ketubah, and list their wedding date as "July 1, 1956, 22nd of Tammuz 5716."

"I'm just warning you," Miller had told Marilyn. "You'll be the most kissed bride in history when my family is there. I'll have to fight the bastards off. I'm going to put up a sign, 'ONE KISS TO A RELATIVE!'"

"Marilyn, if you have a sister, introduce me to her," jokes Goldburg.

But there was nobody from her side there, Marilyn's new father-in-law notes. Still, the mood is of overwhelming happiness as the newlyweds and their guests enjoy a champagne reception on the rolling lawn, complete with lobster and a tiered wedding cake.

"The fairy tale came true," says Norman Rosten. "The Prince appeared, the Princess was safe."

The newlywed couple gifts the rabbi a recording of Arthur Miller's works, with the inscription, "For Bob Goldburg, With all my (our) thanks for a beautiful wedding—July 1, 1956," each signing their names: Arthur Miller, and Marilyn Monroe <u>Miller</u>, her new last name underlined.

* * *

New gold wedding bands come from Cartier. Marilyn lets Susan Strasberg try on her ring, engraved with the wedding date and "A to M, Now is Forever."

"Forever is so romantic...I can't even imagine forever, can you?" sighs the teenager.

I feel like I was at Fox forever, and when I get the blues it feels like I'm in hell forever, Marilyn thinks. "I don't think you can 'think' forever, it's more a feeling," she says.

But she's hoping hard for happily ever after.

On the back of their wedding photograph, Marilyn writes the words, "Hope, hope, hope."

CHAPTER 43

EGGHEAD WEDS HOURGLASS, *Variety* reports as America celebrates the marriage of its greatest playwright and its most famous film star.

In the UK, "Marilyn Mania" has been building in the months since the announcement of *The Prince and the Showgirl*. Before she even arrives, she's received invitations to cricket matches and cream teas. To taste fish and chips on the seafront and shoot grouse in Scotland. Ladies crochet gold and white wool into Marilyn Monroe dolls. Newspapers crowd Prime Minister Sir Anthony Eden's speech about austerity and impending economic disaster to the lower reaches of the front pages in favor of Marilyn's photograph.

On July 14, 1956, two weeks after their wedding, Marilyn and Arthur Miller emerge from a twelve-hour transatlantic flight aboard a piston plane at London Airport.

Miller records his first impressions: "The camera flashes formed a solid wall of white light that seemed to last for almost half a minute, a veritable aureole, and the madness of it made even the photographers burst out laughing."

Sir Laurence Oliver and his wife, Vivien Leigh, are present to greet the newlyweds — but before they can, a photographer is trampled and hospitalized.

"This must be the largest reception and press conference in English history!" Olivier proclaims.

For the duration of the film shoot, Marilyn and Miller will reside at Parkside House, a Surrey country estate covered with creeping vine and backing onto Windsor Great Park, adjacent to Windsor Castle.

The main bedroom is furnished to help ease Marilyn's nightly battle with insomnia. It's fitted with heavy curtains and painted entirely white, with a new white carpet much like the one in Marilyn's New York apartment on Sutton Place.

Miller wakes to the sound of voices. Heavenly voices.

He calls Marilyn to the window. Outside, a boys' choir is harmonizing across every octave.

"What do we do?" Marilyn asks.

"Maybe you put on a robe and just wave down to them," Miller suggests.

"Me?"

"Well, they're not singing to me, darling."

At the Savoy Hotel in London, Marilyn enters in a white cape coat, which she removes to reveal a black sleeveless tea-length dress and tea-length gloves. The crowd gasps in admiration when they see her.

Daily Mirror Hollywood reporter Donald Zec gives Marilyn a once-over.

"Fits a bit tight, Mrs. Miller," he comments.

"It fits," she laughs. When asked how she's feeling, she answers, "All I can say is I've never been happier in my life."

Arthur Miller gives Zec a crushing handshake.

"What do you think of your new bride?" Zec asks him.

"She is the most unique person I have ever met," Miller says.

"What is it like to be married to such a quiet man?" Marilyn is asked.

Miller's eyes narrow. "I'm not so quiet as all that," he replies.

The July 15 press conference for *The Prince and the Showgirl* features a surprise. A London newspaperman wheels in a bicycle, with an oversized tag on it labeled TO MARILYN WITH LOVE FROM THE DAILY SKETCH. It's a gift to Marilyn so that she can explore Windsor Great Park.

A week's rehearsal begins at Pinewood Studios, where the movie will be shot. As director, co-producer, and co-star, Sir Laurence Olivier establishes expectations.

He announces a closed set and assigns a police constable to track Marilyn's movements. The security is to ensure her safety, Olivier insists, but Marilyn chafes at the restrictions.

The gates to Parkside House are kept locked. Still, locals line up for a glimpse inside. Marilyn isn't much more accessible on set.

Colin Clark, a gofer on the film, writes in his diary: "I just can't seem to see enough of her, and perhaps this is because I cannot really see her at all. It is a feeling one could easily confuse with love. No wonder she has so many fans, and has to be careful who she meets. I suppose this is why she spends most of her time shut up in her house, and why she finds it hard to turn up at the studio at all, let alone on time."

On the first day of the shoot, August 7, Marilyn arrives two hours late with Paula Strasberg in tow.

Olivier is taken aback at their Method acting techniques. He comes from the classical school of acting, where the emotions of a character are represented externally—with facial expressions, movements, physical attitudes, even prosthetics.

He gives specific instructions, only to have Paula interject, "Think of Frank Sinatra and Coca-Cola." *What's her motivation?* Marilyn and Paula ask themselves. *What is the character thinking? Where's the vérité?* They workshop the take until Olivier loses the thread entirely.

"Can't you just pretend?" he asks from behind the camera.

"You are the greatest woman of your time," Paula praises Marilyn, to Olivier's annoyance, "the greatest human being of your time; of any time, you name it; you can't think of anybody, I mean—no, not even Jesus—except you're more popular."

Olivier contradicts the acting coach. "All you have to be is sexy, dear Marilyn!" the director declares.

Sexy? Marilyn is deeply offended at Olivier's condescending tone. "He came on like someone slumming," she says. "He upset me a lot."

She immediately retaliates. "I started being bad with him, being late, and he hated it. But if you don't respect your artists, they can't work well. Respect is what you have to fight for."

Miller is on his wife's side, though Marilyn occasionally

accuses him otherwise. "She was generally seen as a very light-headed, if not silly, human being," he says, "some kind of a dancing bear, that she shouldn't be able, for example, to have any interest in anything but sex, showing off or saying dopey things to the newspapers."

He sees her struggle. "I took her at her own evaluation, which very few people did," he says. "I thought she was a very serious girl."

Dame Sybil Thorndike, leading actress of the British theater who's playing the Queen Dowager, urges patience from Olivier. After watching early rushes, she tells him, "Larry, you did well in that scene but with Marilyn up there, nobody will be watching you. Her manner and timing are just too delicious. We need her desperately. She's really the only one of us who knows how to act in front of a camera!"

But the damage is done. The co-stars are soon barely on speaking terms. If Marilyn must address Olivier, she calls him "Mr. Sir."

Hoping to ease tensions, Olivier urges *The Prince and the Show-girl* playwright and screenwriter Terence Rattigan to organize a party. Perhaps they can defuse matters over glasses of champagne.

Rattigan agrees and throws a soiree in Marilyn's honor at his home, hiring a small orchestra to play hits from American musicals.

But even this feels rather double-handed. At the party, Arthur Miller finds himself talking to gossip columnist Louella Parsons, who declares, "We all love Marilyn."

Miller nods, all the while thinking, *Her columns have never been free of a sneering contempt for Marilyn's ambitions to escape the starlet's fate.*

"It's so wonderful to know that she's happy at last. And she does look really and truly happy," Parsons continues.

Is she truly happy?

What Miller doesn't know is that as Marilyn was getting ready for the party, she came across her husband's notebook, left open on his desk. She didn't go looking, she just read what was in front her.

It's a litany of regrets. To Lee and Paula Strasberg, Marilyn distills the essence of Miller's marital complaints. "How he thought I was some kind of angel but now he guessed he was wrong. That his first wife had let him down, but I had done something worse."

"Today is forever," her new husband had promised her less than a month ago.

Forever is apparently fleeting.

But the grudges Marilyn holds when she senses betrayal are not.

Marilyn is further upset by Miller's decision to return to New York after only a month, to tend to his daughter Jane, who's been ill.

The following Monday morning, she fails to turn up on set. She sends word she's feeling poorly. Colitis is cited, but she is nowhere to be seen at Parkside House. She's apparently left Surrey and gone to London. And then on to somewhere else.

*   *   *

In the south of France, Senator Jack Kennedy has chartered a forty-foot yacht. Its ship-shore communications are down and that suits him fine. He's licking fresh political wounds.

The 1956 Democratic National Convention wrapped in Chicago on August 17. It was a wild one. Presidential nominee Adlai Stevenson, the former governor of Illinois, abandoned protocols and left the choice of his vice-presidential running mate to the delegates.

At the end of the vote, Tennessee senator Estes Kefauver was ahead, though he failed to secure the nomination over Kennedy.

The delegates voted again. Kennedy surged ahead, but not enough to convince delegates who valued Kefauver's experience more than Kennedy's relative youth. Kennedy graciously conceded.

After the convention, Jack Kennedy left for Europe. For days, he's completely out of contact. On board, it's just the senator, the skipper, the cook and, according to the *Washington Star*, "blondes." No one—especially not Kennedy's heavily pregnant wife, Jackie—knows if the world's most famous blonde is among them.

On August 23, Jackie Kennedy has an emergency caesarean. The child, a baby girl, is stillborn. Her name is kept private.

Once Kennedy finally gets word, he races to his wife's bedside. Some say Kennedy, or his father, offers Jackie $1 million to stay married to him. "But it was just talk," insists British actor Peter Lawford, who's married to Jack's sister Pat Kennedy Lawford.

*   *   *

Marilyn returns to Pinewood Studios to continue filming, and Miller returns to England.

Olivier's wife, Vivien Leigh, is present on the closed set. Marilyn has stepped into the role Leigh originated on stage, forcing a rivalry between them.

"Marilyn could play this role with her eyes closed," Susan Strasberg says, "but Olivier seemed to feel that she should play it like Miss Leigh and he was infuriating her with his exacting and specific direction."

But Leigh and Marilyn share a tragic common bond.

In early August, forty-two-year-old Leigh had announced a pregnancy to the press, but sadly miscarried soon thereafter. The child would have been her and Olivier's first.

Marilyn suffers a similar trajectory. In early September, not long after joyfully discovering she's pregnant, she loses her and Miller's longed-for baby.

"I'm just Mrs. Miller tonight," Marilyn says on October 11, 1956, at the London premiere of Arthur Miller's play *A View from the Bridge.*

While technically banned from performance in England due to themes of homosexuality, *A View from the Bridge* is instead being staged inside The Comedy Theatre to skirt censorship issues and foil the Lord Chamberlain's "pious attempt...to spare London the shock of this play—a play New Yorkers withstood without pain for some months."

Despite ongoing tension on the set of *The Prince and the*

Showgirl, Olivier and Leigh are seated front and center beside Marilyn and Miller.

Reviews are largely positive. The *Evening Standard* praises the play, though describing it as "so bulging with dramatic muscles that it is constantly on the verge of bursting its seams" — not unlike the *Daily Mail's* comments on Marilyn and her scarlet satin mermaid-tail dress at the premiere.

"How could she walk?" asks the *Daily Mail,* describing the gown as "so tight around the knees that walking was an achievement."

Of the play itself, however, the paper's review says it "will shake you to the core, and should end, once and for all, all that talk of 'Mr. Marilyn Monroe.'"

Throughout her months in England, Marilyn's dreamed of having tea at Buckingham Palace. Her publicist is unable to secure her an invitation to meet Queen Elizabeth II — until the Royal Command Performance on October 29.

The Battle of the River Plate, a film dramatizing Britain's first major naval engagement in World War II, is playing at the Empire, Leicester Square. Before the showing, a select few are invited to meet the queen.

Though the actors and notables have been briefed on protocol — women are to avoid showing cleavage — Marilyn arrives sheathed in a floor-length gold lamé cape. Shrugging off the elegant draping, she reveals a gown of the same fabric, its front cut daringly low.

As the queen makes her way down the receiving line, Marilyn buzzes with nervousness until it's finally her turn to take

Her Majesty's gloved hand and drop into the curtsy she's practiced for hours.

The two women are the same age, both thirty years old, and are neighbors across Windsor Great Park.

"We love it," Marilyn tells the queen. "My husband and I go for bicycle rides in the Great Park."

After the Royal Command Performance, Queen Elizabeth seeks out Marilyn's other films.

"I thought Miss Monroe was a very sweet person," the fascinated queen tells a friend. "But I felt sorry for her, because she was so nervous that she had licked all of her lipstick off."

In November 1956, *The Prince and the Showgirl* wraps under budget and a few days ahead of schedule. It's time to go home.

"England?" Marilyn muses. "It seemed to be raining the whole time ... or maybe it was me."

Privately, Arthur Miller fears the place "had humbled both of us."

CHAPTER 44

MARILYN AND MILLER chase the happiness that eluded them in the first six months of their marriage all the way to the Caribbean island of Jamaica. They'll spend the next sixteen days relaxing at a seaside villa in Ocho Rios on Jamaica's exclusive north coast.

On January 3, 1957, they step onto the tarmac, where Marilyn accepts a rum punch and Miller tells reporters that he's writing something for his wife. "It isn't titled yet. It will be about contemporary life."

From behind dark glasses, Marilyn dodges questions about her next film project, though she softens at a personal one.

"If you had to choose between your husband and your career, which would you pick?" a journalist asks.

"I don't have to choose," she says. "But if I had to, my husband."

*   *   *

Back in New York in their rental apartment on 444 East 57th Street, the Millers enjoy hosting friends and family.

"There was good talk there about books and plays," says Miller's father, Isidore. "Everybody sat on the floor."

Everything in the large living room is white; the carpets, the walls, the furniture, even the marble torso of Aphrodite—and a white-painted piano. It's the same one from Marilyn's child-hood, the one her mother had bought.

"When I was beginning to earn some money modeling," Marilyn explains, "I started looking for the Fredric March piano. After about a year I found it in an old auction room and bought it. It's been painted a lovely white, and it has new strings and plays as wonderfully as any piano in the world."

Miller would write in one room of their Chanel-scented, white-on-white apartment, occasionally interrupting his typing to come gaze upon his bride.

When journalist Donald Zec visits the couple for tea, he notes, "They looked at each with a tenderness that a single sound would have shattered."

Miller turns his attention to Marilyn Monroe Productions (MMP).

Last year, while at Pyramid Ranch awaiting his divorce while Marilyn was filming *Bus Stop*, Miller had promised her, "ALL of these Milton troubles and Josh troubles and all that crap is nonsense that will fade off as soon as I can take charge. You will simply have a business relationship with these people."

Yes, Joshua Logan directed Marilyn to her most acclaimed

performance to date. And Milton Greene inspired Marilyn to challenge the studio system and demand the contract she deserved. But despite Greene's expertise as a celebrity photographer, he has no experience with motion pictures. He's invested what money he could, but he's failed to secure any major backers.

The Greenes seem to live luxuriously, and the fear is that Marilyn is paying. During filming of *The Prince and the Showgirl*, there were rumors of Greene buying a Jaguar and antiques in England and charging the expenses through MMP.

Of the company's one hundred shares, fifty-one are controlled by Marilyn and forty-nine by Greene. Miller begins to edge Greene out, replacing Greene as vice president of MMP.

Marilyn cuts Greene off, ignoring his calls and letters much as she did to Natasha Lytess before him. In a collateral breakup, Marilyn replaces Dr. Margaret Hohenberg—the psychoanalyst she'd previously shared with Greene—with Dr. Marianne Kris, who comes recommended by no less than Sigmund Freud's daughter, Anna.

At Kris's Central Park West office, Marilyn attends up to five sessions a week as the negotiations with Greene progress toward their acrimonious conclusion. Greene accepts a buyout of $100,000, and although he will retain producing credit for *The Prince and the Showgirl*, his Hollywood career is over.

Marilyn takes to calling herself "MMM," for Marilyn Miller Monroe. The couple envisions a summer entwined by the sea in eastern Long Island. "What a lovely place this is—it's got water all around it" is Marilyn's first impression of the area.

They rent Hill House on the private one-hundred-acre oceanfront estate at Stony Hill Farm. "Now we could take easy breaths in a more normal rhythm of life," Miller says.

But on May 31, the House Committee on Un-American Activities finds Arthur Miller guilty of contempt of Congress for his earlier refusal to name names. "Although he testified frankly about his own relationships with persons of Communist bent or membership, he said that his conscience had forbidden him to tell about others," the *New York Times* reports. "At his apartment, 444 East Fifty-seventh Street, Mr. Miller declined yesterday to comment on his conviction."

The consequences of refusing to cooperate with HUAC are harsh. Miller is denied a passport and may face a fine and even a prison sentence. Marilyn's advised to persuade him to comply with the court's demands or risk her own career, but she refuses, saying, "I'm proud of my husband's position and I stand behind him all the way."

The couple slips away. Reporters know the location of Hill House, but not of their second rental retreat at 64 Deep Lane in Amagansett. Marilyn is charmed that a windmill is built into the 1830 house, but privacy is its most valuable feature.

The Prince and the Showgirl—jointly released by Marilyn Monroe Productions and Warner Bros. Pictures—makes its world premiere at Radio City Music Hall on June 13, 1957, as a charity event hosted by Marilyn Monroe Productions to benefit the Milk Fund for Babies.

Marilyn appears at the premiere in a white satin mermaid-tail gown, an evening variation on her most memorable costume in the film. Fans clamor for a glimpse, one getting close enough to brush one of Marilyn's chandelier earrings out of her ear. Arthur Miller, elegant in black tie, replaces the bauble. Photographers never stop shooting, trailing the stars to a gala champagne supper-dance at the Waldorf Astoria.

The film is a light amusement, critics agree, though many lavish Marilyn's performance with praise. "Her best cinema effort" proclaims the *Los Angeles Times*. The *New York Post* says, "Marilyn Monroe has never seemed more as a person and as a comedienne."

Despite the issues during shooting, the film is a financial success. "When you look at the film," Miller's sister Joan Copeland notes, "it is apparent who won the battle, & it wasn't Olivier." Olivier himself agrees, admitting, "Maybe I was tetchy with Marilyn and with myself because I felt my career was in a rut. Her personality was strong on the screen. She gave a star performance." From a distance, the director can admit, "I was good as could be; and Marilyn! Marilyn was quite wonderful, the best of all. So. What do you know?"

To her stepchildren, twelve-year-old Jane and ten-year-old Robert, Marilyn writes warm, funny letters in the voices of Sugar Feeny, the family cat, and Hugo the Basset Hound.

"Hugo" confesses to Bobby: "I made a mistake and I am sorry but I chewed up one of your baseballs. I didn't mean to. I thought it was a tennis ball and that it wouldn't make any difference but Daddy and Marilyn said they would get you another one."

Before they married, Miller wrote Marilyn of the blissful domesticity he imagined they'd share.

"How happy I will make you! What beautiful children I will give you!"

Those are Marilyn's dreams, too.

She's prayed on it over *Daily Prayers,* the book she received from the Avenue N Jewish Center after her conversion.

But faith can't cure her chronic endometriosis. Neither can the surgery she underwent back in 1954, days before she moved to New York. The doctor had cautioned her that endometriosis scarring increased the chances of an ectopic pregnancy occurring outside the uterus. Marilyn is not afraid to take that risk, and she is delighted to become pregnant again in the summer of 1957.

Miller is more tempered in his joy. "The doctor, having administered a series of treatments over a period of weeks, had confirmed that she was pregnant, but could still not rule out the possibility of an ectopic pregnancy," he says. "But she was deaf to this cautionary tone. A child of her own was a crown with a thousand diamonds. I did all I could to throw myself into her anticipatory mood."

To Hedda Rosten, Marilyn confides: "I think I've been pregnant for about three weeks or maybe two. My breasts have been too sore to even touch—I've never had that in my life before—also they ache—also I've been having cramps...I did not eat all day yesterday—also last night I took 4 whole amutal sleeping pills—which was by actual count 8 little amutal sleeping pills.

"Could I have killed it by taking all the amutal on an empty stomach? (Except I took some sherry wine also).

"What shall I do? If it is still alive, I want to keep it."

On August 1, Miller is at his writing desk when he hears screams from the garden. He rushes to Marilyn's side. Her pain is so severe that she briefly loses consciousness.

In the back of the ambulance, she gives way to her agonizing sorrow. All she wants is a family. All she has ever wanted is family. Someone to love. Will she never be allowed that?

Newspapers report: "MISS MONROE was rushed 100 miles to the hospital Thursday afternoon. A hospital spokesman said she was in great pain during the operation and was given a blood transfusion.

"On her admittance to the hospital Thursday afternoon, Miss Monroe's doctor said she was 'five or six weeks pregnant' and that her baby was expected 'around the end of March.'"

The doctors operate, and confirm it was a non-viable ectopic pregnancy. They assure her that she can have more babies. But as Miller tenderly oversees her recovery, he sees how far Marilyn has fallen. Sometimes she cries. Sometimes she sleeps. Mostly, she looks blankly at the wall.

"She lay there sad beyond sadness," Miller observes. "And there were no words anymore that could change anything for her."

Miller has sold his original property on Tophet Road in Roxbury, Connecticut, and purchased land enough for an expansive country estate.

On a spread of over three hundred acres, Miller and Marilyn seed fruit trees and a pine forest. A house built in 1783 still stands, with its massive wood-beamed ceilings.

"All our friends agreed the land was beautiful," Marilyn tells a columnist, "but they said the house was just uninhabitable. I looked at it, and thought how it had been standing there, weathering everything for more than 180 years. And I just hated the idea of its being torn down or even left unoccupied."

She contacts the famed architect Frank Lloyd Wright and drives the ninety-year-old all the way from Manhattan to view the property.

"Ah, yes, the old house. Don't put a nickel in it," the architect immediately pronounces. But his plans to construct a new home in the side of the hill would require, Miller estimates, "heavy construction on the order of the Maginot Line."

Instead, they embark on a modernizing renovation that includes a new writing studio for Miller. They keep company with Hugo the Basset Hound, along with an expanding menagerie, including a mongrel dog called Cindy and Butch the talking parakeet, who repeats, "I'm Marilyn's bird. I'm Marilyn's bird."

But this bucolic life fails to keep her anchored in the physical world.

To temper her wild emotional swings, she drinks champagne and vodka in the morning with whatever pills she needs. Sometimes she cracks open the capsules and pours the powders directly into her drink; other times she sprinkles them under her tongue. At night, she pricks holes into the casings of her barbiturates to speed the effects.

When Miller walks into the sitting room to find Marilyn slumped on the sofa, he's not immediately sure that she's overdosed.

"There's no words to describe her breathing when she is in trouble with pills," he writes. "The diaphragm isn't working. The breathing is peaceful, great sighs. It took me an awfully long time before I knew what was coming on."

An ambulance arrives to revive her once again.

CHAPTER 45

"I'M DYING TO WORK with you again," Billy Wilder writes to Marilyn on March 17, 1958. Wilder, who directed Marilyn in *The Seven Year Itch,* pitches her on his new project, *Some Like It Hot.*

Marilyn hasn't worked on a film since wrapping *The Prince and the Showgirl* in November 1956. Work, Arthur Miller believes, will help Marilyn recover from losing the baby in August. He encourages her to say yes, especially to the lucrative financial offer of $100,000, plus 10 percent of the profits.

She reads the synopsis and sees the comic potential. Wilder's planning to reinvent a 1935 French farce (and a 1951 German remake) into a contemporary love story set in 1929 Chicago. But her part is a supporting role. What's worse, she's once again being cast as a dumb blonde.

Marilyn remains undecided. She writes to her friend the poet Norman Rosten and questions, "Should I do my next picture or stay home and try to have a baby again? That's what I want most of all, the baby, I guess, but maybe God is trying to tell me something, I mean with my pregnancy. I'd probably make a kooky mother; I'd love my child to death. I want it, yet I'm scared. Arthur says he wants it, but he's losing his enthusiasm. He thinks I should do the picture. After all, I'm a movie star, right?"

Her contract specifies that her films must be made in color. This one won't be. Wilder envisions the period piece in black-and-white.

Technicolor would perfectly suit Marilyn as singer and ukulele player Sugar "Kane" Kowalczyk. But Tony Curtis as Joe/Josephine and Jack Lemmon as Jerry/Daphne—two jazz musicians fleeing the mob after accidentally witnessing the St. Valentine's Day Massacre—will play nearly every scene dressed and made up as women.

Lee Strasberg's insight into the character relationships finally unlocks the role. "Sugar's like you," he says to Marilyn. "You've haven't ever had friends who were girls. Now suddenly, here are two women, and they want to be your friend! They like you. For the first time in your life, you have two friends who are girls!"

Curtis and Lemmon do pass as girls—they even go in costume to the women's restroom in the MGM commissary to reapply their lipstick, and the other actresses using the mirror recognize them only as women.

MONROE TO DO "HOT," *Variety* announces in April 1958.

United Artists and the Mirisch Company, which will produce and distribute the film, throw Marilyn a party. Cocktails are called for 7 p.m. and dinner at 9. Most of the A-list guests are gathering their coats to leave the party when Marilyn finally arrives at 11:20.

By August, sixty pages of the script are finished.

"We'll finish the rest while we shoot," Wilder says. He and screenwriter I. A. L. Diamond typically collaborate on the fly. "We sit there and we try to find something," Wilder says. "Sometimes nothing. Sometimes we just sit there and wait."

On July, 14, 1958, "Marilyn Miller" arrives at Dr. Michael Gurdin's office at UCLA. Her appointment with the plastic surgeon is a follow-up.

Under "chief complaint," Gurdin records "chin deformity" on her chart.

"I cannot palpate any cartilage subcutaneously," the doctor notes, referencing the "mild flatness of chin" treated by "Gurdin and Pangman."

Gurdin concludes that the "1950 cartilage implant has slowly been absorbed."

All that's left is the faded scar.

On August 4, 1958, shooting begins on the back lot of MGM. Marilyn and Wilder immediately clash. "I'm not going back into that film until Wilder reshoots my opening," Marilyn says, incensed at what she feels is an overemphasis on Tony Curtis's character.

Her entrance onto a railway platform is reworked. As Marilyn walks by in a black suit, the steam engine puffs two quick blasts of hot air toward her famous legs — a clever nod to the subway grate scene in *The Seven Year Itch.*

Marilyn is understandably emotional. She's just learned that she is once again newly pregnant.

Her husband can't be on set with her because he is — once again — in court. On August 8, the United States Court of Appeals for the District of Columbia rules in his favor. MILLER IS CLEARED OF HOUSE CONTEMPT, the *New York Times* reports. The decision, Miller says in a statement, makes "the long struggle of the past few years fully worth while."

The shoot for *Some Like It Hot* is projected to run fifty days. To Marilyn, it seems doable with Paula Strasberg by her side.

Marilyn will listen only to Paula. Wilder addresses the situation head-on, pausing each take to ask the acting coach, "How was that for you, Paula?"

The tactic helps keep the peace — for a time.

Wilder's also heard all about Strasberg and her bag of pills. Marilyn's pregnancy has put the pills on hold, but without them it's impossible for her to get to sleep until 3 or 4 a.m. With call times as early as 6:30 a.m., Marilyn's paranoid insomnia takes hold.

The shoot is already experiencing costly delays. "Marilyn Monroe was ill again yesterday and unable to report to work in 'Some Like It Hot,' in which she's only appeared on set two hours so far," *Variety* columnist Army Archerd reports on August 21, 1958, adding, "And she's nixed every still taken."

In September, the cast and crew move to the beach at Coronado, California, where the historic Hotel Del Coronado is the stand-in for the film's fictional Florida resort. With jets from the local naval base flying overhead, takes must be carefully timed.

The first day in the new location goes smoothly, with onlookers coming to cheer on Marilyn and Tony Curtis. "Marilyn remembered her lines," Wilder says. "Everything was fine."

Wilder's directing style is to work in master scenes, meaning he captures all of the action in one continuous shot, and then calls "That's a Print!" without running the camera for even an extra moment. Because of that technique, Marilyn is convinced that he's missing the best moments of her performance.

She wards off intense bouts of dizziness and stage fright by sipping from a thermos alternately filled with coffee, vermouth, and a caffeinated, alcoholic mixture of the beverages.

As a stress release, Paula coaches Marilyn to flutter her arms before delivering her lines to the camera. To cast and crew, the gesture resembles a nervous tic. They spend hours on set waiting for Marilyn to emerge from her dressing room.

"Arthur, I don't get my first shot until three in the afternoon. What does she do in the mornings?" Wilder asks Marilyn's husband in frustration.

Back on the MGM lot in October, tensions continue to rise.

Marilyn continues her late arrivals on set. Screenwriter

Diamond attributes it to a power play. "Having reached the top she was paying back the world for all the rotten things she had had to go through," he says.

He's not wrong. *It makes something in me happy—to be late. People are waiting for me. People are eager to see me. I'm wanted. And I remember the years I was unwanted,* Marilyn thinks. *I feel a queer satisfaction in punishing the people who are wanting to see me now. But it's not them I'm really punishing. It's the long ago people who didn't want Norma Jeane.*

"Story of my life. I always get the fuzzy end of the lollypop" is one of Sugar Kane's lines. Marilyn contends that the part is veering too close to the dumb-blonde stereotype, that she's playing the "straight man" to Curtis and Lemmon's leading roles.

They play a scene where Curtis and Lemmon are in their hotel room, out of their disguises. Sugar knocks on the door and they call out in their female voices, "Just a minute."

Her line is "It's me, Sugar."

But Marilyn keeps saying "Sugar, it's me."

"She had only one sentence, she needed eighty-three takes," an exasperated Wilder says.

Her next big line is "Where's that bourbon?" Wilder takes the extreme measure of writing the words in the chest of drawers where her character is searching for the bottle.

After the sixtieth take, Wilder says, "Marilyn, come on. Relax, don't worry."

"Worry about what?" Marilyn says.

"If she gets the line out, absolutely perfect," Wilder says. "Perfect in timing, the sound of her voice. She knew what a joke was. She was not a dilettante. She was born with that kind of gift. Because you can have fifty actresses. They may all be quite good. Some of them might be great technicians, but no one would be better than her."

Yet the fifty-day filming schedule stretches to more than seventy.

As the shoot drags on, Wilder develops nerve damage to his neck that leaves him directing the film lying flat on a board.

The final scene — where Jerry and Osgood Fielding III, his unwitting fiancé, flee the mob on board Osgood's boat — is shot last, with last-minute dialogue drafted into the script.

When Jerry admits, "I'M A MAN!" Osgood shoots back, "Well, nobody's perfect."

The ending sticks.

Producer Harold Mirisch calls United Artists to report: "They didn't do 'too bad' cost-wise although Miss Monroe is impossible to control." They missed thirteen days, which made the costs go up by hundreds of thousands of dollars.

On the other hand, Mirisch can't stop raving about the film's quality, boasting, "We have one of the biggest pictures of the year."

Wilder races to get a first cut ready in a couple of weeks.

In early December 1958, the first preview is held at the Bay Theatre in upscale Pacific Palisades. The theater is full, but the reception is dire — no one laughs except comedian and variety TV show host Steve Allen. Is the audience "really that square?" Allen asks.

Mirisch tells Billy Wilder to cut twenty minutes from the *Some Like It Hot* two-hour running time. Wilder disagrees. He cuts only sixty seconds.

With Wilder aiming to prove it's not the running time but the audience, the next preview takes place later that week in the younger, hipper neighborhood of Westwood Village, home to UCLA.

This time, the theater is filled with screams of laughter.

Marilyn is the one who steals the film. "It takes a real artist to come on the set and not know her lines and yet give the performance she did," Wilder concedes.

Yet the director does not invite her to the wrap party he throws at his home. Through some silver-screen magic, her performance on film reads as nuanced, melancholy, and sublime—but her popularity with the cast and crew is at an all-time low.

During daily rushes, there had been a moment where a frustrated Tony Curtis invoked Marilyn and Hitler in the same breath. "After take forty, kissing Marilyn is like kissing Hitler" is what he claims to have said, though other, unkinder versions of the quote are quickly repeated. Asked if he'd ever make another movie with Monroe, Wilder jokes, "I have discussed this with my doctor and my psychiatrist, and they both tell me I'm too old and too rich to go through this again." Marilyn is hospitalized with exhaustion—for the second time in three months. She is placed on bed rest with a drip for four days, then leaves in an ambulance so as not to "jar the baby" and flies back to New York and to the anxious embrace of Arthur Miller.

On December 17, 1958, there's another private showing of *Some Like It Hot*.

But while the audience is still laughing at the last line of the film, "Well, nobody's perfect," Marilyn, five months pregnant, has another miscarriage.

Neither Miller nor Marilyn's psychiatrist, Dr. Kris, nor the Strasbergs can keep her from falling into a deep depression.

On January 27, 1959, the National Institute of Arts and Letters announces that Arthur Miller will be awarded the Gold Medal for Drama for his career achievements.

As Miller is being elevated, Marilyn is spiraling downward.

That night, Marilyn's maid, Lena Pepitone, discovers Marilyn lying unconscious in bed, her face covered in vomit. With Miller away, she calls the private doctor. Marilyn's stomach is pumped, again.

At 3 a.m., fearful of leaving Marilyn alone, Pepitone calls Norman and Hedda Rosten, who rush to her bedside.

"It's me, Norman, how are you my dear?" he asks, taking hold of her hand.

"Alive," she replies, her eyelids fluttering, her voice gravelly and slowed by the effects of the drugs. "Worst luck. Cruel of them all." She laughs a little. "All those bastards. Oh Jesus... Who'd notice if I went."

"I would," he says. "I would notice very much."

Rosten sits and holds her hand for hours and lets her cry. He knows she's done this before and will probably do it again. It's important to make sure she's found in time. It's a wave of deep sadness, but no one is stuck in a wave forever. It passes. She just has to get through the wave.

On March 29, 1959, barely four months after shooting wraps, *Some Like It Hot* premieres at Loew's State Theatre.

It's been nearly four years since *The Seven Year Itch* debuted in this same location, but the crowds have not diminished in the slightest. Thousands of people line the street in New York City's Times Square.

"Mr. and Mrs. Arthur Miller have arrived," a broadcaster narrates. "Hundreds of photographers out there surround them. They can't even move to get in. They need that police protection, believe me. She looks fantastic. And I'm only looking at her hair."

In its review, *Variety* praises Marilyn as "a comedienne with sex appeal and timing that just can't be beat."

With Marilyn, the professional can never be separated from the personal. "If at the time of filming she was pregnant, and the tight dresses she's asked to wear just don't fit well, never mind," the review continues. "This gal can take it."

Can she?

Not long after the film is released, Marilyn sends Rosten a poem.

Help Help
Help I feel life coming closer
When all I want to do is to die.

CHAPTER 46

SOME LIKE IT HOT makes $13 million in its initial release.

A COMIC MARILYN SETS MOVIE AGLOW proclaims the cover of *Life* magazine's April 20, 1959, issue, which pictures the star clutching a strand of diamonds between her teeth.

Yet despite their combined fame and talent, Marilyn and Arthur Miller are effectively broke.

"All he cares about is himself, his own writing...and money...that's all," Marilyn complains. "It's always money. He's obsessed with money."

Marilyn Monroe Productions has paid him $250,000 for the screenplay for *The Misfits*, which he's yet to complete.

"I would not have written it except for Marilyn," Miller says. He sees *The Misfits* screenplay as a tribute to his "belief in her as an actress."

The character he's writing for her—"Roslyn," a naïve ex-stripper who has come to Reno, Nevada, to get a divorce—wasn't in the short story he earlier published in *Esquire* in October 1957, a fictionalization of the scenes he observed at

Pyramid Ranch while he waited for his own divorce from his first wife.

But the role and partial script bewilder Marilyn. Is this how he sees his wife? Is Miller himself the man who Roslyn says "wasn't there. I mean you could touch him but he wasn't there"?

Marilyn's frequently away from home.

She attends the Chicago premiere of *Some Like It Hot* at the United Artists Theatre and holds a press conference at the Ambassador East. Alfred Hitchcock recently filmed parts of *North by Northwest* at the hotel, where preparations for its "Sky High Soiree" for the July 1 world premiere are already underway when the stars of *Some Like It Hot* arrive.

The hotel is a celebrity mecca, where a US senator on the guest list attracts relatively little notice. There can be no publicity for Marilyn's admirer, political rising star Jack Kennedy— or his clandestine meeting here with Sam Giancana, who since 1957 has led the Chicago Outfit branch of the American Mob.

Rising through the ranks as a getaway driver and hitman for Al Capone, Giancana was disqualified from US military service by a psychologist who classified him as a "constitutional psychopath" with "strong antisocial trends." That diagnosis didn't stop Giancana from forging connections with powerful celebrities and politicians.

One of Giancana's good friends is Frank Sinatra, whom Billy Wilder pursued to play the role of Jerry/Daphne in *Some Like It Hot.* But when Sinatra failed to show for a lunch with

Wilder, the director went with Jack Lemmon, opposite Tony Curtis, who rose to fame as a Universal contract player and as the husband of MGM star Janet Leigh. "You're the handsomest kid in town," Wilder told Curtis. "Who else am I going to use?"

Senator Jack Kennedy won't risk missing a meeting with Giancana, whose Chicago influence he sees as crucial to his upcoming run for the White House.

Kennedy's calendar fills with what by all appearances are soft campaign events that frequently bring him to New York, where he often meets up with Marilyn. On April 30, 1959, he addresses the American Women in Radio and Television. On May 31, he appears on New York senator Ken Keating's television program *Let's Look at Congress.*

"My guest today is Senator John F. Kennedy of Massachusetts, who is generally regarded, as near as I can find out, as the leading candidate for the Democratic nomination for president in 1960—although you can't get him to make any formal announcement of his candidacy."

It's a leading statement, but Kennedy deftly changes topics. The Cold War is an important issue for many voters. "I think it's quite obvious," Kennedy says, "that we're engaged in pretty much of a death struggle with the Soviet Union."

In September 1959, Marilyn and 20th Century-Fox renew negotiations.

Bus Stop premiered three years ago. The studio is pressuring her to honor her 1955 contract and commit to her next picture.

None of the scripts presented to Marilyn appeal to her, but

she agrees to star in the CinemaScope musical comedy *Let's Make Love*—provided her husband, Arthur Miller, is brought in to punch up the script.

Studio head Spyros Skouras agrees to her demand, in part because he desperately needs Marilyn's help on another matter.

President Dwight D. Eisenhower has invited Soviet premier Nikita Khrushchev, who's "curious to have a look at America," on a twelve-day national tour, including a visit to the Fox lot to watch the filming of *Can-Can,* a period musical starring Frank Sinatra and Shirley MacLaine. The day before Khrushchev's Tupolev 114 aircraft lands at Andrews Air Force Base outside Washington, DC, the Soviets land a man-made object on the moon, not only pulling ahead in the space race but also magnifying America's Cold War fears.

Though Arthur Miller was cleared last year of contempt of Congress, his run-ins with the House Un-American Activities Committee keep him off the guest list. Marilyn, however, with her curvaceous figure, baby-soft voice, and fluffy blond hair that has to be bleached on a weekly basis, is at the top of that list.

"She *has* to be there," Skouras says. He tells Marilyn that "in Russia, America meant two things, Coca-Cola and Marilyn Monroe."

She agrees to attend and is instructed to wear a tight dress to meet the Soviet premier. "I guess there's not much sex in Russia," Marilyn tells Lena Pepitone as they choose a black dress with lace cutouts on the chest and shoulder straps.

"Do you think Khrushchev wants to see you?" a reporter asks.

"I hope he does," Marilyn replies.

In Marilyn's bungalow at the Beverly Hills Hotel, Whitey Snyder does her makeup, and she steps into the chosen black dress. For once, she's running ahead of schedule. When her chauffeur delivers Marilyn to an empty parking lot, she says, "We must be *late*! It must be over."

American and Soviet police nearly outnumber the A-listers lunching with Khrushchev at the Fox lot's famed commissary, the Café de Paris, on September 19. Chemists work the kitchen, testing the food for poison, taking special precautions with Khrushchev's plate before it's sent out to the head table.

Marilyn is seated with her *Bus Stop* director Joshua Logan and with actor, Navy veteran, and Dodgers fan Henry Fonda, who's wearing an earplug attached to a transistor radio tuned to the Dodgers-Giants game, where the National League pennant is at stake.

A few tables away, Judy Garland jokes with Shelley Winters, saying, "I think we should all get blind drunk and hiss and boo and carry on." Elizabeth Taylor dares to climb on top of table 15 to get a better look at Khrushchev.

She sees a disappointed man, short in stature and heavy in the belly.

At the start of the meal, Khrushchev's wife, Nina, tells Bob Hope of her excitement to see Disneyland. Midway through lunch, however, the premier learns that the excursion has been canceled because the Los Angeles police chief can't ensure their safety.

The sixty-five-year-old Russian leader's planned speech veers into an angry condemnation of theme-park security.

"Do you have rocket launching pads there?" Khrushchev

demands to know. "What is it? Is there an epidemic of cholera or plague there? Or have gangsters taken hold of the place that can destroy me? And I say I would very much like to go and see Disneyland. For me such a situation is inconceivable."

Elizabeth Taylor and Dean Martin look on, initially laughing at what they believe are jokes—until they realize how serious he is.

"Screw the cops!" Frank Sinatra whispers to actor David Niven. "Tell the old broad that you and I will take 'em down there this afternoon."

Studio head Skouras worries that the situation is escalating, but Marilyn's charms soften Khrushchev. He takes her hand and says, "You're a very lovely young lady," as he looks her slowly up and down.

Khrushchev looked at me like a man looks on a woman, Marilyn thinks, but politely replies, "My husband, Arthur Miller, sends you his greeting."

Skouras leads the premier along to Sound Stage 8, where a costumed Sinatra explains *Can-Can*: "This is a movie about a lot of pretty girls—and the fellows who like pretty girls."

Khrushchev seems to be enjoying himself until Shirley MacLaine starts to dance. The leader's reaction to the can-can is not unlike Joe DiMaggio's when he watched Marilyn dance in *There's No Business Like Show Business,* here on the Fox lot.

"There are moments in this dance that cannot be considered quite decent," the Soviet premier says, amplifying that it was "immoral and tasteless. This is a pornographic film and won't be allowed in Russia."

* * *

"From an entertainer's point of view, what did you think of the show today?" a reporter asks Marilyn afterward.

"Very interesting afternoon," she says.

"What did you find most interesting?"

"Most everything."

"What did you think of the ad libs?" the reporter presses.

"Interesting. Very interesting."

CHAPTER 47

GEORGE CUKOR WILL be leading Marilyn's next production, *Let's Make Love*.

Cukor, celebrated as an actors' director, discovered Katharine Hepburn and directed James Stewart to a Best Actor Oscar for 1940's *The Philadelphia Story*. But no one wants to work with Marilyn. Cukor can't convince either Stewart, or Cary Grant, or Rock Hudson, or Gregory Peck, or any other top actor to play opposite the increasingly unreliable Marilyn.

Her top choice is Yves Montand, a thirty-eight-year-old Frenchman whose career was launched by the beloved Parisian singer Edith Piaf, and whose recent singing tour of the United States caught Marilyn's attention. Arthur Miller is also well acquainted with Yves Montand and his wife Simone Signoret, the leftist, educated, well-read co-stars of the French production of Miller's play, *The Crucible*. Signoret's latest film, *Room at the Top*, premiered the same week as *Some Like It Hot*.

Marilyn overrules the studio's objections—that Montand has never appeared in a Hollywood film and will need to learn

English to play this role—and Montand is eventually cast as her leading man.

In a press conference announcing that rehearsals for the musical comedy will begin in January 1960, Marilyn declares: "Next to my husband and Marlon Brando, I think Yves Montand is the most attractive man I've ever met!"

On January 2, 1960, Senator Jack Kennedy speaks from the US Senate Caucus Room in Washington, DC.

"I am announcing today my candidacy for the Presidency of the United States . . . I have developed an image of America as fulfilling a noble and historic role as the defender of freedom in a time of maximum peril—and of the American people as confident, courageous and persevering. It is with this image that I begin this campaign."

Photographers pose the new candidate next to his beautiful wife, Jackie. Their bright smiles create a portrait of the perfect marriage.

The breaking news takes Marilyn by surprise.

Los Angeles is a long way from Dr. Kris and her New York couch, so an emergency stand-in is called to Marilyn's bedside at the Beverly Hills Hotel.

Like Kris, Dr. Ralph Greenson is a friend of the Freud family. Born Romeo Samuel Greenschpoon in Brooklyn, New York, he graduated from Columbia University, earned his medical degree at the University of Bern in Switzerland, and is now a Professor of Clinical Psychiatry at the UCLA School of Medicine.

Dr. Greenson comes personally recommended. Among his

celebrity clientele is Frank Sinatra. The singer's lawyer, Mickey Rudin, also represents Marilyn, and is married to Greenson's sister, Elizabeth Greenschpoon.

When Dr. Greenson arrives, already briefed on Marilyn's liaisons with Kennedy, she is immediately comforted by the presence of this new doctor who's so very understanding, compassionate, and well-versed in all her problems — almost as if he knows her already.

In slurred, halting words, Marilyn makes a confession. She's taken some pills. She swallowed a few with a large glass of water, though she's not sure which ones or how many.

Dr. Greenson examines the labels on the bottles at her bedside, gently shaking each one to gauge its contents. *How can one person be allowed so many prescriptions?* he wonders.

"Stupid doctors," he mutters. "Stupid, stupid doctors." Supplying a patient, no matter how famous, with whatever she thinks she needs only puts her in danger.

For hours, Greenson listens to his new patient's ramblings. Marilyn describes her husband as a man who is "cold and unfeeling and doesn't love her." Of Jack Kennedy, she speaks animatedly. She envisions running away with the senator as the new Mrs. Kennedy.

America's most famous actress with a man who could be America's next president? Why not? She married America's greatest living sportsman, and then America's greatest living writer.

Greenson's initial assessment of Marilyn is that she suffers from symptoms of paranoia and schizophrenia.

"As she becomes more anxious," he writes, "she begins to act like an orphan, a waif, and she masochistically provokes people to mistreat her and to take advantage of her. As fragments of her past history came out, she began to talk more about the traumatic experience of an orphan child."

Marilyn asks Greenson to return. To her friend Norman Rosten, she describes the doctor as "Jesus — My savior."

"Jesus — How so?" Rosten asks.

"He listens to me."

Sensing that Marilyn is prepared to test the boundaries of doctor and patient, Greenson warns that he will not "help her kill herself, or spite her husband."

Miller, he feels, has "the attitude of a father who had done more than most fathers would do and is rapidly coming to the end of his rope."

Most astonishing to Greenson is Marilyn's tolerance for drugs. "Although she resembled an addict," the doctor observes, "she did not seem to be the usual addict, she seemed to be able to give up the drugs without heavy withdrawal symptoms."

He enlists internist Dr. Hyman Engelberg in his quest to limit her drug usage. Part of the challenge is Marilyn's ongoing obsession with sleep. One afternoon, she begs him for an Amytal intravenous drip, despite having slept some fourteen hours the night before.

Amytal sodium is a powerful barbiturate used as a preanesthetic before surgery.

Greenson tells Marilyn that she's "already received so much medication that it would put five other people to sleep." Sleeping with less medication is possible, he promises, "if she would recognize she is fighting sleep as well as searching for some oblivion which is not sleep."

CHAPTER 48

FOX HAS ALLOTTED ten weeks for rehearsal before shooting of *Let's Make Love* begins on Sound Stage 11.

The plot centers on billionaire Jean-Marc Clément somehow landing an unlikely off-Broadway role playing himself in a musical about his own life. Clement uses his wealth to hire Bing Crosby, Gene Kelly, and Milton Berle — all making cameos as themselves — to polish his singing and dancing enough to impress Marilyn's character, Amanda Dell, a performer who prefers talent to wealth.

In real life, Marilyn is also polishing her skills in a dance studio with Jack Cole, the exacting choreographer who directed the song-and-dance numbers in *Gentlemen Prefer Blondes*.

After they've worked together on six pictures, most recently *Some Like It Hot*, Cole's cues are familiar to Marilyn.

"No, wait. Sharp, I want it sharp!" Cole demands.

"But Jack, I'm supposed to be a sex queen," Marilyn says.

"That's not sexy. That's like a limp fish. Put that arm out there, strong! That's sexy! That's life, that's alive, that's energy!"

Marilyn is not a natural dancer, but Cole maximizes her abilities by teaching her to make small gestures with her head or her hip, trusting her to connect with her instinctual sensuality—and sexuality.

They've become good friends, but Marilyn hasn't been acting like one during this shoot. She's been late to set, distracted, distant. There's much to rehearse, especially on the Cole Porter number "My Heart Belongs to Daddy," where Marilyn will dance among an ensemble in an elaborately choreographed piece Jack Cole envisions rivaling the "Diamonds Are a Girl's Best Friend" number he created for *Gentlemen Prefer Blondes*.

Cukor shares the same frustrations most directors have with Marilyn, but he has more sympathy. "I knew that she was reckless. I knew that she was willful. She was very sweet, but I had no real communication with her at all," he says. "You couldn't get at her...As a director I really had very little influence on her. All I could do was make a climate that was agreeable for her. Every day was an agony of struggle for her, just to get there."

Despite her film-star status, Marilyn still has an odd phobia of the camera—and an inability to remember her lines—but somehow, none of that matters. "She'd do three lines and then forget everything again. You had to shoot it piecemeal. But curiously enough, when you strung everything together, it was complete."

For the duration of the shoot, the studio has booked the co-stars and their spouses into bungalows 20 and 21 at the Beverly Hills Hotel. Yves Montand's wife, Simone Signoret, is amused by Marilyn, who looks like "the most beautiful peasant girl imaginable from the Île-de-France."

Montand is learning English phonetically from the script, but it's a challenge. To spare him the stress of potentially embarrassing himself in front of director George Cukor and the crew, Marilyn suggests that they work on their lines together at the hotel.

Miller is no fan of the script, but he has agreed to do some script doctoring, "to try to save her from a complete catastrophe." Though his marriage to Marilyn is under severe strain, he wants to be a devoted spouse, "giving her the kind of emotional support that would convince her that she was no longer alone in the world—the heart of the problem, I assumed."

But helping with the script doesn't have the effect Miller hoped, leaving him feeling unappreciated. "It was a bad miscalculation, bringing us no closer to each other."

Hollywood awards season opens with the Golden Globe Awards, held at the Cocoanut Grove in the Ambassador Hotel on March 10, 1960. *Some Like It Hot* wins Best Picture–Comedy, Jack Lemmon wins Best Actor in a Comedy, and Marilyn wins Best Actress in a Comedy.

Tony Randall, who's co-starring in *Let's Make Love,* helps Marilyn to the stage to accept the award. Marilyn, a white fur stole over a strapless white dress, beams and holds her trophy high. "Thank you from the bottom of my heart," she purrs.

It's a vindicating moment.

Simone Signoret is also nominated for a Golden Globe, for Best Actress in a Drama for *Room at the Top,* but she doesn't win—yet less than a month later, she beats out Doris Day,

Audrey Hepburn, Katharine Hepburn, and Elizabeth Taylor to win the Oscar statuette for Best Actress.

After a brief acceptance speech, she's off to France to film another picture. Meanwhile, Miller travels to Galway, Ireland, for script meetings with John Huston, who directed Marilyn in *The Asphalt Jungle* and is soon to direct her next film, *The Misfits*.

MARILYN'S HUSBAND IN GALWAY, the newspapers announce.

With their spouses away, Marilyn and her leading man grow closer.

"Tell me," Signoret asks hypothetically, "do you know who could resist if they took Marilyn Monroe into their arms?"

Not Yves Montand.

After missing a day of filming on Sound Stage 11, Marilyn asks Montand back to her room to rehearse. She's been ill, she says, lying in bed with a bottle of cold champagne and a small bucket of caviar, dressed in a transparent night dress. She asks him to give her a kiss goodnight.

Montand moves as if in a reverie. *I bent down to put a good-night kiss on her cheek. And her head turned and my lips went wild. It was a wonderful, tender kiss. A kiss of fire. A hurricane, I could not stop. I was half-stunned, stammering, I straightened up, already flooded with guilt, wondering what was happening to me. I didn't wonder for long.*

Soon it's Montand—not Paula Strasberg on the Fox payroll for $2,000 a week—to whom Marilyn turns for affirmation at the end of each take. Another night, she knocks on his bedroom door, naked but for a mink coat.

Soon the bellboys at the Beverly Hills Hotel, along with Fox hair, makeup, and wardrobe, start to talk. Back from Ireland, Arthur Miller is said to have caught them in bed together.

"An actress whose name came up at this year's Oscars is having marital problems," one gossip columnist reports. Others advise Marilyn to stop sleeping with other people's husbands.

"If Marilyn is in love with my husband, it proves she has good taste," Signoret declares. "For I am in love with him too."

Dr. Greenson's office is nearly equidistant between the Fox lot and the Beverly Hills Hotel, but psychoanalysis can't fill the void that Marilyn feels. "Marilyn had this terrible neediness," Norman Rosten observes. "When she felt insecure, she went with other men simply for something to hold on to, however short-lived."

When the shoot wraps in June, the set lights go dark. Film stops spooling through the cameras. Without the attentions of the director, choreographer, and crew, there is nothing. Silence.

Marilyn and Montand meet once more, this time in New York. The night Montand is to fly back to France, she hires a Cadillac, reserves a hotel room, then drives out to Idlewild Airport with a bottle of champagne chilling in the back seat. His one-hour stopover extends to five, as they sit in the back of the hired car. She begs him to stay in New York. They can leave their spouses and marry each other.

Montand's answer is no, but he's moved by the depths of her feeling.

"I was touched," he says. "Touched because it was beautiful, and it was impossible. Not for a moment did I think of breaking with my wife."

In France, *Paris Match* reports: "The Montands have survived Hurricane Marilyn."

But the eye of the storm is often the most dangerous place to be.

In July, filming begins on *The Misfits*. It's said that Arthur Miller is struggling to finish the script. He doesn't know how the story ends.

CHAPTER 49

FRANK SINATRA IS HOSTING a private screening of his soon-to-be-released movie *Ocean's Eleven* when some unexpected guests show up at his Los Angeles home.

Among them is Peter Lawford, one of the film's co-stars and a newly minted member of the Sinatra-led "Rat Pack" of entertainers known for their spirited carousing. Lawford—known as "Peter Brother-In-Lawford" ever since he married Pat Kennedy in 1954—has brought along the famous Kennedy clan.

The Kennedys are in town for the Democratic National Convention, running from July 11 to 15. Forty-three-year-old Senator Jack Kennedy, a fourteen-year veteran of the US Congress, already has 600 of the 761 delegates needed to secure the party's presidential nomination. Younger brothers Bobby and Ted Kennedy are both working as campaign managers doing their utmost to help Jack over the top.

A little star power might help swing some undecided votes, and Frank Sinatra delivers. On July 10, Sinatra and his "Jack Pack" of entertainers draw two thousand cheering, check-waving donors to the black-tie, $100-a-plate Democratic Committee Dinner at the Beverly Hilton.

To open the convention, the "Committee for the Arts"—Nat King Cole, Tony Curtis, Sammy Davis Jr., Peter Lawford, Shirley MacLaine, Vincent Price, Edward G. Robinson, and Frank Sinatra—file onto the stage at Los Angeles Memorial Sports Arena, known informally as the Coliseum, and sing "The Star-Spangled Banner" to a starstruck crowd of politicians.

What the conventioneers wouldn't give for an invitation to the Jack Pack's favorite party spot—the Spanish-style oceanfront home on 625 Palisades Road in Santa Monica owned by Peter Lawford and Pat Kennedy.

Lawford, a former MGM contract player, bought the place directly from studio founder Louis B. Mayer, who famously hosted a 1939 pool party there for Judy Garland's seventeenth birthday.

These days, Marilyn is a frequent guest of Lawford's too—and with Arthur Miller away working on *The Misfits* script, she's alone in LA and her evenings are free.

Jack Kennedy is also without his wife on this trip. Following the advice of her doctors, a pregnant Jackie Kennedy remains at home in Massachusetts, answering campaign mail and writing a syndicated column called "Campaign Wife."

On July 12, Marilyn joins Kennedy and Peter Lawford for dinner at Puccini. Frank Sinatra and Lawford co-own the Beverly Hills restaurant, where menus and matchbooks are illustrated with their famous faces. Kennedy's is soon blushing with embarrassment. He's run his hand so far up Marilyn's leg that he's made a discovery. There's truth in the rumor that she prefers to go without underclothes.

On July 13, the Kennedy campaign surges forward, steam-rolling the competition, among them Texas senator Lyndon B. Johnson and Adlai Stevenson, the party's losing candidate in 1952 and 1956.

His triumph assured, Kennedy addresses the delegates. "With our devotion to this country, we wish to keep it strong, and we wish to keep it free. It requires at this critical time the best of all of us. And I can assure all of you who have confidence in me that I will be worthy of your trust, that we will carry the fight to the people in the fall, and we shall win!"

Like every director who chose Marilyn for a role, Kennedy has a momentous casting decision to make as he selects his vice-presidential running mate. JOHNSON IS NOMINATED FOR VICE PRESIDENT; KENNEDY PICKS HIM TO PLACATE THE SOUTH the *New York Times* reports of Kennedy's selection on July 14.

The Coliseum holds one hundred thousand people, and the space is filled to capacity on July 15 as Kennedy and Johnson accept their nomination at the top of the ticket. "The New Frontier is here whether we seek it or not," the new party leader intones in a speech that electrifies the audience.

The energy carries late into the night at a private celebration at the beach house on 625 Palisades Road. Marilyn is among the attendees, escorted by Kennedy pal Sammy Davis Jr. Tonight, the man of the hour treats Marilyn like the star she is. They drink and dance and retire to the pool house in the pink light of dawn.

CHAPTER 50

TRUMAN CAPOTE DEMANDS that Marilyn Monroe be cast as Holly Golightly in *Breakfast at Tiffany's,* the film that director Blake Edwards is adapting.

Capote wrote the novella more or less envisioning his good friend Marilyn as Holly, a charming socialite-escort, describing the character as having "strands of albino-blonde and yellow hair" and "large eyes, a little blue, a little green."

Marilyn, Shirley MacLaine, and Audrey Hepburn are all shown the script. Paula Strasberg strongly advises Marilyn, who is desperate to escape "dumb blonde" stereotypical roles, to pass on the part, convincing her that it would damage her reputation to play a "lady of the evening."

MacLaine also passes. "I turned it down because I didn't want to have to worry about my weight to be able to wear all those outfits and do all those fittings," she says. "I also didn't think it was a very good script."

Hepburn has concerns of her own, worrying, "This part called for an extroverted character. I am not an extrovert...It called for the kind of sophistication I find difficult. I did not think I had enough technique for the part."

Capote makes his case to studio executives, but he loses. "Paramount double-crossed me in every way and cast Audrey," he complains, though it is a small victory that the film will be the first ever shot on location at the famous Fifth Avenue jewelry store.

In Reno, Nevada, the desert sun beats down relentlessly, pushing the thermometer over the 100-degree mark as filming begins on *The Misfits* in July 1960.

When her plane lands in Reno, Marilyn hangs back, waiting for the crowds to disperse. She waits half an hour in the heat, preparing herself, adjusting the wig Whitey Snyder has suggested she wear to hide the diminished state of her natural hair. Years of bleaching have destroyed it, and during the filming of *Let's Make Love* it became impossible to work with. In this oppressive heat, the hairpiece only adds to her discomfort.

Marilyn checks in to her sixth-floor suite in the Art Deco–style Mapes Hotel, one of the few in Reno with its own casino and nightclub. The studio has rented air-conditioned Cadillac limousines to drive Marilyn and Paula Strasberg to set.

Onto a dry lakebed outside Reno steps Marilyn, costumed by designer Jean Louis in a white sundress printed with a cherry pattern. Her skin and hair are so pale and luminous that she does not look of this world. The awestruck crew watch her rehearse with Paula Strasberg, the acting coach clothed in her traditional all-black outfits despite the heat.

But the crew's infatuation doesn't last. Soon they take to

calling Paula "the Witch" or "Black Bart" and wondering of the perpetually absent star, "Is Marilyn working today?" A pattern emerges: Whitey and his co-workers make "a beeline for the bar at the end of the day to offset the horrors and the heat of the day," he says. Then they'd "wake up in the morning with screaming headaches, hoping to God Marilyn would be late again."

Miller's script follows wide-eyed divorcee Roslyn Taber, who forms a business capturing wild horses with a hard-bitten trio of cowboys: gambler Gay Langland, former pilot Guido Racanelli, and ex-rodeo rider Perce Howland. Miller calls it "a story of three men who cannot locate a home on the earth for themselves and, for something to do, capture wild horses to be butchered for canned dog food; and a woman as homeless as they, but whose intact sense of life's sacredness suggests a meaning for existence."

Marilyn's emotional temperature is a mix of pain, misery, and exhaustion. Her affair with Yves Montand has left her hurt, her affair with Jack Kennedy makes her feel used, and her husband Arthur Miller is barely speaking to her.

Yet she can't deny that the Pulitzer Prize–winning Miller and Oscar-winning Huston have secured stellar co-stars— Clark Gable, the King of Hollywood, as Guy; Montgomery Clift, the three-time Academy Award nominee for *The Search, A Place in the Sun,* and *From Here to Eternity* as Perce; and Marilyn's Actors Studio pal Eli Wallach as Guido.

Miller spends every night rewriting the script. It's the first screenplay he's ever written, and he lacks confidence in it.

"It's supposed to be a Western, but it's not, is it?" Gable asks Miller.

"It's sort of an Eastern Western," Miller replies. "It's about our lives' meaninglessness and maybe how we got to where we are."

Will Marilyn's character end up with Gable or Clift? To Marilyn, her husband's indecision is a sad indictment of their marriage. In the script she recognizes far too many lines of dialogue from arguments that the two of them have had.

But there's one burden she alone must carry. *She was "Marilyn Monroe" and that was what was killing her.*

The Misfits is Marilyn's twenty-ninth film. Fourteen years have passed since she first signed with Fox in 1946, and more than a decade since John Huston first directed Marilyn in *The Asphalt Jungle*. That shoot was in 1949, before Marilyn's stardom, before the Method, before the pills took over.

Here in Reno, the set doctor has refused to write her any more prescriptions, but there's a local doctor who comes to her hotel suite to inject the Amytal she craves to help her sleep.

The effects of medication and alcohol show in her face. Huston has chosen black-and-white film to convey the bleak Western location. Now he adds a soft-focus lens to hide the wear to Marilyn's features and reluctantly resigns himself to her late starts. "Sometimes we'd wait the whole morning," he says.

When the director looks into Marilyn's glassy eyes, he estimates she's taking twenty Nembutal a day, downing the capsules with vodka or champagne. The sedation is so extreme that Whitey Snyder must do her makeup while she's lying flat rather than seated in a chair.

"If she goes on at this rate, she'll be in an institution within two or three years, or dead. Anyone who allowed her to take narcotics ought to be shot," Huston tells Miller.

Dr. Ralph Greenson had successfully begun to wean her off medication, but when in-person sessions in Los Angeles give way to telephone calls from Reno, Marilyn slips back into destructive patterns.

She's not the only one. Over a cocktail in a local bar, Montgomery Clift confides to W. J. Weatherby, a British journalist covering *The Misfits* on assignment. "I have the same problem as Marilyn," says Clift, who's recovering from a near-fatal car accident. "We attract people the way honey does bees, but they're generally the wrong kind of people. People who want something from us, if only our energy. We need a period of being alone to become ourselves. To be an actor, you can't afford defenses, a thick skin. You've got to be open, and people can hurt you easily."

Clift orders another drink. Gable sips from pints of whiskey. Huston brings his glass of scotch to the craps table at the hotel casino, losing $25,000, then winning it all back and more. All the while, Miller continues to write and rewrite the script.

Frank Sinatra cuts through the gloom with an invitation to Cal Neva, fourteen acres straddling the California and Nevada border along the north shore of Lake Tahoe. Sinatra and other investors have recently bought and renovated the Cal Neva Lodge & Casino, called the "Lady of the Lake" or "Castle in the Sky," originally built in 1926. The grand reopening is set for September 1960, so in mid-August he invites *The Misfits* principals to christen the new "Celebrity Room," a place for him and others to perform. He's also eager to show off how he's had the building's old Prohibition underpasses turned into carpeted privacy tunnels that can be used to shield the Rat Pack and other famous friends from photographers' lenses.

But Marilyn can't get happy. Jack Kennedy is nothing more than a flickering image on television. And her lifelong crush and father figure, Clark Gable, is complaining to John Huston, "What the hell is that girl's problem? Goddamn it, I like her, but she's so damn unprofessional."

It doesn't help that Miller's falling in love with set photographer Inge Morath. He's come to realize that there is nothing he can do to salvage his marriage to Marilyn, writing, "If it was plain that her inner desperation was not going to let up, it was equally clear that literally nothing I knew to do would slow its destructive process."

Director John Huston makes a decision. He sends Marilyn to Los Angeles for treatment at the private Westside Hospital.

Officially, Marilyn is being treated for exhaustion, but unofficially, psychiatrist Ralph Greenson and internist Hyman Engelberg are attempting to end her dependence on barbiturates. Columnist Earl Wilson visits her, looking for a quote on her health. But Marilyn buys his silence with a promise of an even bigger story after *The Misfits* wraps.

Marilyn returns to Reno to finish the film. October 17 is Arthur Miller's forty-fifth birthday. But instead of toasting her husband at the cast dinner at the Christmas Tree Inn, Marilyn joins John Huston at the craps table.

"What should I ask the dice for, John?"

"Don't think, honey, just throw," Huston tells her. "That's the story of your life. Don't think, do it."

Marilyn makes a lucky roll, then falters. She doesn't know her next play.

Clark Gable does. The fifty-nine-year-old actor is soon to be a first-time father with wife Kathleen "Kay" Williams. "When

I wind up this picture I'm taking off until after the baby is born. I want to be there and I want to be there a good many months afterward."

Screenwriter Miller has finally decided that Marilyn's Roslyn belongs with Clark Gable's Gay. In the final scene, the pair drives off together in a truck and exchanges their last lines.

Roslyn: "How do we get home?"

Gay: "We'll follow that star and we'll get there."

"Cut! Fine!" Huston calls on November 4. "Thanks, Clark; thanks, Marilyn."

As the shoot wraps, Gable is pleased with the film. After seeing a rough cut, he tells Miller it's "the best picture he had made in his life."

On November 8, 1960, sixty-nine million Americans turn out to cast votes in the presidential election. The popular vote is initially too close to call. But Senator Jack Kennedy edges Vice President Richard Nixon by just 118,550 votes and prevails in the Electoral College 303 to 219. Kennedy will be the first US president born in the twentieth century.

On November 11, Marilyn delivers to columnist Earl Wilson her promise of an exclusive.

"The marriage of Marilyn Monroe and Arthur Miller is over," Wilson writes, "and there will soon be a friendly divorce."

Mr. and Mrs. Miller leave Reno in separate cars and return to New York on separate flights.

CHAPTER 51

ON NOVEMBER 16, 1960, a journalist rings Marilyn with terrible news. Clark Gable has died at Hollywood Presbyterian Hospital, following a series of heart attacks that began ten days earlier on November 6, two days after *The Misfits* wrapped. Gable did not live to see his unborn son.

She is speechless with grief. The man who'd looked so like her father, with his wry smile and his rakish mustache, is gone.

The Misfits, filmed over months in the extreme desert heat and involving the unlawful capture of wild mustangs, was a physical, exhausting shoot. Stunt men took many of the risks, but in the climactic action scene Gable himself was dragged by the stallion he was trying to wrestle down.

"I felt guilty when he died," Marilyn tells journalist W. J. Weatherby, "in case I put too much strain on him while we were making the movie. But that was stupid. He had a bad heart. No one can give you that. But he was such a strong, upright man—a real gentleman—that it was a great shock.

301

Like your father dying. I wept all night. I'd have gone to his funeral, but I was afraid of breaking down."

To Dr. Greenson, Marilyn muses, "Maybe it was subconscious. Maybe I kept him waiting, punishing him like my father, getting even for having kept me waiting my entire life."

Weatherby recalls Clark Gable's words on the set of *The Misfits*, "She's worth waiting for."

In New York, Marilyn returns to her studies with Lee Strasberg at the Actors Studio. She also agrees to a series of conversations with Weatherby. "Don't write about it now," she tells him. "Do it when I retire!"

They meet in a nondescript bar on Eighth Avenue, not far from the Greek Revival church building that houses the Actors Studio.

"Apologies, apologies, apologies," she says when she arrives late. "I was sleeping. I took some pills. Will you forgive me?"

Dressed in pants that hide her shape, her hair covered in a scarf, Marilyn sits in a back booth without being recognized.

"Sometimes it would be a big relief to be no longer famous," she says. "But we actors and actresses are such worriers — such, what is your word? — Narcissus types. I sit in front of the mirror for hours looking for signs of age."

Weatherby listens with rapt attention, committing her words to memory.

"Sometimes I think it would be easier to avoid old age, to die young but then you'd never complete your life, would you?"

That includes new love.

"Have you someone in mind?" Weatherby asks. "Is there a leading candidate?"

"Sort of," Marilyn says, running a finger along her glass of gin and tonic. "Only problem is, he's married right now. And he's famous; so we have to meet in secret."

Weatherby doesn't press and Marilyn keeps talking.

"He's in politics."

"In Hollywood?" Weatherby asks.

"Oh, no," Marilyn giggles. "In Washington."

On Christmas Eve, a lonely Marilyn sits on a windowsill in her New York apartment at 444 East 57th Street, the one she used to share with Arthur Miller. Despite the wintry air, she's opened her bedroom window wide so she can stare out at the city lights.

Her maid, Lena Pepitone, enters the room and sees Marilyn poised on the edge, as if she is going to jump, dropping thirteen stories into the street below. Pepitone sprints across the room to grab Marilyn by the waist.

"Let me die!" Marilyn cries, as Pepitone struggles to pull her back to safety. "I want to die. I deserve to die. What have I got to live for?"

And yet, on Christmas Day, someone remembers her fondly. Several scarlet poinsettias are delivered in full bloom — a gift from Joe DiMaggio. Later that day, the man himself arrives. It's as if he's heard her clarion call of sadness. On several occasions over the next few days, he discreetly uses the service elevator to reach her apartment unseen. They have supper together, they watch television together. Sometimes he stays the night. His company is comforting.

*   *   *

There's still the unresolved matter of Marilyn's divorce from Arthur Miller. She's not disputing his keeping the Connecticut house and Hugo the Basset Hound, but they need to make it legal. She's hired a new personal publicist who devises a brilliant plan.

Pat Newcomb of the Arthur P. Jacobs public relations firm is a sharp strategist. The daughter of a Washington judge, Newcomb is equally well-connected in Hollywood and Washington, and is a friend of the Kennedy clan.

January 20, 1961, will be president-elect John F. Kennedy's Inauguration Day.

That's exactly when Newcomb suggests that Marilyn travel to Mexico to finalize her divorce paperwork.

"It's the best day," Newcomb insists. "The eyes of the world will be elsewhere."

The movie star and her publicist fly out of New York on January 19, ahead of the winter storm that's blanketing Washington, DC, in over eight inches of snow.

At the National Guard Armory in Washington, Frank Sinatra has organized a fundraising gala to balance out the $2 million Kennedy campaign debt. Thousands of supporters brave the weather, paying $100 per ticket—$10,000 per box—to see Nat King Cole, Gene Kelly, Jimmy Durante, Ethel Merman, and Sinatra himself perform.

"We are all indebted to a great friend, Frank Sinatra," President-elect Kennedy says. "Long before he could sing he was pulling in votes in a New Jersey precinct...Tonight, we saw excellence."

That's what Kennedy's supporters see the next day in the smiling man in the top hat, formal day dress, and striped trousers as he walks alongside Jackie Kennedy from the White House to the Capitol. In subfreezing temperatures, he receives the oath of office from Supreme Court Justice Earl Warren and becomes the thirty-fifth president of the United States.

In a small, hot office in Ciudad Juárez, Mexico, a local judge presides over the dissolution of the four-and-a-half-year marriage between Arthur Miller and Marilyn Monroe on the grounds of "incompatibility of character."

She signs the papers without even reading them.

In the thirty minutes it takes Marilyn to become the ex–Mrs. Miller, photographers surround the building.

Flashbulbs pop, capturing the image of a despondent woman with unwashed hair dressed in a black suit. She battles her way to the waiting car, unable to escape the sound of her name until she shuts the door and blocks everything out.

CHAPTER 52

"I DON'T THINK *The Misfits* is going to knock 'em over," Marilyn tells journalist confidant W. J. Weatherby. "First reactions are very mixed."

"Wait and see. It's too early," he says.

"Maybe I didn't have enough—you know—distance from the character. Arthur wrote me into it and our marriage was breaking up during that period. Maybe I was playing *me* too much, some ideal me—"

To a remarkable degree, Marilyn predicts the reaction of film critics.

"The casting of the film is almost impeccable," says *The New Yorker* in its review on January 27, 1961. "In a part literally made for her, Miss Monroe displays a gentleness and a tired, childlike grace that are appropriate and moving, and, very evidently, a reflection of herself."

On January 31, Marilyn appears at the world premiere at the Granada Theater in Reno, Nevada, on the arm of co-star Montgomery Clift.

"Gable has never done anything better on screen," raves the *New York Daily News*, "nor has Miss Monroe." The *Hollywood Reporter* states, "Miss Monroe has seldom looked worse," but softens the blunt assessment with praise for her acting: "But there is a delicacy about her playing, and a tenderness that is affecting."

The film is on track to cover its $4 million budget, hardly a commercial success.

Since *The Misfits* wrapped, Marilyn has visited her New York psychiatrist forty-seven times, leading Dr. Marianne Kris to believe her patient is suicidal.

On Sunday, February 5, Kris drives Marilyn to Weill Cornell Medical Center on the Upper East Side.

She has persuaded Marilyn that she needs to check herself in for a good rest and some good meals to restore some of the weight that has tumbled off her lately.

After signing the admission papers as "Faye Miller" to avoid publicity, Marilyn is taken through the cavernous hospital corridors to the Payne Whitney Psychiatric Clinic.

A male doctor gives Marilyn a gratuitous breast examination under the guise of looking for cancerous lumps in her bosom. She is then ushered on to the floor for "disturbed patients." Her clothes are taken from her, and she is given a hospital gown to wear. Then she is placed in a padded room, where the door is slammed shut and locked from the outside.

She's alone.

Marilyn starts to panic. It's as if all the nightmares that she had at the orphanage have come true. All her life, she's feared inheriting her mother's insanity. It feels like it's finally come for her. She is Gladys.

It's all happening so quickly, so suddenly, that she goes into shock. She's hysterical. Screaming, she pounds on the metal door with her bare hands. Her fists are raw and bleeding, and still no one comes, no one answers.

"I'm not crazy," Marilyn yells, her face pressed against the small glass window. "Open the door, open the door. I won't make trouble. I'll be good. I promise. Just open the door!"

She paces around the cell like a caged tiger. She shakes her head, pulling at her hair. Suddenly, she gets an idea from her film role in *Don't Bother to Knock*. She picks up the room's only chair and hurls it at the door, repeatedly.

Eventually the small window in the steel door shatters. The staff at last comes running—with a straitjacket. After securing Marilyn in the restraint, four male nurses carry her to a more secure unit on the ninth floor, where she is sedated.

The true identity of patient "Faye Miller" spreads throughout the hospital. During the night, doctors and nurses form a procession. One by one, they peek through the small window at Marilyn Monroe, bound up in a straitjacket, screaming, crying, and rolling around on the floor of her cell.

None of her friends know where she is.

Three days later, a sympathetic nurse loosens the jacket and gives her a pen and paper, which she uses to write to Lee and Paula Strasberg, begging them to get her out. Her handwriting is spiky, the spelling is erratic, but her terror at the captivity is obvious.

Dear Lee and Paula,

Dr. Kris has had me put into the New York Hospital —
pstikiatric division under the care of two idiot doctors.
They both should not be my doctors.
   You haven't heard from me because I'm locked up
with all these poor nutty people. I'm sure to end up a
nut if I stay in this nightmare. please help me Lee, this
is the last place I should be — maybe if you called Dr
Kris and assured her of my sensitivity and that I must
get back to class . . . Lee, I try to remember what you
said once in class 'that art goes far beyond science'
   And the science memories around here I'd like to
forget — like screaming women etc.
   please help me — if Dr. Kris assures you I am all
right you can assure her I am not. I do not belong here!

I love you both
Marilyn

P.S. forgive the spelling — and theres nothing to write
on here. I'm on the dangerous floor its like a cell.
can you imagine — cement blocks they put me in her
because they lied to me about calling my doctor and Joe
and they had the bathroom door locked so I broke the
glass and out side of that I havnt done anything that is
uncooperative

But her message goes unanswered; no help comes.

The press gets a tip that Marilyn Monroe's been admitted to a clinic. The doctors deny that she's schizophrenic like her mother. One says that she is "psychiatrically disconnected in an acute way because she works too hard."

Eventually, she is allowed one telephone call. Only one person is strong enough to get her out of this situation.

Joe DiMaggio.

DiMaggio is in Florida. He has signed on as a spring training instructor with the Yankees, who are practicing at Huggins-Stengel Field in St. Petersburg. He catches the next flight to New York and comes directly to Payne Whitney Psychiatric Clinic.

"I want my wife," DiMaggio demands, with all the might of a former professional athlete.

Behind the reception desk, the staff quakes at his forcefulness.

"I want my wife," he repeats. "And if you do not release her to me, I will take this place apart—piece of wood, by piece... of...wood."

Out of loyalty, guilt, love, or perhaps a mixture of all three, Marilyn's second husband has never remarried.

According to one friend, "He carried a torch for Marilyn that was bigger than the Statue of Liberty." Another echoes, "He deeply loved that woman."

Marilyn is released. She leaves the hospital via the service entrance in the basement and straight into Dr. Kris's waiting car.

DiMaggio is waiting at Marilyn's apartment, where he and a furious Marilyn hear the doctor's regretful confession.

"I did a terrible thing," Kris says. "I really didn't mean to, but I did."

Marilyn refuses to accept any apology. She eliminates Dr. Kris from her life.

CHAPTER 53

"ALL'S WELL WITH THE WORLD, men, so fear not, fear not," reports the *New York Journal-American*. For the past three weeks, Marilyn Monroe has been in a private room at Columbia-Presbyterian Medical Center, recovering from the disastrous time she endured at the Payne Whitney. "Marilyn's face still has the ethereal rose-petal texture, the smile's as delicately soft as ever, the figure — ah yes — the figure — and best of all they've untied the knots in her nerves."

Joe DiMaggio visited Marilyn daily and filled her hospital room with bouquets of roses. While hospitalized, she gets word that her former mother-in-law, Augusta Miller, has suddenly passed away, and after she's discharged on March 6, 1961, Marilyn makes sure to attend the funeral on March 8. She sits with the family, holding hands with Isidore.

Afterward, she accepts DiMaggio's invitation to visit him in Florida. He's attentive and kind, and in his off-hours from coaching the Yankees through spring training, they have quiet dinners and look for shells on the beach.

DiMaggio does everything he can to prevent Marilyn from slipping back into the dungeons of loneliness and misery, and she is grateful. But she just can't help herself.

At the White House, Jack Kennedy has informed the switchboard that if a "Miss Green" calls, she is to be put straight through. Almost as soon as Marilyn leaves the hospital, she's on the telephone whispering and giggling to "The Prez."

Marilyn has never lost her anxiety about sounding unintelligent. Though obviously smart—and well-read these days, despite her early lack of education—she prepares pertinent questions to ask Kennedy during their phone conversations: What went wrong during the Bay of Pigs invasion on April 17? Should the US have withheld air support? And why is Castro such a bad, bad man?

She jots down everything the president tells her in the little red book she uses as a memory aid. CIA counterintelligence knows all about what they call Marilyn's Book of Secrets. Given the heightened threat of nuclear war, they deem it a matter of concern.

At FBI headquarters in Washington, DC, J. Edgar Hoover sits at his desk, staring at Marilyn Monroe's "105" file. The designation indicates that its contents are political. The file is further flagged "SM-C" for "Security Matter-Communist." He sighs and pushes the pages across his desk. How is he going to solve the Marilyn Monroe Problem?

*   *   *

After her recuperation in Florida, Marilyn decides she is strong and well enough to return to Hollywood and the California sunshine.

New York holds too many painful memories of padded cells and straitjackets, and besides, it is more Arthur Miller's town. According to Dr. Greenson, her relationship with Miller is at the heart of all her problems.

"As a great intellect and playwright, he was too big a challenge for her" is Greenson's opinion. "In trying to win Miller's respect, she had become obsessed with the 'serious dramatic actress' goal. This was false, it wasn't her." He tells her that "she should continue her acting lessons, and gradually improve her skills, but the movies she should concentrate on now were those that came most naturally to her—comedies, musicals, 'fun' movies, nothing too serious."

Greenson advises, "Above all, you have to be yourself."

"Whoever that is," Marilyn replies.

CHAPTER 54

MARILYN RETURNS TO CALIFORNIA and moves into a West Hollywood triplex, two apartments off of a main house. She takes one apartment. The other apartment's tenant is Frank Sinatra, who's been using the place as a getaway since he and Ava Gardner divorced in 1957.

With Marilyn also newly single, the old friends begin a casual affair. Sinatra's been busier than ever with his music career in the aftermath of another divorce, this one professional. He's left Capitol, his longtime record label, to establish his own label, Reprise, where he records Reprise's first album, *Ring-a-Ding-Ding!* It's released on May 7, 1961.

Rat-Packer Dean Martin's forty-fourth birthday is June 7. Sinatra decides to throw him a party at the Sands in Las Vegas. It's the perfect venue to showcase the twelve songs off the new album.

Sinatra's press agent has issued a memo: "Under no circumstances is any backstage photographer permitted to photograph Mr. Sinatra and Miss Monroe together at the cocktail reception to follow the performance on June 7th." Hotel staff receive their own strict instructions not to disturb the VIP guests "by telephone call or visitors before 2 pm."

Marilyn and Pat Kennedy Lawford, eight months pregnant with a fourth child due in early July, spend the day having manicures, pedicures, and massages. Marilyn chooses the same black lace dress that she wore to meet Soviet premier Nikita Khrushchev on the Fox lot.

She starts drinking champagne at noon. By the time Sinatra takes the stage, she is already drunk. Marilyn steps into the Copa Room and takes her seat at a stage-side table alongside two famous couples. As Elizabeth Taylor and her fourth husband, Eddie Fisher, as well as birthday boy Dean Martin and his second wife, Jeanne, enjoy the show, Marilyn edges closer and closer to the stage, hooking her arm over the edge and gazing up at Frank.

It's only been three months since she was released from Columbia-Presbyterian.

"From a distance, it was wow, she's a knockout. But close up it was...oh no, she's knocked out. She didn't look well, and she also acted very strangely. She seemed a little crazy to me," says one of the photographers.

"Frank Sinatra, 'The Voice,' swung into the Sands hotel last night and the affair lasted until all hours and ended with the 'Clan'—Sinatra, Sammy Davis Jr., Peter Lawford and Joey Bishop—singing 44th birthday greetings to Dean Martin," United Press International reports on June 8. "The Maitre D' said 2000 persons were turned away."

*   *   *

"Dearest Marilyn," Clark Gable's widow, Kay, writes. "How about our little 'carbon copy lover boy'—I am certain you have seen his press pictures. Just exactly like Clark..."

Clark Gable's son was born on March 20, 1961. In Encino, California, Marilyn is among the invited guests at the June 11 christening of ten-week-old John Clark Gable. She climbs the steps to St. Cyril's Church dressed in a black suit, her hair covered by a sheer scarf patterned with black hearts.

Her attire might be more fitting for a funeral than a christening, but an air of tragedy lingers over today's happy occasion.

I feel certain his dearest father is watching his every move from heaven.

CHAPTER 55

ON JUNE 28, Marilyn is back in New York—and admitted to another hospital.

The doctors assess her condition. She's poorly nourished, her skin is dehydrated, her hair is unwashed, and she has seemingly long since abandoned the practice of one ounce of Chanel No. 5 in every bath. The nausea and chronic pain in her side are symptoms of a diseased gallbladder. She's wheeled into surgery to have the organ removed.

On July 11, Marilyn is well enough to be discharged.

"How are you, Marilyn?" the assembled crowd shouts at her, upping the intensity as they push closer. "Give us a smile, Marilyn!" "Feel any better?" "Are you remarrying Joe DiMaggio?" "Did Arthur Miller visit you?"

Pat Newcomb fights her way through the throng to get Marilyn into the waiting car.

Marilyn is frightened by the jostling of the crowd. "I thought they were going to pull me to pieces!" she exclaims as she falls back into her seat, tentatively holding her abdomen. Her surgical wound has started to bleed; it's still raw and hasn't yet formed a protective scar.

Fox has been patient, but Marilyn still owes the studio two films on her 1955 contract.

In December 1961, the studio pitches her *Something's Got to Give*, a zany comedy inspired by the 1940 Cary Grant and Irene Dunne picture *My Favorite Wife*. Marilyn would earn her contractual rate of $100,000 and reprise Dunne's role as Ellen Wagstaff Arden, aka Eve, a wife rescued after years stranded on an island. George Cukor, who directed Marilyn in *Let's Make Love*, agrees to lead the production, which will co-star Dean Martin and Cyd Charisse.

It's the kind of light fare that meets Dr. Greenson's approval. Marilyn books daily appointments, staying at the doctor's office for at least an hour and sometimes two, so she can review with him everything she's written in her little red book.

Greenson begins to cancel sessions with his other clients in favor of spending more time with Marilyn. He has been collecting newspaper cuttings about her. He has boxes of them, piles of photographs. There are well-thumbed interviews and posters from her films.

Marilyn's friends are skeptical of the doctor. There's "something sinister about Ralph Greenson," her makeup artist, Whitey Snyder, thinks. He worries that the doctor exerts "enormous influence over her."

*　　*　　*

A knock sounds on Marilyn's apartment door. She answers, barefoot, in a red kimono, her unbrushed hair falling over her face. In front of her is a short middle-aged woman with cropped gray hair, in a sensible white shirt and winged spectacles.

"Good day to you," the woman says, with a tight smile. "My name is Eunice Murray. Dr. Greenson said you'd be expecting me."

Marilyn hadn't exactly been expecting Mrs. Murray, whom Dr. Greenson has hired to be her new housekeeper. But "it wasn't hard to understand," says Pat Kennedy Lawford. "Eunice was simply Greenson's spy, sent down to report back on everything Marilyn did."

"How can I put it?" asks Marilyn's hairdresser George Masters. "She was terrifically jealous of Marilyn, separating her from her friends. She was a divisive person."

Joe DiMaggio turns up on December 23 with a Christmas tree, lights, and presents. He fills Marilyn's refrigerator with her favorite champagne and caviar.

Four weeks pass. The pine needles have long since dropped, the lights are broken, and the ornaments are hanging limply from the bent branches. Mrs. Murray keeps suggesting they tidy up and take down the tree, but Marilyn won't have it. She wants to keep a little bit of DiMaggio in the apartment.

Reliable, kind Joe. He spent Christmas Day eating turkey at the Greensons', despite his innate dislike of strangers and Dr. Greenson's evident dislike of him.

Also, extremely generous Joe. He's offered to help her buy a home of her own. Her first.

A movie star as famous as Marilyn would be expected to buy a home as chic and glamorous as the Lawfords' beach house in Santa Monica. But what Marilyn craves is privacy.

Mrs. Murray finds a listing for 12305 Fifth Helena Drive in Brentwood. The property at the end of a cul-de-sac is a single-story home with a tiny guest house, high white walls, and a lush garden. With pretty floor tiles, it looks and feels like a Spanish hacienda, just like the Greensons' nearby house.

"And look, Marilyn," says Mrs. Murray as they tour the grounds around the "cute little Mexican-style house with eight rooms," with Dr. Greenson walking behind, nodding his approval. "A swimming pool!"

Everything Mrs. Murray says to Marilyn has a patronizing edge, a tone exacerbated by their chosen forms of address. To Marilyn, the housekeeper is "Mrs. Murray," yet Mrs. Murray calls her employer only by her first name.

"Oh, an actual swimming pool, Mrs. Murray!" enthuses Marilyn. "What do you think, Maf?" she asks the little dog in her arms. The white Maltese that she sometimes calls a poodle was a present from Frank Sinatra. Marilyn named him Maf, short for Mafia, as a little joke between the two of them. "Imagine how athletic I would be if I swam every morning."

They walk the garden, taking in the abundant planting and the beautiful fruit trees, before returning to the porch at the front of the house.

"*Cursum Perficio,*" she says slowly, reading out the letters in the tilework. "*Cursum Perficio*—what does that mean?"

"It's Latin," says Dr. Greenson. "It means 'I complete the race,' or journey's end, the end of the road. Something like that."

"The end of the road?" Marilyn asks, wrinkling her nose. "As in your final resting place?"

"Or 'welcome,' " chips in Mrs. Murray. "As in, you've reached the end of your journey. You're here."

"I am here," agrees Marilyn. "I like it! Let's buy it!"

The house costs $77,500. Marilyn might be the world's most famous movie star, but she hasn't got that level of cash at her disposal. Generous Joe lends her the money for the down payment, as promised. It's now February. She'll pay him back in April, as soon as she starts shooting *Something's Got to Give.*

On February 12, Fox sends over the latest version of Nunnally Johnson's script, bound in blue paper and stamped with the studio's corporate logo. Using pen and pencil, Marilyn marks up the script with her notes on blocking and dialogue.

Marilyn plays Ellen Arden. But her character's entrance strikes her as under-written. "The only people on earth I get on well with are men," she notes in the margin of page 12, "so let's have some fun with this opening scene."

In the script, Nick Arden (Dean Martin) has married Bianca (Cyd Charisse), believing his first wife, Ellen, died in a shipwreck years earlier. Once Ellen returns, very much alive, Bianca questions Ellen's sanity, calling her "psychosomatic."

"Would she come right out with this sort of thing?" Marilyn questions on page 7. "Gives away what she will be saying later... No! She is not a Nut but a cold Hard dame."

With notes on 32 of its 108 pages, Marilyn returns the script for rewrites.

*   *   *

Screenwriter Budd Schulberg, who won an Oscar for *On the Waterfront,* is also struggling with a different Fox script—the adaptation of *The Enemy Within,* Bobby Kennedy's account of corruption within the Teamsters.

How does one write honestly about the attorney general, brother of the president, without compromising the script? How does one write honestly about labor racketeering without being considered anti-labor?

It's been a year since the *New York Times* announced: ATTORNEY GENERAL ROBERT KENNEDY'S BOOK SOLD TO FOX STUDIO, naming the author as a producer on the film.

The attorney general is highly involved with the script, conferring frequently with Schulberg.

Isn't it exciting that the president's brother has a reason to be on the Fox lot? Maybe the president, too?

CHAPTER 56

"ARRIVING EASTERN AIRLINES FLIGHT 505 at 9:05 tonight," the telegram to Isidore Miller reads. "Have reservations at Fontainebleau. Love you. Marilyn."

On February 17, 1962, Marilyn is en route to Florida to visit two of her favorite exes: Joe DiMaggio, who's there as a spring training coach helping the Bronx Bombers prepare to defend their 1961 World Series title, and Isidore Miller, her beloved former father-in-law, whom she still calls "Dad."

Miller waits for her at the Miami International Airport, clutching the telegram with the details of her arrival. Over dinner and a show at the Hotel Fontainebleau's Club Gigi, Marilyn gently points out, "You know, Arthur's getting married tonight."

Isidore didn't know. Arthur Miller and Inge Morath wed quickly up in New York. Marilyn reassures him, "I'm sure a letter must be on its way."

Marilyn wants to make me feel right, her former father-in-law realizes. *She wants me to protect her, but she also protects me.*

Later that evening, after returning to his own hotel, he puts a hand in his coat pocket and finds that Marilyn has slipped in $200.

"I can't tell you in mere words just how much your trip to Florida meant to me," he writes her on Sea Isle stationery. "I don't ever remember having such a good time!" He signs the letter "Love Dad."

After leaving Miami, Marilyn travels up to see DiMaggio in Fort Lauderdale at a beachfront resort constructed to resemble an ocean liner. The Yankee Clipper Hotel has quickly become the favorite of the New York Yankees near their new spring training facility, Fort Lauderdale Stadium.

DiMaggio and Marilyn spend the night of February 19 in his hotel suite. The next morning, he sees Marilyn back to Miami International Airport and kisses her good-bye as she boards a Pan Am flight to Mexico City.

The shopping trip in Mexico from February 20 to March 3 to furnish the new house at 12305 Fifth Helena Drive is another suggestion of Dr. Greenson's, who's overseeing her move and some home repairs.

Marilyn's personal publicist Pat Newcomb and hairdresser George Masters are irritated that housekeeper Eunice Murray is joining the trip. But Dr. Greenson insists.

At the Hilton Continental Hotel in Mexico City, Newcomb has organized an informal press conference. Marilyn has her next film to promote, along with a local itinerary that includes a visit to the country's most important film set, Churubusco Studios, where she'll meet famous Spanish director Luis

Buñuel and the cast of his surrealist dinner-party comedy, *The Exterminating Angel*.

As Marilyn dresses, selecting an aqua-colored three-quarter-sleeve Pucci knit, she enjoys some champagne. When she arrives at the event, she smiles and blows kisses to the reporters and photographers she's kept waiting for two hours, then sits down in an armchair with a fresh bottle of champagne on the side table.

Questions come fast and thick. All of them are personal.

Her measurements?

"I never measure myself," Marilyn answers. "It's other people who measure me."

Why isn't she wearing stockings?

"Don't you like my skin?"

Does she wear underwear?

Marilyn gives her stock answer: "I only wear Chanel Number Five."

Bitter about her failed marriages?

"No way, I still haven't given up hope that I'll find happiness."

A fling with a Mexican actor?

"Why does he have to be an actor?" she asks. "Just being Mexican is enough for me."

Marilyn finds a fling quickly. She chooses José Bolaños, a handsome Mexican screenwriter. They're photographed dancing in a tight embrace at a Mexico City nightclub.

Bolaños makes Marilyn feel loved, showering her with flowers and gifts and affection. One evening he hires a mariachi band and stands outside her hotel room window, serenading her to sleep.

An old friend of Dr. Greenson, American expat Frederick Vanderbilt Field and his fourth wife, Nieves Orozco, are Marilyn's cultural guides to Mexico. Field, now an amateur archaeologist, and Orozco, once a favorite model of the artist Diego Rivera, live in the Zona Rosa section of Mexico City, an informal collective of leftist Americans.

Field is known as "the Reds' pet blueblood," having cast his vote in the 1928 US presidential election for the Socialist Party candidate. That decision cost him more than $70 million — the amount his industrialist uncle Frederick Vanderbilt was planning to leave Field before Vanderbilt disinherited his namesake nephew.

Field advises Bolaños to avoid being photographed with Marilyn.

The FBI has marked Field as a Comintern operative for the Russians, and they surveil and bug his home — where Marilyn and Mrs. Murray are out dining with Field.

A charming and affable host, Field pours champagne for Marilyn, keeping her talking about American political news. Her views, she explains, are informed by her friendships with Kennedys. How President Kennedy and his brother Bobby, the US attorney general, are dedicated to winning the space race, promoting global service through the Peace Corps, and monitoring the country's slowly escalating involvement in Vietnam. There's also Jack and Bobby's intense dislike for that awful FBI chief, J. Edgar Hoover.

"His goons follow everybody, all the time. They'd like to get rid of him," she explains. "But apparently, it's politically not the right time. Although I have no idea why not. Surely, as I said to Jack the other day, if you're President of the United States of America, you can do what you like?"

The file about Marilyn Monroe's champagne-fueled indiscretions, including the private thoughts of the president and the attorney general and her meetings in the Zona Rosa, quickly reaches the FBI director's desk.

Hoover is alarmed at the extent to which the president's affairs have become a national security risk. His movie star mistress is gossiping with a known Soviet agent who briefs other foreign intelligence operatives.

And then there's José Bolaños. Hoover's information suggests that the screenwriter is "deeply distrusted by the real left" because he has a close friend who works for the CIA, and he has been seen walking in and out of the CIA station in Mexico City.

Now Marilyn has invited Bolaños to Beverly Hills. She's asked him to escort her to the Golden Globes.

CHAPTER 57

MARILYN SPENDS $3,000 on a green sequined halter-neck gown with a mermaid-tail hem designed by Norman Norell, who also made the dress she wore to marry Arthur Miller.

The dress is an investment in her career. At the 1960 Golden Globes, she took home the trophy for Best Actress in a Comedy or Musical for *Some Like It Hot*. Tonight, March 8, 1962, Rock Hudson will be presenting her with a Henrietta Award as World Film Favorite.

Being Marilyn Monroe is becoming increasingly expensive and time-consuming. The hair takes longer to style and the makeup takes longer to apply. But when she makes the effort, the effect is as hypnotically beautiful as always.

She hasn't had a bite to eat today, reminding herself, *I have to be skinny for Frankie.* Instead, she sips champagne.

Frank Sinatra, in the apartment next door, has promised to come see her new dress before she leaves for the ceremony at the Beverly Hilton. He says he has a surprise for her.

"Hi, baby," she whispers breathlessly.

Sinatra is beguiled by the platinum hair, the sparkling sequins.

"Close your eyes."

From his dinner jacket, Sinatra removes a leather box, saying, "Now you can look!"

Resting on a velvet cushion is not the large, hoped-for engagement ring but a pair of emerald earrings to match her bright green dress. Emeralds and diamonds. He clips one to each ear.

"Thank you, Frankie," she whispers. "They're very beautiful."

"I should hope so," he replies. "They cost me thirty-five thousand dollars."

Nearly half the price of her new house.

Marilyn's red-carpet look is among the most elegant at the Golden Globes. Reporters buzz about her emerald gown and matching earrings. Photographers can't take enough pictures.

Marilyn and her screenwriter escort, José Bolaños, exchange intimate glances, and, as the A-list crowd celebrates with champagne and cocktails, they dance as close as they did in Mexico City.

Peter Lawford invites Marilyn to New York City, where a dinner is to be held in President Kennedy's honor in a private apartment on Park Avenue.

At 9 p.m., Marilyn is already an hour late and still not quite ready. Milt Ebbins, Peter Lawford's talent manager, has been waiting outside her room for almost two hours. Finally, he bursts through the door to find Marilyn sitting at her dressing table, applying makeup to her famous beauty mark.

"Please, Marilyn! We can't keep the president waiting!"

"Oh," she greets Ebbins. "Can you help me with this dress?" She pulls a black beaded sheath from its hanger.

"It just needs a little tug!"

So I'm watching this giant international movie star standing there stark naked in her high heels, Milt thinks. *She puts a scarf over her hair so it won't get mussed and pulls this beaded dress over her head. This dress was so tight it took me ten minutes to pull it down over her ass!*

"Take it easy," Marilyn says. "Don't tear the beads."

When Marilyn is finally ready, Ebbins is astonished at the transformation, enthusing, "Jesus Christ, you sure are pretty."

"Thank you," she replies, coolly, disguising her famous blond hair in a red wig for the drive uptown.

The Secret Service clears them into the party that's already well underway.

Among the twenty-five guests is Arlene Dahl, a former MGM contract player who now runs her beauty company Arlene Dahl Enterprises from the Upper East Side.

Dahl instantly notices the president's attraction to Marilyn. She's not alone.

"Marilyn walked in and everything stopped, everyone stopped. It was magical, really. I've never seen anyone stop a room like that."

"Finally! You're here," the president says. "There are some people here who are dying to meet you."

They talk and flirt all night long. Kennedy ends the night

with a whisper in her ear. Would she like to join him for a weekend in Palm Springs? Frank Sinatra's invited him for March 24.

Marilyn doesn't answer right away.

"Jackie won't be there," he adds.

Sinatra spends over half a million dollars doing up his Palm Springs estate for the presidential visit. On the grounds, he builds a helicopter pad along with several guest cottages. The presidential flag will fly from a giant flagpole. Portraits of the Kennedys are newly hung on the interior walls, and twenty-five extra telephone lines put in for the security detail. Sinatra even installs a gold plaque in the bedroom where "TP" — Sinatra's shorthand for "the president" — will sleep, announcing JOHN F. KENNEDY SLEPT HERE.

Except he doesn't.

In the Justice Department, Bobby Kennedy calls a meeting on the proliferation of organized crime. One lawyer blurts out, "We are out front fighting organized crime on every level and here the president is associating with Sinatra, who is associating with all those guys."

The room falls silent, and everyone looks at the attorney general.

"Give me the facts," Kennedy says. "I can't do anything without the facts."

A few days later, the file that arrives on his desk makes for enlightening reading. Sinatra, the report alleges, "has a long and wide association with hoodlums and racketeers," including the cousin of Al Capone.

Scanning further down the document, he reads that Sam Giancana has made numerous visits to Sinatra's estate in Palm

Springs. The president and the Don of Dons, actual bedfellows? Absolutely not.

Bobby calls the president and tells him that the optics are terrible. Doesn't Bing Crosby have a house nearby? He's nearly as famous as Sinatra, and he won an Oscar for *Going My Way.*

"You can handle it, Peter!" President Kennedy tells his brother-in-law, assigning him to break the bad news to Sinatra.

The scorned host is furious.

Lawford listens as Sinatra calls Bobby "every name in the book."

Revenge will come quickly. It's too late for Sinatra to cut Lawford from *Sergeants 3,* last month's Rat Pack release, but he'll make sure that Lawford has made his last appearance with the group, on film or in person.

Lawford is stunned to learn what happens next. "When he got off the phone Frank went outside with a sledgehammer and started chopping up the concrete landing pad of his heliport. He was in a frenzy."

Sinatra's wounds are personal and political. How could the president choose to spend the weekend with Bing Crosby? A Republican!

At the White House, J. Edgar Hoover has a private lunch with the president, during which he bluntly informs his boss that his private life risks going dangerously public. He must keep his trousers zipped.

Kennedy cuts the lunch short, telling aide Kenneth O'Donnell, "Get rid of that bastard. He's the biggest bore."

*   *   *

"I'm going on a trip," Marilyn tells Mrs. Murray.

When Peter Lawford arrives to pick her up, Marilyn keeps him waiting until she perfects a disguise that includes a writing pad and a fistful of sharpened pencils. Dressed in a sharp black suit, a brunette wig, and a pair of spectacles, Kennedy's "new secretary" is ready to drive the hundred or so miles to an important presidential meeting in Palm Springs.

Bing Crosby's estate is in Silver Spur, a mountainous area that was once a ranch. Marilyn wears a flowing, robe-like dress to dinner and at the after-party is casually intimate with Kennedy, linking her arm through his.

She's promised him a private massage later. He has constant back pain, incurable even after four surgeries. Recovering from a 1954 spinal fusion procedure, Kennedy, then a senator, chose a color poster of Marilyn posing in blue shorts, legs planted in a wide V, and hung it upside down above his hospital bed.

Tonight, Marilyn pauses her ministrations to telephone an expert.

It's 3 a.m. in New York and Marilyn's masseur Ralph Roberts is half asleep. "I've been arguing with my friend about the major muscles of the back. I'm going to put him on the phone, so you can tell him."

Roberts jolts awake at the sound of the famous voice with its unmistakable accent. Suddenly, he finds himself discussing anatomy with the President of the United States.

"I think I made his back feel better," Marilyn laughs.

CHAPTER 58

AFTER THE WEEKEND in Palm Springs, the Secret Service becomes watchful of Marilyn's interest in the president.

"She was calling him a lot. She wanted to see him. Everyone knew it," one agent says.

Kennedy tells his friend George Smathers, Democratic senator from Florida, that he had dismissed Marilyn with an offhand remark. "You're not really First Lady material, anyway, Marilyn."

Yet her infatuation continues.

In April, Marilyn places a call to the Kennedy Compound at Hyannis Port, Massachusetts. When she reaches First Lady Jackie Kennedy, she doesn't identify herself but says only that she's "looking for Jack."

Alone in her bedroom, Jackie recognizes the voice of the woman who's looking to take her place. Jackie has heard that Marilyn's a bit troubled, so she keeps it light.

"Marilyn, you'll marry Jack, that's great," she says. "And

you'll move into the White House, and you'll assume the responsibilities of the First Lady. And I'll move out, and you'll have all the problems."

Fred Otash makes his living as a "fact verifier" for gossip magazines. Three years ago, the former LAPD vice detective lost his license to run the Fred Otash Detective Bureau due to a conviction in a Santa Anita racetrack conspiracy.

Now he keeps tabs on celebrities as well as Democratic politicians. Former vice president Richard Nixon and Howard Hughes, the reclusive industrialist who once controlled RKO Pictures, want to know what the Kennedys are up to.

Otash is the one who installed the bugs, first in Peter and Pat Kennedy Lawford's place, and more recently in Marilyn's house. He parks his van down the road and listens in.

Rewrites on the script for *Something's Got to Give* push back the start date for shooting to April 23.

Marilyn decides to visit the Strasbergs in New York. She offers Paula $5,000 a week to be her acting coach on the new picture. But Marilyn has caught Lee Strasberg's cold, making the return trip to Los Angeles disastrous. She is shivering and feverish, and, by the time the plane touches down, seriously unwell.

On Fox Stage 14, the cast and crew of *Something's Got to Give* are waiting for their star. Director George Cukor flashes back to *Let's Make Love* and Marilyn's chronic lateness to set. He should never have agreed to work with her again.

Three days later, Marilyn's cold has developed into chronic sinusitis. Studio doctors are dispatched to 12305 Fifth Helena Drive, where Mrs. Murray eyes them suspiciously before escorting them to the door of the blacked-out bedroom. Marilyn has a temperature of 101, a severe cough, and a throat infection. She is barely able to open her eyes, such is the pain in her head.

Every day without Marilyn sends the production costs spiraling. The insurers are called in. More doctors are sent, reporting to Fox that it will take a good "two weeks to cure this infection." But it's easier to believe that she's once again suffering the ill effects of alcohol and pills rather than her actual diagnosis.

She is still too ill to work, but she does try. She books limousines to drive her to set, then leaves the chauffeurs waiting for hours until she finally fails to appear. One day she passes out in the bath. An hour and a half of filming proves so exhausting that she faints in her dressing room.

"Dearest Marilyn," Joe DiMaggio writes a postcard on May 6 from Denmark on his way to Moscow. "Have a short stop here in Copenhagen en route to 'long underwear country.'"

The retired New York Yankee is earning a $100,000 annual salary as executive vice president of V. H. Monette & Co., supplier to US military bases worldwide. Company founder Val Monette has sent DiMaggio, his top field representative, on a European goodwill tour.

DiMaggio drops the postcard in the mailbox.

Monette, who's often on the road with DiMaggio, notices his dedication to his ex-wife. "He was never a man to write letters to anyone, not even to his family. But wherever he goes, he always finds time to drop her a note or a card or send her flowers."

On Monday, May 14, 1962, Marilyn returns to Stage 14.

The gossip begins immediately. Is Marilyn leaving on the seventeenth to fly to New York? Is she really abandoning the shoot before the week is out?

This Saturday night in New York City, the Democratic Party will host a fundraising dinner and birthday salute to President John F. Kennedy. After a four-course dinner at the Four Seasons, America's top entertainers will perform at Madison Square Garden. The red-white-and-blue event program is already printed with "Happy Birthday, Mr. President" on the front cover—and Marilyn is among the list of performers.

Envisioning a gown "only Marilyn Monroe would wear," she's worked with Jean Louis, her costume designer on *The Misfits* and *Something's Got to Give,* on a creation of sheer souffle fabric the same color as her skin and hand-sewn with thousands of rhinestones. Standing up on the stage under the spotlights, she'll appear to be covered in shimmering stars. The gown is said to be worth $12,000.

When it's delivered to her house, the material is so light and delicate that Marilyn can lift it in the palm of one hand—and so thin she won't be able to wear any undergarments.

On May 16, a certified letter on 20th Century-Fox Film Corporation letterhead is sent to Marilyn Monroe Productions, Inc.

According to Fox, her planned absence from the set "for the purpose of attending a social function being held outside the State of California...will constitute a willful failure to render services...will result in serious loss and material damage to the undersigned corporation."

The following day, the letter is refused receipt, and it is returned to the studio.

CHAPTER 59

ON MAY 18, Marilyn arrives for rehearsal at Madison Square Garden in a pair of dark sunglasses. She's tied a scarf over her hair and dressed in a lime-green Pucci blouse, light-colored pants, and white Ferragamo pumps.

Even after practicing her number for weeks, she can never quite shake the inevitable stage fright, especially when she'll be performing among musical greats Ella Fitzgerald, Peggy Lee, Harry Belafonte, and Maria Callas.

It was Peter Lawford who put the idea in her head to sing "Happy Birthday" to the president. Tomorrow night the fifteen thousand people who've paid up to $1,000 for a ticket will see how she's made it her own.

"Life's too short to worry about Marilyn Monroe," Jackie Kennedy says to her sister, Leigh.

The First Lady spends May 19 in Leesburg, Virginia, at the Loudoun Hunt Horse Show, winning a third-place ribbon on her show-jumping horse Ninbrano.

In Marilyn's dressing room backstage at Madison Square Garden, Mickey Song is styling her hair with a flip curl.

It's the first time Marilyn is meeting Song, a hairdresser for the Kennedys. He's cut Jack and Bobby Kennedy's hair for tonight's event. "She didn't want me to work on her, because she didn't know me," Song says. "But Bobby convinced her."

Song is excited to work with the movie star, but he senses that she's "extremely nervous and uptight."

That might be because Bobby Kennedy is pacing back and forth outside her dressing room.

"Would you step out for a minute?" the attorney general asks Song.

The hairdresser waits in the corridor. From what he can hear, Marilyn and Kennedy are arguing. Voices are raised. The exchange is growing more intense.

Fifteen minutes later, Kennedy emerges. He looks at Song. "Do you like her?" he demands.

When Song nods his head yes, the attorney general declares, "Well, I think she's a rude fucking bitch."

Kennedy stalks off and Song returns to Marilyn.

She's all disheveled but giggles and says, "Could you help me get myself back together?"

* * *

Twelve feet from the stage, the president steps into his private box, signaling the start of the show to be emceed by his brother-in-law Peter Lawford.

Bobby and Ethel Kennedy are sitting nearby. So are Marilyn's good friend Pat Kennedy Lawford and her publicist, Pat Newcomb. Harry Belafonte sings a moving interpretation of "Michael Row the Boat Ashore."

Marilyn is scheduled to perform next, but she misses her first cue.

Lawford jokes into the microphone, "Mr. President, on this occasion of your birthday, this young lady is not only pulchritudinous but punctual."

A spotlight pans to the corner of the stage. It's empty.

Laughing, Lawford gives her a second cue. "A woman about whom it truly may be said, 'She needs no introduction.' Let me just say, 'Here she is.'"

From the band, a drumroll. Again, the flash of the spotlight to reveal blank space.

The audience laughs along. *It's all part of the show, isn't it?*

Lawford is riffing now but gears up for a final introduction. "In the history of show business, perhaps there has been no one female who has meant so much...who has done more... Mr. President, the *late* Marilyn Monroe!"

To thunderous applause, the famously "late" Marilyn finally appears. She crosses the stage in tiny, geisha-like steps, the top of her magnificent dress concealed by a hip-length short-sleeved white ermine coat.

As Lawford helps Marilyn out of her wrap, the audience inhales sharply, and neither Jack nor Bobby can take his eyes off her. No one can.

341

Marilyn flicks the microphone with her finger. It pops. She's had nightmares that she'd start to sing but no sound would come out.

"Happy biiiiiirthday to youuuu..."

She performs a breathy rendition of the classic song, with the gentlest hint of innuendo that is smartly judged and perfectly knowing. It's just as she rehearsed it.

After the briefest of pauses, she launches into a familiar tune. "Thanks for the Memory" may be best known as Bob Hope's theme song, but tonight the lyrics have been cleverly rearranged. Leo Robin, who wrote "Diamonds Are a Girl's Best Friend" for Marilyn, has created "Thanks, Mr. President."

She sings the lines through, and then exhorts the audience, "Everybody! Happy Birthday!"

The band once again strikes up the song as Marilyn bounces to the beat, waving her arms in time to the music and encouraging the audience to join in the serenade as two men in chef's toques carry a litter bearing an enormous multitiered birthday cake.

Watching from the wings is Isidore Miller, Marilyn's former father-in-law. He and Marilyn have remained close since the divorce. Bringing the Austrian-born Miller as her proud escort to this All-American gala, Marilyn thinks, will be "one of the biggest things of his life."

She's right.

After the show, President Kennedy takes the microphone to thank all the performers. "We're grateful to Miss Monroe, who left a picture to come all the way east," he says, "and I can now retire from politics after having had 'Happy Birthday' sung to me in such a sweet, wholesome way."

The president, the attorney general, and Marilyn all sign the guestbook at the Upper East Side townhouse where Arthur Krim, chairman of United Artists, is hosting a private after-party for leading Democrats and celebrities who performed at the gala.

Marilyn arrives on the arm of Isidore Miller.

Her one-of-a-kind rhinestone dress continues to attract attention. "She was wearing skin and beads," says Adlai Stevenson. "I didn't see the beads!"

As White House photographer Cecil Stoughton snaps candids, he captures the two Kennedy brothers listening intently as Marilyn speaks.

"There was something at once magical and desperate about her," historian and Kennedy campaign aide Arthur Schlesinger Jr. observes from across the room. "Robert Kennedy, with his curiosity, his sympathy, his absolute directness of response to distress, in some way got through the glittering mist as few did."

The next day, Jackie Kennedy is furious—not with the president, but with his brother. "My understanding of it is that Bobby was the one who orchestrated the whole goddamn thing," Jackie tells her sister-in-law over the telephone. "The attorney general is the troublemaker here, Ethel. Not the president. So it's Bobby I'm angry at, not Jack."

CHAPTER 60

"IT WAS MARILYN who was the hit of the evening," *Time* magazine reports on the gala.

That's scant consolation for how little she means to the studio. "Fox should start paying as much attention to me as they are paying to Elizabeth Taylor," Marilyn tells Lawrence Schiller, a photographer she befriended in 1960 on the set of *Let's Make Love.*

Taylor's salary for the Fox period drama *Cleopatra,* currently shooting in Rome, is $1 million. Marilyn is making one tenth of that — $100,000 — for *Something's Got to Give.*

Marilyn's personal publicist, Pat Newcomb, has an idea how to close the gap.

The whirlwind cross-country trip has exhausted Marilyn, but she makes her 6:15 a.m. call time on Monday, May 21. A studio doctor examines her and pronounces her vulnerable to a relapse of sinusitis.

But he does clear her to shoot a solo sequence. *Something's*

Got to Give screenwriter Nunnally Johnson calls it the "midnight skinny dip."

When director George Cukor calls "Action," on Tuesday, May 22, Marilyn, costumed in a flesh-colored bikini that's meant to make her appear nude, cavorts in the pool. The ruckus is intended to wake her on-screen ex-husband, Dean Martin. But Martin's out sick himself, and not on set.

The cameras shoot close-ups, long shots, wide shots. In the rushes, though, it's revealed that the bathing suit straps are visible across the shoulders.

"That's easily solved," Marilyn calls from the pool. "I'll just take it all off."

The "spontaneous" declaration is part of Newcomb's plan. Yesterday, the publicist had telephoned Schiller, who's booked to be on the lot shooting a story for *Paris Match*.

"I would plan to be on the set all day tomorrow if I were you, Larry, and bring plenty of film," Newcomb told him. "Marilyn has the swimming scene tomorrow and, knowing Marilyn, she might slip out of her suit!"

Marilyn adds her own instructions. "Larry, if I do come out of the pool with nothing on, I want your guarantee that when your pictures appear on the covers of magazines Elizabeth Taylor is not anywhere in the same issue."

Newcomb tips off two other photographers: William Reed Woodfield of Globe Photos and Fox photographer Jimmy Mitchell.

Schiller selects a long lens and focuses his camera on Marilyn as she moves through a series of poses. One leg over the edge of the pool. Laughing and splashing in the water. Lying on the pool deck under artfully draped towels. It's as Marilyn glides through the water that the photographer suddenly realizes "she didn't have the top of her swimming suit on."

He keeps shooting. Eleven. Twelve. Thirteen rolls of film. And when he finishes working in black-and-white, he does four rolls of color.

Westfield, too, gets a shot of Marilyn shedding her suit poolside.

Marilyn Monroe is taking her clothes off on Stage 14! Security is posted at the doors to keep out Fox employees eager for a look.

Marilyn doesn't mind the commotion. She's taken uppers for mood and painkillers for her thumping earache, and she can't feel a thing. Least of all how cold the water is.

The shoot goes on for four hours.

"I had been wearing the suit, but it concealed too much," Marilyn says afterward, "and it would have looked wrong on the screen...The set was closed, all except members of the crew, who were very sweet. I told them to close their eyes or turn their backs, and I think they all did. There was a lifeguard on the set to help me out if I needed him, but I'm not sure it would have worked. He had his eyes closed too."

It's a marketing masterstroke. What the Taylor-Burton affair has done for publicizing *Cleopatra,* Marilyn's nude photo shoot will do for *Something's Got to Give.*

While the rolls of film Mitchell snapped are studio property—a show is made of placing them in a bank vault to signal their immense value—Schiller suggests to Woodfield that the two of them combine forces. "Bill, two sets of photos will just drive down the price. One set, and we control the market for these pictures."

Marilyn personally reviews every image. She's "a very intelligent businesswoman about these things," Schiller observes. She approves the ones she likes and cuts through the ones she doesn't with a pair of scissors.

Hugh Hefner offers $25,000 for a single shot, shattering the ceiling of what *Playboy* magazine has ever paid for an image. The photos sell to seventy magazines worldwide. *Life* chooses a rather demure snap—Marilyn poolside in a blue robe—for the cover of its June 22 issue.

Twenty-four-year-old Schiller thanks Marilyn for engineering the biggest payday of his career so far. "See what tits 'n' ass can do?" he jokes.

"That's how I got my house and swimming pool," Marilyn says, laughing along with Schiller. "There isn't anybody that looks like me without clothes on."

Yet she hardly feels secure.

It's still about nudity. Is that all I'm good for?

CHAPTER 61

THE SKINNY-DIPPING PHOTO SHOOT leaves Marilyn with an ear infection. She's treated at home on Sunday, May 27. On Monday, she's in too much pain to work and she's given an injection of penicillin.

Though Marilyn sang "Happy Birthday" to President Kennedy on May 19, his actual birthday is May 29. She's been wanting to wish him the best for his forty-fifth. But when "Miss Green" telephones the White House, her calls no longer go through.

What she doesn't know is that the switchboard has been duly informed that neither "Miss Green" nor the president's other *close* friends should be put through any longer. Kennedy's private number has also been disconnected.

On Friday, June 1, 1962, Marilyn celebrates her thirty-sixth birthday by going to work. She's on the Fox lot by six a.m.

Marilyn's stand-in, Evelyn Moriarty, convinces a studio artist to draw a funny "Happy Birthday (suit)" card sending up last week's skinny-dip.

But when Moriarty returns from the Los Angeles Farmers Market with a cake she's bought with $5 from the cast and crew, she's told, "You hide that cake and don't bring it out until 6:00. We are going to get a full day's work out of that dame."

They do, and the mood brightens when the cake is lit with sparklers at the end of the day. After it's cut, Marilyn playfully feeds George Cukor a piece. The director had bristled earlier when Dean Martin brought bottles of Dom Perignon to set, but Marilyn has done well filming her scene today, so why not raise a toast?

Marilyn's evening is just getting started. She's next due at Dodger Stadium.

Two local Major League teams, the Dodgers and the Angels, call the brand-new facility home. Tonight the Angels are playing the defending World Series champion New York Yankees—Joe DiMaggio's old team.

"I have to go," she tells producer Henry Weinstein. "I promised the people at Muscular Dystrophy." She's making an appearance to help the charity raise money.

The evening temperature is hovering around fifty-five degrees. To keep warm, she asks to borrow her Jean Louis–designed movie costume—a cream-colored fur-trimmed suit. Then she's driven to Beverly Hills to pick up Dean Martin's ten-year-old son, Dean Paul Martin. She's known "Dino" since he was a toddler, even babysitting him from time to time.

The game is a big draw. Both teams are in contention for the American League pennant. A record-setting crowd of 51,584 ticket holders is about to see a celebrity more famous than any player on a roster that includes Mickey Mantle, Roger Maris, Yogi Berra, and Whitey Ford.

When Angels outfielder Albie Pearson reports to the home-team dugout, the "Littlest Angel," as he's called for his five-foot-five-inch frame, knows only that he's drawn escort duty for the pregame charity presentation.

"So I go out to the dugout," Pearson says, "and they tell me the person I'm going to walk to home plate is Marilyn Monroe."

The player, who's in his second season with the Angels, is suddenly nervous. "Where is she?" he asks, looking around the dugout.

He finally spots her in the far corner, standing completely in shadow, "pale and shaking and I'm thinking this can't be Marilyn Monroe, the famous movie star." Marilyn is "the most famous yet loneliest person I ever saw in my life," Pearson thinks. "She was a beautiful shell."

She's also a professional. Pearson watches in amazement as Marilyn taps into that spark that made her famous. As they climb the steps of the dugout, the actress is suddenly smiling, waving, and sparkling. She's transformed into Marilyn Monroe.

Standing at home plate, Marilyn asks the crowd to consider a donation to the muscular dystrophy fund. But the Angels haven't forgotten that it's her special day. The acclaimed Robert Mitchell Boys Choir, which frequently appears in movies, sings "Happy Birthday" to her.

Pearson sees Marilyn safely back to the dugout. Though they haven't exchanged a word, he's feeling protective of her. He's a religious man, and Bible verses run through his head.

Suddenly, she turns to him, asking, "What? What is it you want to tell me?"

Pearson is too tongue-tied to answer.

Someone else is looking out for Marilyn tonight—her favorite limo driver, Rudy Kautzsky. She climbs into a rented Cadillac, returning to the Fox lot to return her costume. Then it's on to dinner at La Scala, the Beverly Hills restaurant where, *Variety* columnist Army Archerd notes, Marilyn often "dines alone, late."

Shortly after midnight on Saturday, June 2, it's finally time to go home.

Within hours, she's gripped by a fever and a chill she caught at the baseball game. The symptoms of her acute sinusitis come rushing back. But her mind is whirring with the feelings that wash over her every year around her birthday, feelings of sadness and regret over being alone.

Marilyn's telephone rings. She can tell it's long distance by the clicking sounds when she picks up the phone. She's brimming with hope when the operator connects her with Hyannis Port.

"Jack?"

"It's me, Peter. Peter Lawford."

Lawford has once again been pressed into doing Jack's dirty work. "You can handle it, Peter," his brother-in-law had told him.

Lawford does the president's bidding. Clearly and firmly, he tells Marilyn that she will never again hear from Jack Kennedy. The president was *never* going to divorce his wife to marry her. Marilyn was never going to be First Lady.

To drive the point home, Lawford gets crude. "You're just another one of Jack's fucks."

Lawford ends the call, then makes another one to Marilyn's publicist.

"Get to Brentwood as soon as you can," Lawford tells Pat Newcomb, knowing the damage his call has inflicted. "Marilyn needs you."

Pat Newcomb hurries over to comfort her friend, who is deeply distraught. Penicillin cured the ear infection Marilyn suffered after filming the swimming scene, but there's no cure for the twin afflictions of humiliation and heartbreak the Kennedys have so cruelly administered. But she can always sedate herself.

On Sunday morning, a shaft of light pierces Marilyn's new blackout blinds. No matter how many times she tugs at the curtains, the room is simply not dark enough to sleep.

By the afternoon, Marilyn is begging for relief. She asks Mrs. Murray to call Dr. Greenson, who's been away in Germany for four weeks.

"Bring him back!" she cries, collapsing to her knees.

Mrs. Murray calls Dr. Greenson's children, Joan and Danny. Danny is now a medical student.

The three of them enter Marilyn's dark room and find her wrapped in a bedsheet. Her masked face looks to Danny like "the Lone Ranger," but when he looks beneath it, he sees that her face is white with anxiety and damp with sweat, classic signs of a Dexamyl overdose. After consulting with their father by telephone, they summon a local doctor, who clears Marilyn's nightstand of all drugs.

"I can't sleep. I'm ugly. Nobody loves me. People are only nice to me when they want something I can give them."

Listening to her expressions of hopelessness and rejection, Danny grows increasingly concerned. *This woman is desperate.*

"My life isn't worth living," she insists.

CHAPTER 62

MONDAY, JUNE 4. Marilyn is once again absent from Stage 14. The studio's insurance doctor is dispatched. Her temperature is 100 degrees, yet her lawyer, Mickey Rudin, encourages her to go back to work. Marilyn lashes out, angrily accusing him of being "with them," taking Fox's side against her.

Co-star Dean Martin has also had enough. When, on June 5, Marilyn is once again a no-show, he declares, "That's it!"

Production is suspended and it becomes a legal matter.

Rudin places an urgent call to Dr. Greenson, who flies back to Los Angeles on Wednesday and goes straight to Marilyn's bedside. Mrs. Murray and Pat Newcomb have no idea how to help her. Maybe the doctor can.

Thursday, June 7. Marilyn makes an emergency visit to Michael Gurdin, a UCLA plastic surgeon, seeking treatment for "an accidental fall." She'd seen him previously in 1958, under her then married name, Miller.

With her hair covered in a scarf and dark glasses over her face, "Joan Newman" arrives at Dr. Gurdin's office accompanied by Dr. Greenson.

When Gurdin examines her face, he observes black-and-blue marks around her nose and a bruised left cheekbone.

"Marilyn had a small accident in the shower," Greenson says, explaining that she fell and hit the tiles.

Gurdin orders X-rays to determine the extent of the damage.

The doctor is skeptical of the situation. He tells a colleague that he thinks Marilyn "was beaten up." Who did this to her? He's suspicious of Greenson, who "did all the talking" and "didn't seem anxious for Marilyn to speak."

But while they're waiting for the X-rays, Marilyn does speak, asking the doctor, "If my nose is broken, how quickly can we fix it?"

When a nurse delivers the films, Dr. Gurdin diagnoses "a minute fracture of the tip of the nasal bone."

"Thank goodness!" Marilyn exclaims, sinking into Greenson with obvious relief.

Marilyn has missed seventeen of thirty shooting days on *Something's Got to Give*. Still, Dr. Greenson and Rudin are determined to save her job. On Friday, June 8, Greenson makes Fox executives a promise that he'll have Marilyn back on set by Monday.

"I can persuade Marilyn to go along with any reasonable request," Greenson brags. "While I don't want to present myself as a Svengali, I can convince Marilyn to do anything I want her to do."

*   *   *

While the negotiations are happening, Marilyn musters the energy to attend to another pressing piece of business.

She contacts celebrity investigator Fred Otash and asks him to install a bug on her telephone. She wants to record her own calls—as insurance against potential threats or blackmail.

The mini listening device is so small, Otash explains, "You could hide it in your bra." What he doesn't tell her is that recording devices have already been installed throughout 12305 Fifth Helena Drive...by Otash himself.

A letter on 20th Century-Fox Film Corporation letterhead is sent to Marilyn Monroe Productions, Inc., putting her on notice that, effective Friday, June 8, she's been terminated from *Something's Got to Give* for "the willful failure and refusal on Miss Monroe's part to perform and render services in said motion picture."

That same day, Fox announces: "Marilyn Monroe has been removed from the cast of 'SOMETHING'S GOT TO GIVE.' This action was made necessary because of Miss Monroe's repeated willful breaches of her contract. No justification was given by Miss Monroe for her failure to report for photography on many occasions. The studio has suffered losses through these absences and the Twentieth-Century Fox Film Company will take legal action against Miss Monroe."

Dr. Greenson is stunned to hear the news over his car radio. He rushes to check on his patient. Marilyn is shocked. She's going to need careful monitoring to get through these next critical hours.

To Mrs. Murray, Greenson rails against the studio's harsh actions. His patient has been ill. "You know, it isn't as if she was goldbricking or out partying. They have acted in bad faith!"

Marilyn's next visitor is makeup artist and friend Whitey Snyder, who observes, "She had never been fired before, so she was devastated. She couldn't understand it."

Less than a month ago, Marilyn's picture was on the front page of every paper for bringing down the house at Madison Square Garden when she sang "Happy Birthday" to President Kennedy.

Now her name is linked with failure and the threat of a lawsuit from her employer for the better part of fifteen years.

In a further betrayal, Fox names Marilyn's replacement, Lee Remick, who starred in the 1960 Fox adventure drama *Wild River* and is billed as "America's answer to Brigitte Bardot."

But Dean Martin will accept no substitute. He voices his support for Marilyn: "I have the greatest respect for Miss Lee Remick and her talent and all the other actresses who were considered for the role, but I signed to do the film with Marilyn Monroe and I will do it with no one else."

Even Elizabeth Taylor is sympathetic. Marilyn is surprised to receive a long-distance telephone call from her Fox rival expressing support.

"I know we're not friends," Taylor says, "but what's happening to you now has been happening to me for a long time over this *Cleopatra* situation."

The cost overruns on Taylor's film have famously threatened

to collapse the entire studio. Nevertheless, the *Cleopatra* star offers Marilyn financial help. "If you're in a bad position and you need any help," Taylor says, "I will send some money to you. If there is anything you need—anything at all—call me and you will have it within twenty-four hours."

Marilyn is touched by Taylor's offer, as well as her willingness to stage a walk-out on Marilyn's behalf.

"Well, thank you so much, Elizabeth. I'm okay financially. I don't need money, although I really appreciate the offer. And I don't want you to walk out of the movie. Neither one of us should damage our career any more than the studio already has."

At the news of Marilyn's dismissal, Joe DiMaggio leaves his European tour on behalf of V. H. Monette & Co. and on June 10 flies to be by her side. Though Marilyn is distraught that this may spell the end of her career, DiMaggio sees it as an opportunity, the removal of an obstacle that was preventing them from being together.

"He loved her a great deal," Val Monette says. "He had decided to remarry her. He thought things would be different than they had been before, and that everything would work out well for them now."

Marilyn isn't expecting DiMaggio, but she's delighted when he arrives, dropping her shopping and throwing herself into his arms.

She proudly shows him around her new house. He's seen the house before—he helped her with the down payment, after all—but not the progress she's made with her herb and flower gardens.

"I don't know why but I've always been able to make anything grow," she says.

If Marilyn has it in her to cultivate a healthy garden, what does she need with Dr. Engelberg and the "youth shots" Dr. Greenson has instructed him to administer nightly at 6 p.m.?

DiMaggio wants to know what's in the shots, but Marilyn doesn't know or care. They perk her up, make her more talkative, keep her going until about midnight, even when she's tired or fearful.

As of Monday, June 11, *Something's Got to Give* is canceled.

"Dear George," Marilyn telegrams director Cukor, "please forgive me, it was not my doing. I had so looked forward to working with you."

CHAPTER 63

THE STALEMATE BETWEEN Fox and Marilyn stretches for sixteen days.

On Thursday, June 28, Marilyn receives an important guest—Fox's chief of production, Peter Levathes.

Marilyn has arranged every detail, from caviar-and-cocktail refreshments down to a costume reminiscent of the executive look she devised when she founded Marilyn Monroe Productions, Inc., in 1955.

She's had help from top stylists, some of her closest friends in Hollywood. Norman Norell, who designed the dress she wore to marry Arthur Miller and the emerald-green gown she wore last year to pick up her Golden Globe trophy, makes a beige dress in a tailored style. Makeup artist Whitey Snyder and hairstylist Sydney Guilaroff create a sleek yet serious look, accessorized with horn-rimmed glasses.

Although Levathes was quoted days earlier as questioning Marilyn's mental state—"Miss Monroe is not just being temperamental, she's mentally ill, perhaps seriously"—those words were part of a calculated smear campaign from the studio rather than a legitimate sentiment.

Today, he is nothing but complimentary of the "astute businesswoman."

"You couldn't have had a better meeting with an actress," Levathes says. "She had a kind of renewed interest in the project that was infectious. I was finally confident that the picture would be made. In fact, I even authorized a new rewrite of the script incorporating Marilyn's ideas."

By the end of the month, Marilyn is negotiating for a seven-figure, two-picture contract in the realm of what Elizabeth Taylor commands.

Exactly what prompted the studio's reversal is unclear. But Marilyn suspects that someone she fondly calls "the General" is watching out for her.

That would be Bobby Kennedy—US attorney general and producer of the Fox property *The Enemy Within,* based on his 1960 book of the same name.

Bobby's been spending a lot of time in LA recently. It's a notable event when the attorney general arrives in his official car at his sister and brother-in-law's Santa Monica beach house.

And when the Lawfords throw dinner parties, they always invite Marilyn.

"Then the help would come in and say, 'Marilyn's arrived,'" one of their neighbors remarks. "Sometimes I'd notice Bobby and Marilyn go out through the patio to the beach to walk."

One night during one of these parties, Bobby's bodyguard

cautions a young parking attendant. "You have eyes but you can't see, you have ears but you can't hear, and you have a mouth but you can't speak. You're gonna see a lot of things, but you have to keep quiet."

Marilyn could use that caution herself. She tells dozens of friends about her burgeoning relationship with the president's brother.

According to a friend, "It wasn't a physical attraction for her. It was more mental. Because she was depicted as a dumb blonde. You always want what you don't have, and Bobby was a bright guy. That's what turned her on."

"I like him," Marilyn tells her masseur Ralph Roberts, "but not physically."

Bobby on the other hand is dazzled by Marilyn. His interest in her is validating, especially after Jack's rejection. But she desperately wants him to take her seriously.

She even starts taking notes on their conversations in her little red diary, she tells her friend Bob Slatzer, because "Bobby liked to talk about political things. He got mad at me one day because he said I didn't remember anything he told me."

"I think she made those notes when he was talking on the telephone, in the hope of having something to talk to him about later," another friend says. "It probably never occurred to Bobby that she was listening to his conversations."

CHAPTER 64

THERE'S RENEWED INTEREST in the star who challenged 20th Century-Fox not once but twice. Photographers and reporters clamor for access.

Photographer Bert Stern has been in Rome on the set of *Cleopatra*, shooting Elizabeth Taylor in a pleated Fortuny dress and a gold serpent belt to promote the Fox film in *Vogue*.

The magazine next sends Stern to Los Angeles to photograph Marilyn for its August issue, her first-ever appearance in the fashion magazine.

"You're beautiful" is Stern's opening line upon Marilyn's arrival in Suite 261 in the Hotel Bel-Air, only five hours late.

"Really? What a nice thing to say," she replies.

On the way to creating something "pure Marilyn," they have a lighthearted and intimate sitting, just the two of them, a hairdresser, an assistant—and three bottles of Dom Perignon.

"Can you get me some scarves?" Stern had asked *Vogue*. "Scarves you can see through—with geometrics. And jewelry. Jewelry doesn't need too many clothes, right?"

It doesn't take long to get Marilyn on board with the idea of a near-nude shoot. Her only concern is the noticeable reminder of her June 1961 gallbladder surgery. "What about my scar?" she asks. "Will it show?"

Stern assures her they can retouch the photos if necessary, though personally he prefers seeing a small imperfection. After that, Marilyn is unselfconscious, happily shedding clothes, frolicking with sheer scarves, flowers, and jewelry. The shoot lasts twelve hours, ending around seven in the morning.

Vogue commissions an eight-page editorial and sends Stern back to shoot three more days to fill the space. This time, it's about the clothes.

Marilyn poses first in a backless black Dior gown, then in a column dress, but it's not until she's undressed and again rolling around in the crisp white hotel linens that Stern gets the images he really wants.

When Stern later sends her his negatives, Marilyn sends them back with orange *x*'s through the ones she dislikes. She is a woman in control.

Richard Meryman, *Life* magazine's human affairs editor, initially requested an interview with Marilyn after meeting her in New York earlier that year. Now Marilyn sets strict parameters. Meryman must provide the interview questions, as well as the transcript, and must grant her approval over the content before it's printed. "You can have all the clearance rights you wish," he assures her. "And, yes, you can destroy negatives."

Marilyn has had plenty of reasons to mistrust the press. "They go around and ask mostly your enemies," she explains. "Friends always say, 'Let's check and see if this is all right with her.'...Most people don't really know me."

Meryman wants to get to know her. He's especially interested in Marilyn's experiences with fame. "I do hope that you might find it an interesting topic to explore." He agrees to her conditions and on Wednesday, July 4, brings his tape recorder to 12305 Fifth Helena Drive.

She looks great but is clearly troubled, the journalist thinks when she greets him.

A tour of the house is Marilyn's version of a personality test. She loves the home she's chosen, but she requests that photos of it be minimal.

"I don't want *everybody* to see exactly where I live, what my sofa or my fireplace looks like. Do you know the book *Everyman*? Well, I want to stay just in the fantasy of Everyman." She's only got one major regret about the house. "I live alone and I hate it!"

She's still waiting for the furnishings she chose in Mexico to arrive, but she's added some decorative touches. Meryman admires a leather-covered coffee table, a tin candelabra, and wooden folding stools.

"Good," Marilyn says, "anybody who likes my house, I'm sure I'll get along with."

Negotiations about restarting the production of *Something's Got to Give* are still ongoing. She's weary of conflict.

"Have many friends called up to rally round when you were fired by Fox?" Meryman asks.

Marilyn sits in silence, finally looking Meryman full in the face.

"No," she all but whispers.

People can be so unkind. Even her stepchildren have been taunted because of their relationship to her. Arthur Miller's son Bobby once tried to hide from her a magazine article he worried would hurt her feelings. Joe DiMaggio Jr. endured cruel teasing, "Ha, ha, your stepmother is Marilyn Monroe, ha, ha, ha."

It's no surprise that Marilyn is wary of being a punch line.

"I hope you got something here," she says to the journalist, "but please don't make me look like a joke!"

On Saturday, July 7, Richard Meryman returns to Marilyn's Brentwood home with his colleague, *Life* photojournalist Allan Grant. Grant is well-regarded, especially among celebrities— he's "very handsome and glamorous, two virtues that made him popular in Hollywood."

Though the shoot is meant to start at noon, it's four o'clock before Marilyn is ready. Not due to the vanity or arrogance she's been accused of, so much as a complete inability to stay on task. "There was none of the fearful moping and preening in front of mirrors I had heard so much about. She was entirely cheerful and utterly disorganized," Meryman observes. "The necessary mechanics of daily living were beyond her grasp; she always started out behind and never caught up."

Once she's finally ready—casually dressed in slim capri trousers and a soft, dark sweater—Grant selects an Italian-style carved chair with light green velvet upholstery and positions it under a window to catch the best light and the thick foliage outside.

Marilyn is in a playful mood, posing on and around the chair, at one point piercing the seat's fabric with one of her spike heels, and causing a small crack in the wood when she poses on the chair back.

"Forget Monroe the movie star," Grant's been instructed, *"and simply photograph Marilyn the person."*

Meryman is interested in both.

On why she became an actress: "I didn't like the world around me because it was kind of grim, but I loved to play house...Some of my foster families used to send me to the movies to get me out of the house and there I'd sit all day and way into the night. Up in front, there with the screen so big, a little kid all alone, and I loved it."

On being objectified: "Sometimes I'm invited places to kind of brighten up a dinner table like a musician who'll play the piano after dinner, and I know you're not really invited for yourself. You're just an ornament."

On respecting the artistry of her craft: "An actor is not a machine, no matter how much they want to say you are. Creativity has got to start with humanity and when you're a human being, you feel, you suffer."

"I was never used to being happy, so that wasn't something I ever took for granted," she tells Meryman. "Fame to me certainly is only a temporary and a partial happiness, even for a waif and I was brought up a waif. But fame is not really for a daily diet, that's not what fulfills you. It warms you a bit but the warming is temporary. It's like caviar, you know, it's good to have caviar but not when you have it every meal every day."

And if fame leaves her?

"If it goes by, I've always known it was fickle. So at least it's something I experienced, but that's not where I live."

Two days later, as agreed, Meryman brings over the final draft of his story, "Marilyn Lets Her Hair Down About Being Famous," for approval. Marilyn has it ready when he returns later that day, with only a few small changes penciled in.

She's pleased with the story and appreciates how Meryman's captured her voice. "Hey, thanks," she calls out as he departs.

George Barris and Marilyn first met on the set of *The Seven Year Itch*, when he photographed her in and around New York City.

Now *Cosmopolitan* magazine has commissioned a photographic essay, and he approaches Marilyn about collaborating on a series of sessions and interviews.

"Are you happy or unhappy?" Barris asks.

"I think I'm human," Marilyn says. "I have my down moments, but I'm also robust. I think I'm more robust than down...I'm human."

Barris makes her words the theme of the shoot. "She would hide nothing in our photos. No magic, no makeup or retouching of our finished photographs."

She asks Barris to select some costumes and props.

"Off to Saks," he writes, "for a bulky sweater, terry cloth three quarter hooded beach jacket, a blanket, a large towel for those peek-a-boo beach shots, and a sexy bikini. I did not buy Marilyn any undergarments — she never wore them."

Marilyn also brings some of her own clothes, including a sweater that she purchased in February at a market in Toluca, Mexico.

Friday, July 13, is the final day of the shoot. This time on Santa Monica Beach at sunset.

The low-lying gray clouds create a moody, almost mysterious effect. And the shifting natural light should perfectly capture an enigmatic movie star in the throes of a metamorphosis.

The real Marilyn Monroe, the real Norma Jeane. That's who Barris is looking to meet on the beach that day.

And he does.

She projects such joy when the camera's on, Barris muses. *The world can't forget her face.*

The sun is setting and the temperature dropping as he shoots down to his very last roll of film. Even the champagne he's brought as fortification is losing its effect. He sees Marilyn shivering but she never complains.

The last photo he takes is of Marilyn bundled in her Mexican sweater, her blond hair blowing in the sea breeze.

Her face softens with affection, and her lips pucker, as if to blow him a kiss.

"This one's for you, George," she says.

* * *

When Marilyn and George Barris meet at her home to review the photos he's taken, she spends five hours looking carefully at each one, using a red pencil to cross through her rejections.

"I'm in your hands now," Marilyn says. "I trust you."

"Don't worry," Barris says. "I'll never hurt you. When this is published, there won't be any changes."

CHAPTER 65

ON THE SAME Friday the thirteenth as the Santa Monica Beach photo shoot, a report lands on FBI Director J. Edgar Hoover's desk from the FBI office in Mexico City.

The memo is labeled "MARILYN MONROE — SECURITY MATTER — C [Communist]."

It details information passed along by an unnamed source claiming that Marilyn had information about political matters overheard while she was at Peter Lawford's residence with one of the Kennedy brothers a few days earlier.

The only Kennedy brother who's recently been in Los Angeles is Bobby. And the most likely informant to the Mexican FBI is Marilyn's lover José Bolaños.

"She was very pleased, as she had asked the President a lot of socially significant questions concerning the morality of atomic testing," the report notes. "Subject's views are very positively and concisely leftist; however, if she is being actively used by the Communist Party, it is not general knowledge among those working with the movement in Los Angeles."

The FBI is already alarmed to know of Marilyn's continued connection to suspected agent Frederick Vanderbilt Field, who is currently staying with his wife Nieves in Marilyn's New York apartment at 444 East 57th Street. Field writes Marilyn a letter thanking her and calling her apartment "the key to the success of the whole expedition."

"We hope you are winning your battles in Hollywood," he writes. "We kind of figure being who and what you are you will come out on top."

But Marilyn isn't feeling victorious.

Days after the FBI report, Bobby stops taking her calls.

The sudden cold shoulder—so reminiscent of what happened recently with Jack—leaves Marilyn furious.

"He should face me and tell me why," she rants to friends. "Or tell me on the phone. I don't care. I just want to know *why*."

When Marilyn can't get through to the attorney general, she turns to his sister for help.

"Forget it," Pat Lawford tells her. "Bobby's still just a little boy. But you have to remember he's a little boy with a wife and seven kids." Not only that, but a staunch Catholic who'd been named "Father of the Year" just two years earlier. There's simply no way he's ever going to sacrifice his career and reputation to leave his wife for Marilyn.

But Marilyn is deeply hurt and can't let it go.

"He owes me an explanation!" she complains to her friend Bob Slatzer. "I want to know what happened, and I want Bobby to tell me himself!"

She continues unsuccessfully trying to reach him: on his private number, at the Justice Department, and even at home in Hickory Hill. If Bobby Kennedy keeps ignoring her, she tells Slatzer, "I might just hold a press conference. I've certainly got a lot to say!"

CHAPTER 66

MY GOD, WHAT a beautiful woman, thinks Buddy Greco. On Saturday, July 28, the pianist is at the Cal Neva Lodge in Lake Tahoe. He's sitting outside Frank Sinatra's bungalow when a limousine pulls up and "this gorgeous woman in dark glasses steps out."

It's Marilyn, of course, though Greco doesn't immediately recognize her.

She's dressed head-to-toe in green: a lime-green long-sleeved silk jersey Pucci blouse with a boat neck, green shoes, green trousers, and a green headscarf.

"Before I realized who it was, I thought: 'My God, what a beautiful woman. No taste in clothes, but what a beautiful woman!'" Greco laughs.

He's met Marilyn only briefly, so he's delighted to see her again. She greets him with a big hug around the neck. She and Greco, along with Peter and Pat Lawford, are guests of Sinatra. A number of Sinatra's other Hollywood friends and Mob associates, like Sam Giancana, are there that weekend too. Greco will be performing his rendition of "The Lady Is a Tramp," his big 1960 hit, in Sinatra's Celebrity Room.

Both Sinatra and the Lawfords, aware of what's been going on with the Kennedys, hope that getting Marilyn out of Los Angeles will distract her.

Over the last few weeks, Marilyn has become deeply depressed and withdrawn. She's seen few people except Mrs. Murray and her doctors—Dr. Greenson, whom she's seen twenty-eight times in the last thirty-five days—and Dr. Engelberg, whom she's seen thirteen times.

After she and Dean Martin finish *Something's Got to Give*, Sinatra might co-star with Marilyn on her next film, *What a Way to Go!*, which has been written specifically for her. So why not celebrate in advance?

But it's far from the "magical weekend" that Greco describes having.

Shortly after the pianist walks off stage Saturday night to join Sinatra at his red velveteen booth in the lounge, Greco spots an unsteady Marilyn standing in the doorway, "still in the same green outfit she'd worn all day."

But the "smart, funny, intelligent, fragile" woman he'd spent time with earlier in the day has disappeared.

In her place is a clearly intoxicated, defiant, and angry woman.

"Who the fuck are they all staring at?" Greco hears her say.

This is not the star we're used to seeing, he thinks.

Sinatra is quick to react. He calls over his bodyguard, former USC football star Ed Pucci, to escort Marilyn out. Pucci takes no chances, scooping up the tiny blonde and carrying her away.

Greco's upset. He doesn't know Marilyn well, but he's heard stories about her previous issues, and he's worried enough to follow her outside to make sure she's all right.

He finds Marilyn sitting alone by the pool in the moonlight, looking pale and out of it, so he escorts her back to her bungalow.

Marilyn doesn't want to be alone. She calls the front desk and keeps the line open all night. The operator can hear her breathing.

Marilyn passes the next hours suspended in a fog. She may have nearly OD'd. She may have fallen out of bed. She may have been unknowingly assaulted.

Whatever it was, maybe it's best if she just blocks it out.

"I have the most wonderful memory for forgetting things," Marilyn once told Hollywood journalist Sidney Skolsky.

That talent is convenient now.

What's certain is that the "relaxing" weekend in the Sierras is cut short. By Sunday afternoon, Marilyn is flown back to Los Angeles with Peter Lawford on Frank Sinatra's private plane.

She stumbles off the plane, barefoot and bedraggled, and walks straight to a limo waiting to take her home.

Lawford is driven home by the pilot, Frank Lieto. En route, Lawford insists that they stop while he makes a twenty-minute phone call from a pay phone.

Marilyn's a loose cannon, and there are people he has to warn.

CHAPTER 67

NOW THAT *Something's Got to Give* is set to resume production, Hollywood reporters are willing to put a more positive spin on their coverage.

In the *New York Journal-American,* Dorothy Kilgallen writes:

> Marilyn Monroe's health seems to be much improving. She's been attending select Hollywood parties and has become the talk of the town again. In California, they're circulating a photograph of her that certainly isn't as bare as the famous calendar, but is very interesting...And she's cooking in the sex-appeal department, too; she's proved vastly alluring to a handsome gentleman who is a bigger name than Joe DiMaggio in his heyday. So don't write off Marilyn as finished.

Marilyn would agree. She's nowhere near finished. She's busy working the phones.

"They are not calling back," she says of the Kennedys, when

she telephones her friend Bob Slatzer in Ohio. "Bobby and Jack used me. They used me."

I'm not going to stand for that. I'm going to tell everyone about us.

When Marilyn hears that Bobby will be attending a legal conference in San Francisco this weekend, she works the problem. Surely Pat Lawford will tell her where he's staying. San Francisco is 350 miles north of Los Angeles, but the distance is not important. She has to see Bobby.

A big confrontation is looming. Surely the journalists will be on her side. Walter Winchell, Dorothy Kilgallen, they're always looking for a scoop. What could be bigger than the true story of Marilyn Monroe and the Kennedys?

She calls her friend Henry Rosenfeld in New York. She asks the dress manufacturer, an early investor in Marilyn Monroe Productions, to meet her in Washington, DC, next month and escort her to the premiere of the new Irving Berlin musical, *Mr. President*. Joshua Logan, who directed Marilyn in *Bus Stop*, is also directing this stage production.

More crucially, she's heard that John and Jackie Kennedy will be attending the party. She wants to make sure Jack knows what he's missing. And she has just the designer to create a new evening look: Jean Louis, who created the "skin and beads" gown she wore to serenade the president at his birthday gala. She's already put in an order at a cost of $6,000.

Why not make a hair appointment, too? She books Mickey Song to come to her house. *Who would know more about the Kennedys' private life than their hairdresser?*

Has Song seen Bobby or Jack with "other women"? Marilyn wants to know.

She doesn't get many answers, but that's all right. Peter Lawford is having a dinner party at his beach house tonight. Surely, she'll pick up some information there—especially if she brings drinks to share.

She greets Lawford's friend Dick Livingston with a bottle of Dom Perignon.

"Champagne is so zestful," Marilyn says, pouring herself a glass over ice cubes and breathing into the glass as if ingesting the elixir of life. She's in good spirits and has spent the morning at a nearby nursery ordering citrus plants and flowers for her garden.

Livingston eyes Marilyn's odd outfit—"a pair of hip-huggers with a bare midriff that revealed her gallbladder-operation scar, and a Mexican serape wrapped around her neck"—but focuses on her unhealthy pallor, "absolutely white, the color of alabaster."

"My God, Marilyn, you ought to get some sun," he advises.

"I know," she replies, looking at him over her champagne glass. "What I need is a tan...and a man."

Bobby Kennedy arrives in San Francisco with Ethel and four of their children on Friday, August 3, the same day that Marilyn's story in *Life* hits newsstands. They have weekend plans at Bates Ranch before the attorney general is scheduled to speak at the American Bar Association on Monday.

Marilyn tries several times to contact Bobby at his hotel, the St. Francis, but he's not answering or returning her calls.

She calls Bob Slatzer again, fuming.

"I'm going to blow the lid off this whole damn thing! I'm

going to tell everything!" Marilyn tells him. "That the Kennedys got what they wanted out of me and then moved on!"

Slatzer attempts to calm her down and talk her out of holding a press conference.

Try to be a little more discreet, he cautions.

"Well, I've told a couple of people already," she admits.

Everyone is worried about Marilyn's state of mind. No one wants her talking to the press in her current state. Who knows *what* she'll say?

Dr. Greenson has been coming over once, even twice, a day. Peter Lawford invites her to near-daily gatherings. Pat Newcomb finds pretexts to sleep over at Marilyn's house.

Newcomb takes her out to La Scala. Marilyn drinks too much, then swallows sleeping pills in an attempt to get some rest.

But sleep is elusive. Throughout Friday night and into Saturday morning, Marilyn is repeatedly woken by the shrill ringing of the white telephone by her bed, her personal line.

"Leave Bobby alone, you tramp. Leave Bobby alone," an unknown woman repeatedly curses at her.

"Ethel?" asks Marilyn.

The line goes dead.

Was that Bobby's wife on the telephone? Did she imagine it?

It's a hot night, the baking heat is blowing off the Mojave Desert, and her little dog, Maf, is barking into the darkness, as Marilyn tries, once more, to sleep.

CHAPTER 68

MARILYN AND SID Skolsky have been friends for decades, ever since the days at Schwab's.

She's never been a political person. Until lately, when she's gotten involved with America's leading political family.

It's one thing to attend parties at the beach house of Peter and Pat Kennedy Lawford. They're Hollywood types.

But her association with, as she calls them, "extremely important men in government...at the highest level" is another matter entirely.

It's Saturday, August 4, and Skolsky calls to check on Marilyn.

She starts in on her problems with the Kennedys. She's seeing one of them, she insists. Tonight.

Skolsky's journalistic instincts kick in.

He motions to his daughter Steffi, asks her to pick up a telephone extension. Steffi is hit with the same shock and disbelief her father is experiencing.

Marilyn is adamant about her plans. And she seems to be telling the truth.

Marilyn calls Dr. Greenson to come over for an emergency afternoon session.

"Here I am, the most beautiful woman in the world, and I do not have a date for Saturday night."

Investigator Fred Otash is reviewing his surveillance notes. The tape recordings from the "grain of rice" microphone run about forty minutes.

Seems like Marilyn was right about seeing a Kennedy tonight. Only, not in the way she had planned.

The recordings place both Peter Lawford and Bobby Kennedy at 12305 Fifth Helena Drive, deep in conflict with a highly emotional Marilyn, who's demanding "an explanation as to why Kennedy was not going to marry her."

"It was a violent argument about their relationship and the commitment and promises Bobby made to her," Otash writes in his notebook. "She said she was passed around like a piece of meat." The attorney general loses control of his tone of voice, which becomes "screeching, high-pitched."

He's not leaving without finding what he came for—Marilyn's diary. The little red book where she kept all her notes about "political things."

"Where is it? Where the fuck is it? We have to know. It's important to the family. We can make any arrangements you want, but we must find it."

Marilyn refuses to answer.

"She was really screaming...Bobby gets the pillow and he muffles her on the bed to keep the neighbors from hearing. She finally quieted down and then he was looking to get out of there."

Marilyn lies in bed with her white telephone. She's calmed herself with some pills. Talking to friends might make her feel better.

She holds it together when Joe DiMaggio Jr. calls — she's so proud of Joey, now a twenty-year-old military private — but by the time she reaches her friend and hairdresser Sydney Guilaroff after 8 p.m., she's rambling.

"Danger...betrayals...men in high places...clandestine love affairs," she says, before finally declaring, "I know a lot of secrets about the Kennedys. Dangerous ones."

When José Bolaños telephones at 9:30, Marilyn claims to have news for him that "will one day shock the whole world."

She sets the phone down. *Is someone at the door?*

Eventually, Bolaños ends the call.

Marilyn picks up the telephone again. She was supposed to go over to Peter Lawford's again for dinner tonight, but he'd made excuses on her behalf.

"Marilyn's not coming, she's not feeling well," he'd told the other guests.

Now Lawford is alarmed by the drifting quality of her voice on the phone. He shouts at her, desperately trying to draw her focus.

Marilyn answers sweetly, "Say good-bye to Pat, say

good-bye to Jack, and say good-bye to yourself, because you're a nice guy."

Is he?

Silence is his only answer.

Marilyn is too far gone.

CHAPTER 69

MARILYN MONROE DIES; PILLS BLAMED the *Los Angeles Times* announces on August 6.

At the County Morgue, Coroner Theodore J. Curphey gives his "presumptive opinion," pending an autopsy, that "death was due to an overdose of some drug."

The case is assigned to a "suicide team."

In a 1954 interview Marilyn gave to journalist-turned-screenwriter Ben Hecht at the Beverly Hills Hotel, she had said, "There was something special about me, and I knew what it was. I was the kind of girl they found dead in a hall bedroom with an empty bottle of sleeping pills in her hand."

Now her prediction has become eerily, horribly true.

Was it an accidental overdose? Or was it deliberate? And if so, was it suicide . . . or murder?

Says LAPD homicide detective Sergeant Jack Clemmons, "It was the most obviously staged death scene I had ever seen. The pill bottles on her bedside table had been arranged in neat order and the body was deliberately positioned."

Peter Lawford quickly instructs investigator Fred Otash to "do anything to remove anything incriminating" at Marilyn's house that could connect her to Jack and Bobby Kennedy.

But "incriminating" covers a lot of potential ground.

During an interview with the BBC, Mrs. Murray says words to the effect of "Oh, why do I have to keep covering this up?"

"Covering what up, Mrs. Murray?"

"Well of course Bobby Kennedy was there [on August 4], and of course there was an affair with Bobby Kennedy."

On the other hand, Mrs. Murray was on the verge of losing her job. Marilyn had been trying to get rid of her.

"I can't flat out fire her," Monroe had told Dr. Greenson. "Next thing would be a book—*Secrets of Marilyn Monroe by Her Housekeeper*. She'd make a fortune spilling what she knows and she knows too damn much."

The Associated Press reports, 2 CLOSE TO MARILYN LEAVE HOLLYWOOD.

Eunice Murray leaves town with no forwarding address.

The Arthur Jacobs Agency acknowledges that Pat Newcomb, formerly employed as Marilyn's personal publicist, "is no longer with us." According to the *Hollywood Reporter*, she's accompanied Peter and Pat Kennedy Lawford to the Kennedy Compound in Hyannis Port.

At the autopsy, John Miner, who heads the medical-legal section in the Los Angeles DA's office, wants to know more. It is established protocol for the chief medical examiner to conduct celebrity autopsies, but inexplicably, junior medical examiner

Dr. Thomas Noguchi performs the procedure on the five-four, 118-pound actress.

Dr. Noguchi's examination is meticulous, and his subject clearly makes an impression, stirring the pathologist to quote the Italian poet Petrarch: "It's folly to shrink in fear if this is dying. For death looked lovely in her lovely face."

Bearing in mind that "when you are a coroner, you start from the assumption that every body you examine might be a murder victim," Dr. Noguchi examines Marilyn and detects neither needle marks indicating a drug injection nor signs of physical violence beyond a fresh bruise just above her left hip.

The autopsy confirms blood toxic with barbiturates, and also a stomach empty of food particles, even the yellow dye that coats Nembutal capsules. But Dr. Noguchi never performs the full range of organ tests, stopping short after analyzing the blood and the liver. "I am sure that this could have cleared up a lot of the subsequent controversy, but I didn't follow through as I should have."

The forensic pathologist Cyril Wecht interprets the autopsy as "acute combined drug toxicity, chloral hydrate and Nembutal."

Miner is convinced that someone administered an enema to Marilyn containing the lethal combination of Nembutal and the sedative chloral hydrate.

Ralph Greenson is also an unofficial "suspect." Miner claims that the psychiatrist allows him to listen to sessions Greenson has taped with Marilyn, sessions filled with conflicting references to a hopeful future and unresolved feelings for both of the Kennedy brothers.

"I tell you, doctor," Marilyn says in one session. "I'm glad he [Jack] has Bobby. It's like the Navy—the president is the captain and Bobby is the executive officer. Bobby would do absolutely anything for his brother and so would I, I will never embarrass him. As long as I have memory, I have John Fitzgerald Kennedy."

Marilyn asserts, "As you see, there is no room in my life for him [Bobby]. I guess I don't have the courage to face up to it and hurt him. I want someone else to tell him it's over," she says. "I tried to get the president to do it, but I couldn't reach him."

But Greenson then destroys the tapes, so there is only Miner's recollection to go on.

"When they found Marilyn Monroe," the *Los Angeles Times* reports, "one of her hands grasped a telephone. Perhaps she had called for help. She'd been calling for help all her life."

It may have provided some vestige of comfort.

Not long before she died, she'd confided in the journalist W. J. Weatherby. "Do you know who I've always depended on? Not strangers, not friends. The telephone! That's my best friend."

EPILOGUE

CHAPTER 70

"THE EARTHLY REMAINS of Marilyn Monroe are left to the ultimate loneliness," British Pathé news service reports in a newsreel titled "The Final Farewell to Marilyn Monroe."

"I don't believe it—I don't believe it," says Dean Martin, who'd successfully lobbied for Marilyn to return as his leading lady in *Something's Got to Give*. The film will never be completed.

One week earlier, on August 1, Joe DiMaggio had quit his job as a traveling executive to relocate to the West Coast. He was worried about Marilyn and wanted to be near her.

Now she is dead.

On the night of August 5, Joe DiMaggio grieved next to Marilyn's body, having flown from San Francisco to Los Angeles after hearing the news. There were rumors that he'd proposed marriage to Marilyn for a second time. Instead, he's overseeing her funeral.

It's a simple, private service.

Among the twenty-five mourners invited are her half sister, Berniece; studio workers; her favorite limo driver, Rudy Kautzsky; Ralph Roberts, her masseur; Miss Emmeline Snively, who first contracted Marilyn for the Blue Book Modeling School; the Strasbergs; Dr. Greenson and his family; Eunice Murray; Pat Newcomb; and Grace Goddard's family. They file into the chapel where eulogies and Scripture passages are read over her flower-draped coffin.

DiMaggio puts out word that no members of the Rat Pack—or the Kennedy family—would be allowed entrance. Marilyn's attorney Mickey Rudin complains that it's unfair that DiMaggio keep all her friends away, to which DiMaggio answers: "If it weren't for those friends, she would still be alive."

Whitey Snyder acts as a pallbearer, but first he fulfills his long-ago promise to Marilyn that he would do her makeup while she was "still warm." He applies eyeliner. Blush to her cheeks. A red lip. He and his wife dress her in the aqua Pucci dress that she wore to greet the press at the Continental Hilton Hotel in Mexico City.

But her body doesn't look right. *Marilyn without a bust—she'd have freaked,* Synder thinks, adding bits of cushions and newspaper to give her the perfect shape.

Hairstylist Sydney Guilaroff, who'd spoken to Marilyn on the night she died, is too overcome to dress her platinum hair one last time. She's buried in the wig she wore to film *The Misfits.*

Before the casket is closed, Joe DiMaggio kisses his ex-wife on the forehead. "I love you, I love you," he repeats. He attends alongside his son Joe Jr., in military dress. Joe Jr. had been one of the last people to speak to Marilyn on the night she died. "If anything was amiss, I wasn't aware of it," he says. "She sounded like Marilyn."

Marilyn's most recent ex-husband, Arthur Miller, doesn't attend the funeral. He can't leave his heavily pregnant third wife, Inge Morath. He instead sends flowers on behalf of him and his two children, Jane and Bob, whom Marilyn also adored.

His sentiments mirror DiMaggio's. "Instead of jetting to the funeral to get my picture taken I decided to stay home and let the public mourners finish the mockery," Miller writes on August 8, in an unpublished essay about the anticipated mourners "weeping and gawking" over "this lovely girl who at last you killed." "Not that everyone there will be false, but enough. Most of them there destroyed her, ladies and gentlemen."

Truman Capote pens a tribute to the friend who'd inspired his classic character, Holly Golightly. On the day of Marilyn's funeral, Capote writes to literary critic Newton Arvin, "She was such a good-hearted girl, so pure really, so much on the side of the angels."

Says Billy Wilder, "Nobody else is in that orbit; everyone else is earthbound by comparison."

"M.M. was late for everything—but much too early for death," *Variety* mourns.

The Vatican City weekly, *L'Osservatore della Domenica*, writes that "for all the million words written about the death of

Marilyn Monroe, perhaps few people said the prayer for repose of her soul."

Albie Pearson does say a prayer.

The Los Angeles Angels outfielder who escorted Marilyn to the Dodgers Stadium home plate on her recent birthday is on a road swing in New York.

"I go down to the lobby to get a morning paper and there's the headline, MARILYN MONROE COMMITS SUICIDE.

"I didn't save Marilyn but I could save others. I had to save others. So I prayed and turned my life over to God."

"I feel I'm just getting started; I want to do comedy, tragedy, interspersed," Marilyn had told George Barris in July.

"The happiest time of my life is now. As far as I'm concerned, there's a future and I can't wait to get to it—it should be interesting!"

SOURCES

The authors wish to convey thanks to the sources below:

BOOKS

Blonde by Joyce Carol Oates (Ecco, 2000)

Cary Grant: The Making of a Hollywood Legend by Mark Glancy (Oxford University Press, 2020)

Conversations with Marilyn by W. J. Weatherby (Mason/Charter, 1976; reprinted by Paragon House, 1992)

Dressing Marilyn: How a Hollywood Icon Was Styled by William Travilla by Andrew Hansford (Applause Theatre & Cinema Books, 2012)

Fragments: Poems, Intimate Notes, Letters by Marilyn Monroe (Farrar, Straus and Giroux, 2010)

Goddess: The Secret Lives of Marilyn Monroe by Anthony Summers (Macmillan, 1985)

The Last Days of Marilyn Monroe by Donald H. Wolfe (William Morrow, 1998)

Marilyn and Me: Sisters, Rivals, Friends by Susan Strasberg (Grand Central, 1992)

Marilyn: A Very Personal Story by Norman Rosten (Millington Books, 1967)

The Marilyn Encyclopedia by Adam Victor (Overlook Press, 1999)

Marilyn Monroe by Barbara Leaming (Crown Publishers, 1998)

Marilyn Monroe: The Biography by Donald Spoto (HarperCollins, 1993)

Marilyn Monroe: The Private Life of a Public Icon by Charles Casillo (St. Martin's Press, 2018)

Marilyn's Last Sessions by Michel Schneider (Canongate, 2013)

My Story by Marilyn Monroe with Ben Hecht (Taylor, 2006)

The Secret Life of Marilyn Monroe by J. Randy Taraborrelli (Grand Central, 2010)

The Strange Death of Marilyn Monroe by Frank A. Capell (The Herald of Freedom, 1964)

Timebends: A Life by Arthur Miller (Grove, 1987)

Newspapers, Magazines, and Websites

"The Actress and the Goddess: Joan Copeland and Marilyn" (TaraHanks .com, January 12, 2022)

"An Adorable Child" by Truman Capote (from *Music for Chameleons*, April 28, 1955)

"Arthur Miller Once Wrote of Marilyn Monroe, His Wife from 1956" (*Times Leader* [Wyoming], October 31, 2010)

"Arthur Miller on His Divorce from Marilyn Monroe: 'Everything Was Coming Together in an Explosion'" by Myles Burke (BBC, January 22, 2024)

"Arthur Miller's Refuge Amid the Pines" by Elizabeth Maker and Bruce Weber (*New York Times*, February 20, 2005)

"Auction of Marilyn Monroe's Jewish Prayer Book Puts Her Conversion Story on Display" by Julia Jacobs (*New York Times*, October 18, 2018)

"Barney Ruditsky, Detective, Dead" (*New York Times*, October 19, 1962)

"Barney Ruditsky: 'Wrong Door Raid' Leader Dies" (*Los Angeles Times*, October 19, 1962)

"Before Taylor and Travis, There Was Marilyn Monroe and Joe DiMaggio" by Frederic J. Frommer (*Washington Post*, February 6, 2024)

"Behind-the-Scenes of Marilyn Monroe's Iconic Flying Skirt" by Melissa Stevens (Biography.com, September 10, 2020)

"Ben Lyon, 78, Silent-Screen Star Who 'Discovered' Marilyn Monroe" (*New York Times*, March 26, 1979)

"'Blonde': The True Story of Arthur Miller's Relationship with Marilyn Monroe" by Laura Martin (*Esquire*, September 27, 2022)

"*Blonde*: Who Were Marilyn Monroe's Troubled Mother and Mysterious Father?" by Savannah Walsh (*Vanity Fair*, September 28, 2022)

"The Breakup with Marilyn" by Dennis Gaffney (*American Experience*, PBS .org, *Joe DiMaggio: The Hero's Life*, May 8, 2000)

SOURCES

"Brilliant Stardom and Personal Tragedy Punctuated the Life of Marilyn Monroe" (*New York Times*, August 6, 1962)

"Cinema: The Dostoevsky Blues" (*Time*, January 24, 1955)

"Cinema: To Aristophanes & Back" (*Time*, May 14, 1956)

"Clark Gable Dies at 59" (*Los Angeles Times*, November 17, 1960)

"Constance Collier (1878–1955)" by Sydney Higgins (*The Golden Age of British Theatre [1880–1920]*, Plus.net, 2009)

"The Curious Case of Marilyn Monroe's Missing 'Heirloom' Engagement Ring" by Emily Chan (*Vogue*, December 22, 2022)

"Did Marilyn Have Surgery? Medical Records and X-RAYS Under the Hammer for £20,000" (London *Express*, October 9, 2013)

"DiMaggio and Sinatra: The Feud Between Two Italian-American Pathbreakers" by Michael Beschloss (*New York Times*, June 13, 2014)

"Disturbing Note Marilyn Monroe's Doctor Found Taped to Her Stomach Just Before Surgery" by Kathleen Boyle (*Daily Express US*, May 11, 2024)

"Donald Zec's Incredible Memories of Showbiz Legends from Marilyn Monroe to Elvis Presley" by Donald Zec (*Daily Mirror*, September 10, 2021)

"Don Murray: 'I Never Understood Why Marilyn Monroe Was Not Nominated for *Bus Stop*" (*Film Talk*, December 11, 2014)

"Don Murray, Oscar-Nommed for His 'Bus Stop' Role Opposite Marilyn Monroe, Dies at 94" by Carmel Dagan (*Variety*, February 2, 2024)

"Dr. Hyman Engelberg, 92; Marilyn Monroe's Personal Physician" by Myrna Oliver (*Los Angeles Times*, December 21, 2005)

"Eleanor Goddard; Monroe Companion" by Myrna Oliver (*Los Angeles Times*, February 17, 2000)

"Elia Kazan's Private Letters: Marilyn Monroe Affair Detailed" by Andy Lewis (*Hollywood Reporter*, April 10, 2014)

"Excerpts from Arthur Miller's Testimony before the House Un-American Activities Committee" (*American Masters*, PBS.org, *Arthur Miller: Private Conversations*, April 8, 2020)

"Files: FBI Kept Watch on Arthur Miller" (CBS News, June 20, 2006)

"First Scene Put Her in Limelight" (*New York Times*, August 6, 1962)

"Five Things: Marilyn Monroe" by More Intelligent Life, A.R. (*The Economist*, November 2, 2010)

"Forever Marilyn Part 1: The Second Fox CinemaScope Film: How to Marry a Millionaire" by Robert Siegel (Blu-ray.com, July 31, 2012)

"For Her Birthday, Mapping Marilyn Monroe's 43 Homes" (Curbed.com, May 30, 2014)

"A Friendship in the Crucible" by Judith S. Gillies (*Washington Post,* August 30, 2003)

"The Grey Fox and the Platinum Blonde: Marilyn Monroe in Howard Hawks' *Monkey Business* (1952)" by Andréas Giannopoulous (*CTEQ Annotations on Film,* issue 105, April 2023)

"Hal Schaefer, Jazz Pianist and Marilyn Monroe Friend, Dies at 87" by Bruce Weber (*New York Times,* December 12, 2012)

"Handsome Johnny Roselli: The Hollywood Mobster" by Sam Moore (WhyNow, July 27, 2021)

"Happy Birthday, Mr. President: The Story of Marilyn Monroe and That Dress" by David Thomson (*The Guardian,* November 3, 2016)

"Hello, Norma Jeane" by Susan King (*Los Angeles Times,* December 2, 2002)

"He's Her Joe DiMaggio!" (*Photoplay,* July 1952)

"Hollywood Legends: Cary Grant and Marilyn" (The Marilyn Report, February 2, 2021)

"How Marilyn Monroe and Joe DiMaggio's Tumultuous Marriage Began in San Francisco" by Rae Alexandra (KQED.org, January 10, 2023)

"How Married and Bored Norma Jeane Became Sex Bomb Marilyn Monroe" by Michelle Morgan and Astrid Franse (*New York Post,* November 21, 2015)

"How Norma Became Marilyn" by Charles Casillo (TheHistoryReader .com, 2020)

"'I'll Never Forget My Honeymoon—with the 45th Division'" by Richard Ben Cramer, from *Joe DiMaggio: The Hero's Life* (Simon & Schuster, 2000), reprinted in ESPN.com

"Inside DiMaggio and Monroe's Twisted Love" by Maureen Callahan (*New York Post,* June 8, 2014)

"Inside Marilyn Monroe's Summer of Love in Amagansett" by Isabelle Canelli (*Hamptons,* July 22, 2020)

"In Those Years Joe's Reputation Was the Big Lover" by Richard Ben Cramer, from *Joe DiMaggio: The Hero's Life* (Simon & Schuster, 2000), reprinted in ESPN.com

"James Dougherty, 84; Was Married to Marilyn Monroe Before She Became a Star" by Dennis McLellan (*Los Angeles Times,* August 18, 2005)

"Jean Negulesco; Directed 'How to Marry a Millionaire'" by Myrna Oliver (*Los Angeles Times,* July 22, 1993)

"Joe DiMaggio and Marilyn Monroe's Central Coast Honeymoon" by David Middlecamp (*Tribune,* March 25, 2016)

"Joe DiMaggio's Last Hurrah: The 1951 Lefty O'Doul Tour" by Rob Fitts

(Society for American Baseball Research, published in *Nichebei Yakyu: US Tours of Japan, 1907–1958*)

"John Huston, Film Director, Writer and Actor, Dies at 81" by Peter B. Flint (*New York Times*, August 29, 1987)

"Last Talk with a Lonely Girl" by Richard Meryman (*Life,* August 17, 1962)

"The Legendary Ghosts of 625 Beach Road, Hearst's Gargoyle and Citizen Kane" by Alicia Mayer (HollywoodEssays.com, September 9, 2012)

"'Lost' Report on Monroe's Death Issued" (*Los Angeles Times,* September 23, 1985)

"Lucille Ryman Carroll, 96; MGM Talent Manager Mentored Actors" by Mary Rourke (*Los Angeles Times,* November 2, 2002)

"The Man Who Kept Marilyn's Secrets" by James Spada (*Vanity Fair,* May 1991)

"The Man Who Minted Style" by Peter Biskind (*Vanity Fair,* April 2003)

"Marilyn: Behind the Icon—The Asphalt Jungle" (*Classic Movie Hub,* June 22, 2020)

"Marilyn: Behind the Icon—Clash by Night" (*Classic Movie Hub,* June 15, 2020)

"Marilyn: Behind the Icon—How to Marry a Millionaire" (*Classic Movie Hub,* September 21, 2020)

"Marilyn: Behind the Icon—The Prince and the Showgirl" (*Classic Movie Hub,* July 21, 2020)

"Marilyn and Her Monsters" by Sam Kashner (*Vanity Fair,* October 5, 2010)

"Marilyn and Joe, et al. a 70 Year Saga" by Jack Doyle (PopHistoryDig.com, February 2022)

"Marilyn & Lauren Bacall" by Tara Hanks (ImmortalMarilyn.com, June 9, 2015)

"Marilyn and Me: Mirror Showbiz Legend on His Amazing Friendship with the Sex Goddess Movie Icon Who Died 50 Years Ago" by Donald Zec (*Daily Mirror,* August 3, 2012)

"Marilyn & Truman: Beautiful Children of NYC" by Elizabeth Winder (The HistoryReader.com)

"Marilyn Is Getting Married" by Guillaume Hanoteau (*Paris Match,* June 29, 1956)

"Marilyn Monroe, Arthur Miller Married in White Plains Court" (*New York Times,* June 30, 1956)

"Marilyn Monroe and the Prescription Drugs That Killed Her" by Dr. Howard Markel (*PBS NewsHour,* PBS.org, August 5, 2016)

"Marilyn Monroe Broke Protocol with Her Dress When She Met Queen Elizabeth" by Erin Hill (*People,* May 6, 2022)

"Marilyn Monroe Dead, Pills Near" (*New York Times,* August 6, 1962)

"Marilyn Monroe Dies; Pills Blamed" by Howard Hertel and Don Neff (*Los Angeles Times,* August 6, 1962)

"Marilyn Monroe Found Dead of Suspected Overdose" (*Variety,* August 6, 1962)

"Marilyn Monroe Loses Baby, Undergoes Operation" (*Desert Sun,* August 2, 1957)

"Marilyn Monroe Loved Brooklyn and 'Walking Around'" (*Brooklyn Magazine,* August 6, 2012)

"Marilyn Monroe Marries Arthur Miller" (*History Today,* June 2006)

"Marilyn Monroe Mystery Persists: 23 Years After Her Death Questions Continue to Generate Controversy" by Robert Welkos and Ted Rohrlich (*Los Angeles Times,* September 29, 1985)

"Marilyn Monroe: Rare Early Photos, 1950" by Ben Cosgrove (*Time,* November 1, 2014)

"Marilyn Monroe: Rare Photos of an Up-and-Coming Star, 1952" by Ben Cosgrove (*Time,* December 24, 2013)

"Marilyn Monroe's Bra, Love Letters from Joe DiMaggio and Arthur Miller Up for Auction" by Lindsey Bever (*Washington Post,* November 12, 2014)

"Marilyn Monroe's Death: Her Sudden Passing and Its Aftermath" by Alex Gurley (*People,* September 22, 2022)

"Marilyn Monroe's Early Career" by Susan Doll (HowStuffWorks.com)

"Marilyn Monroe's Only Oscars Appearance Featured a Major Fashion Mishap" by Hayley Maitland (*Vogue,* March 11, 2023)

"Marilyn Monroe's 1955 Resolutions" by Joanna Robinson (*Vanity Fair,* January 4, 2015)

"Marilyn Monroe's Sadness Was Deeper Than Anyone Knew (And Owed to Her Mother) — Here's the Story of Their Relationship" by Karen Sheedy (*Woman's World,* April 3, 2023)

"Marilyn Monroe's World War II Drone Program" by Michael Beschloss (*New York Times,* June 3, 2014)

"Marilyn Monroe vs. Hollywood" by Helen O'Hara (*Sunday Telegraph,* reprinted in *Vancouver Sun,* June 6, 2015)

"Marilyn Monroe Was Married 3 Times: All About Her Husbands" by Joyann Jeffrey (*Today,* September 6, 2022)

"Marilyn Monroe Was 'Never a Victim': Seven Ways She Masterminded Her Career" by Julie Miller (*Vanity Fair,* January 17, 2022)

SOURCES

"Marilyn Monroe—Wolves I Have Known" by Marilyn Monroe, as told by Florabel Muir (*Motion Picture and Television* magazine, January 1953)

"Marilyn Studying, Enjoys Anonymity" by Hedda Hopper (*Los Angeles Times,* April 27, 1955)

"Marilyn (Swinging a Hip) Monroe Is Here" (*Jamaica Gleaner,* January 4, 1957)

"Medical Issues on Marilyn Monroe's Life and Death: A Retrospective—Part I" by Sachi Sri Kantha (*International Medical Journal* 29, no. 2, April 2022)

"Meeting Marilyn and the Wedding" by Dennis Gaffney (*American Experience,* PBS.org, *Joe DiMaggio: The Hero's Life,* May 8, 2000)

"The Mentor and the Movie Star" by Patricia Bosworth (*Vanity Fair,* June 1, 2003)

"Miller Convicted in Contempt Case" by Joseph A. Loftus (*New York Times,* June 1, 1957)

"'Misfits' Writer Arthur Miller Dead at 89" (*Nevada Appeal,* February 10, 2005)

"The Monroe Doctrine" (*Life,* April 1952)

"Moving Marilyn Monroe" by Debra Levine (*Los Angeles Times,* August 9, 2009)

"Mrs. and Mr. Marilyn Monroe Honeymoon in Japan" by Patrick Parr (*Japan Today,* August 23, 2018)

"The Mystery of Marilyn Monroe's Plastic Surgery" by Joan Kron (*Allure,* October 9, 2013)

"New Inquiry Rejected in Marilyn Monroe's Death" by Robert Lindsey (*New York Times,* November 23, 1985)

"Nikita Khrushchev Ogles Marilyn Monroe" by Peter Carlson (History .net, June 12, 2017)

"Now We Get the Mmmm Girl" by Earl Wilson (*New York Daily News,* August 14, 1949)

"Nude Calendar Beauty at Last Is Identified: Marilyn Monroe" by Aline Mosby (United Press, March 13, 1952)

"Paparazzi Have Feeding Frenzy with Miller and Monroe in the 1950s" by Susan Tuz (*NewsTimes,* March 22, 2010)

"Physician Emerges as Seller of Marilyn Monroe Plastic Surgery Notes" by Eric Kelsey (Reuters, October 9, 2013)

"Playboy Founder Hugh Hefner, Who Shook Up American Morality with an Ideal of Swinging Singlehood, Dies at 91" by Elaine Woo (*Los Angeles Times,* September 27, 2017)

"Playwright Arthur Miller Refused Visa for a Visit to Brussels to See His Play" (*New York Times,* March 31, 1954)

401

"The Playwright, the Starlight, and the Rabbi: A Love Triangle" by Lila Corwin Berman (*AJS Perspectives,* spring 2013)

"'Please Don't Make Me a Joke,' review of *Marilyn* by Gloria Steinem" by Diana Trilling (*New York Times,* December 21, 1986)

"Portrait of an Icon: Never Before Seen Images of Injured Marilyn Monroe Taken on the Set of River of No Return" by Maysa Rawi (*Daily Mail,* October 20, 2011)

"The Press: Out at Home" (*Time,* October 18, 1954)

"The Prince, the Showgirl, and the Stray Strap" by Pat Ryan (*New York Times,* November 11, 2011)

"Publisher's Letter, May 14, 1956" (*Time,* May 14, 1956)

"Read Arthur Miller's Steamy Love Letter to Marilyn Monroe" by Walker Caplan (*Literary Hub,* January 24, 2022)

"Remembrances of Marilyn" by Flora Rheta Schreiber (*Good Housekeeping,* January 1963)

"Revisit Marilyn Monroe's Country Retreat in Connecticut and Spanish Colonial-Style Home in Los Angeles" by Jeffrey Meyers (*Architectural Digest,* September 23, 2016)

"Rita Hayworth: Don't Put the Blame on Me, Boys" by John Hallowell, author of *The Truth Games* (*New York Times,* October 25, 1970)

"Rita Hayworth, Movie Legend, Dies" by Albin Krebs (*New York Times,* May 16, 1987)

"Robert Mitchum Was Mr. Bad Taste and Trouble Himself" by Robert Ward (*Daily Beast,* March 10, 2020)

"Roy Craft, Ex-Publisher, Hollywood Publicist, Dies" (Associated Press, December 28, 1989)

"'The Seven Year Itch': Marilyn Monroe, Tom Ewell Star at State" by Bosley Crowther (*New York Times,* June 4, 1955)

"She Wears a Borrowed Dress to Her Party" (*Life,* November 29, 1954)

"She Wore a Black Wig, Ray-Bans, and Called Herself Zelda Zonk" by Caroline Howe (*Daily Mail,* January 6, 2017)

"Some Speculate Marilyn Monroe Died at Lake Tahoe Resort" (CBS News, May 12, 2012)

"Something's Got to Give: The Story of the Marilyn Monroe Film That Never Got Made" by Alexandra Pollard (*The Independent,* March 29, 2019)

"Susan Strasberg, 60, Actress Lauded in 'Anne Frank,' Dies" by Mel Gusow (*New York Times,* January 23, 1999)

"Throwback Thursday: When Marilyn Monroe's Mom Was the Bombshell" by Bill Higgins (*Hollywood Reporter*, May 14, 2015)

"The True Story of How Marilyn Monroe Met Queen Elizabeth" by Michelle Morgan (*Town & Country*, May 3, 2022)

"The True Story of the Night Marilyn Monroe Died" by Lauren Kranc (*Esquire*, April 27, 2022)

"Vet Snaps Shot with Marilyn Monroe in Korea" (The American Legion, Legion.org, November 12, 2013)

"A View from the Bridge, October 1956" by Samantha Ellis (*Guardian*, July 16, 2003)

"Weeping Marilyn Gets Divorce after Telling Judge Joe Was 'Cold,' 'Indifferent' to Her" by Aline Mosby (United Press, October 27, 1954)

"What Did Queen Elizabeth and Marilyn Monroe Really Think of Each Other After They Met in 1956?" by Erin Hill (*People*, May 5, 2022)

"When Marilyn Monroe Interrupted Her Honeymoon to Go to Korea" by Liesl Bradner (History.net, December 3, 2019)

"The White Mask: Marilyn Monroe and 'Some Like It Hot'" (*San Diego Reader*, September 4, 2003)

"Why I Wrote 'The Crucible'" by Arthur Miller (*The New Yorker*, October 13, 1996)

TELEVISION AND VIDEO

"Almanac: Marilyn Monroe's Dress" (*CBS Sunday Morning*, September 15, 2019)

"Arthur Miller Announcing He Will Be Marrying Marilyn Monroe June 21, 1956" (Marilyn Monroe Video Archives)

"Arthur Miller Interviewed about Marilyn Monroe in 1987" (Marilyn Monroe Video Archives)

"G.I.'s Are a Girl's Best Friends" (Marilyn Monroe Video Archives)

"Grace Goddard Train Trip 1944" Interview with Marilyn Monroe (Marilyn Monroe Video Archives)

"Groucho Marx Talking About Marilyn Monroe, *Love Happy*, 1949" (Marilyn Monroe Video Archives)

"Marilyn Monroe Archive Footage — Press Conference at the Savoy Hotel London, 1956" (Marilyn Monroe Video Archives)

"Marilyn Monroe in Korea 1954 — 'The Highlight of My Life'" (Marilyn Monroe Video Archives)

"Marilyn Monroe at Press Conference in Support of Her Husband Arthur Miller—'Contempt of Congress'" (Marilyn Monroe Video Archives)

"Marilyn Monroe Presented with a Bike 1956 Footage" (Marilyn Monroe Video Archives)

"Marilyn Monroe Rare Footage and Interview on Arrival at Los Angeles Airport, February 1956" (Fox Movietone News)

"Marilyn Monroe RARE Press Conference Footage—Outside Her Apartment June 21, 1956" (Marilyn Monroe Video Archives)

Marilyn: Something's Got to Give (documentary by Henry Schipper, 1990)

"'The Prince and the Showgirl' Movie Premiere 1957, Interview" (Marilyn Monroe Video Archives)

"Rare Interview with Emmeline Snively (Blue Book Modeling Agency) About Marilyn Monroe in August 1962" (Marilyn Monroe History, YouTube.com)

Auction Items/Memorabilia

"Arthur Miller Passionate Love Letter in Which He Bears His Soul to His New Love and Future Wife, Marilyn Monroe" (Heritage Auctions, "Profiles in History: Hollywood Summer 2015 #997027," Lot #2185, September 29, 2015)

"Billy Wilder *Some Like it Hot* Synopsis Sent to Marilyn Monroe" (Julien's Auctions, "Property from the Estate of Lee Strasberg," Lot #411, November 17, 2016)

"A Charles Feldman Letter to Marilyn Monroe and Joe DiMaggio Pertaining to *The Seven Year Itch*" (Bonhams, "Pop Culture Then & Now," Lot #3, June 4–14, 2024)

"Laurence Olivier Floral Arrangement Card to Marilyn Monroe" (Julien's Auctions, "Property from the Estate of Lee Strasberg," Lot #371, November 17, 2016)

"Laurence Olivier Letter to Marilyn Monroe" (Julien's Auctions, "Property from the Estate of Lee Strasberg," Lot #370, November 17, 2016)

"A Marilyn Monroe and Arthur Miller Signed Record Album to Their Rabbi on Their Wedding Day" (Bonhams, "Entertainment Memorabilia Including Animation Art," Lot # 1002, December 17, 2006)

"Marilyn Monroe Gifted Money Clip" (Julien's Auctions, "Hollywood Legends," Lot #521, March 31, 2012)

"Marilyn Monroe Gladstone Hotel Statement" (Julien's Auctions, "Property from the Estate of Lee Strasberg," Lot #380, November 17, 2016)

SOURCES

"A Marilyn Monroe Group of Telegrams from Elia Kazan" (Bonhams, "TCM Presents...the Dark Side of Hollywood," Lot #321, November 20, 2018)

"Marilyn Monroe Letter from Cary Grant" (Julien's Auctions, "Icons and Idols 2014: Hollywood Featuring Property from the Life and Career of Marilyn Monroe," Lot #725, December 5, 2014)

"Marilyn Monroe Letter from John Steinbeck" (Julien's Auctions, "Property from the Estate of Lee Strasberg," Lot #259, November 17, 2016)

"Marilyn Monroe Letter to Her Stepchildren from the Cat" (Julien's Auctions, "Property from the Estate of Lee Strasberg, Lot #318," November 17, 2016)

"Marilyn Monroe Letter to Jane Miller as Hugo the Dog with Photographs" (Julien's Auctions, "Property from the Estate of Lee Strasberg," Lot #316, November 17, 2016)

"Marilyn Monroe Letter to Robert Miller as Hugo the Dog with Photographs" (Julien's Auctions, "Property from the Estate of Lee Strasberg," Lot #314, November 17, 2016)

"Marilyn Monroe: A Model Release Form for Tom Kelley Studio" (Christie's, "Film and Entertainment Including Vintage Film Posters," Lot #164, June 16, 2005)

"Marilyn Monroe: Paula Strasberg Annotated 'Bus Stop' Script" (Julien's Auctions, "Hollywood: Classic & Contemporary," Lot #127, April 22–23, 2023)

"A Marilyn Monroe-Received Letter from Isidore Miller, 1962," (Bonhams, "Entertainment Memorabilia," Lot #1017, December 21, 2008)

"Marilyn Monroe Received Letter from Patricia Newcomb" (Julien's Auctions, "Legends Auction," Lot #666, June 13, 2019)

"Marilyn Monroe Received Letter from Richard Meryman" (The Marilyn Monroe Collection, MarilynMonroeCollection.com, March 2, 2013)

"*Playboy* Issue #1 [December 1953], With Marilyn Monroe Cover" (Sotheby's [London], "Erotic: Passion & Desire," Lot #74, February 15, 2018)

"*The Seven Year Itch,* Extensive Archive of Marilyn Monroe Agent Charles K. Feldman's (1,000+) Items" (Heritage Auctions, December 11, 2018)

"A Twentieth Century-Fox Letter Ordering Marilyn Monroe to Return to Work" (Bonhams, "Pop Culture Then & Now," Lot #2, June 4–14, 2024)

ABOUT THE AUTHORS

James Patterson is one of the best-known and biggest-selling writers of all time. Among his creations are some of the world's most popular series, including Alex Cross, the Women's Murder Club, Michael Bennett and the Private novels. He has written many other number one bestsellers including collaborations with President Bill Clinton, Dolly Parton and Michael Crichton, stand-alone thrillers and non-fiction. James has donated millions in grants to independent bookshops and has been the most borrowed adult author in UK libraries for the past fourteen years in a row. He lives in Florida with his family.

Imogen Edwards-Jones is the bestselling author of *Hotel Babylon*, *Air Babylon* and *Fashion Babylon*, as well as novels such as *The Witch's Daughter* and *Have You Got Anything Stronger?* A broadcaster, columnist and journalist for over twenty-five years, she lives in London.

Also By James Patterson

ALEX CROSS NOVELS

Along Came a Spider • Kiss the Girls • Jack and Jill • Cat and Mouse • Pop Goes the Weasel • Roses are Red • Violets are Blue • Four Blind Mice • The Big Bad Wolf • London Bridges • Mary, Mary • Cross • Double Cross • Cross Country • Alex Cross's Trial (*with Richard DiLallo*) • I, Alex Cross • Cross Fire • Kill Alex Cross • Merry Christmas, Alex Cross • Alex Cross, Run • Cross My Heart • Hope to Die • Cross Justice • Cross the Line • The People vs. Alex Cross • Target: Alex Cross • Criss Cross • Deadly Cross • Fear No Evil • Triple Cross • Alex Cross Must Die • The House of Cross

THE WOMEN'S MURDER CLUB SERIES

1st to Die (*with Andrew Gross*) • 2nd Chance (*with Andrew Gross*) • 3rd Degree (*with Andrew Gross*) • 4th of July (*with Maxine Paetro*) • The 5th Horseman (*with Maxine Paetro*) • The 6th Target (*with Maxine Paetro*) • 7th Heaven (*with Maxine Paetro*) • 8th Confession (*with Maxine Paetro*) • 9th Judgement (*with Maxine Paetro*) • 10th Anniversary (*with Maxine Paetro*) • 11th Hour (*with Maxine Paetro*) • 12th of Never (*with Maxine Paetro*) • Unlucky 13 (*with Maxine Paetro*) • 14th Deadly Sin (*with Maxine Paetro*) • 15th Affair (*with Maxine Paetro*) • 16th Seduction (*with Maxine Paetro*) • 17th Suspect (*with Maxine Paetro*) • 18th Abduction (*with Maxine Paetro*) • 19th Christmas (*with Maxine Paetro*) • 20th Victim (*with Maxine Paetro*) • 21st Birthday (*with Maxine Paetro*) • 22 Seconds (*with Maxine Paetro*) • 23rd Midnight (*with Maxine Paetro*) • The 24th Hour (*with Maxine Paetro*) • 25 Alive (*with Maxine Paetro*)

DETECTIVE MICHAEL BENNETT SERIES

Step on a Crack (*with Michael Ledwidge*) • Run for Your Life (*with Michael Ledwidge*) • Worst Case (*with Michael Ledwidge*) • Tick Tock (*with Michael Ledwidge*) • I, Michael Bennett (*with Michael Ledwidge*) • Gone (*with Michael Ledwidge*) • Burn (*with Michael Ledwidge*) • Alert (*with Michael Ledwidge*) • Bullseye (*with Michael Ledwidge*) • Haunted (*with James O. Born*) • Ambush (*with James O. Born*) • Blindside (*with James O. Born*) • The Russian (*with James O. Born*) • Shattered (*with James O. Born*) • Obsessed (*with James O. Born*) • Crosshairs (*with James O. Born*) • Paranoia (*with James O. Born*)

PRIVATE NOVELS

Private (*with Maxine Paetro*) • Private London (*with Mark Pearson*) • Private Games (*with Mark Sullivan*) • Private: No. 1 Suspect (*with Maxine Paetro*) • Private Berlin (*with Mark Sullivan*) • Private Down Under (*with Michael White*) • Private L.A. (*with Mark Sullivan*) • Private India (*with Ashwin Sanghi*) • Private Vegas (*with Maxine Paetro*) • Private Sydney (*with Kathryn Fox*) • Private Paris (*with Mark Sullivan*) • The Games (*with Mark Sullivan*) • Private Delhi (*with Ashwin Sanghi*) • Private Princess (*with Rees Jones*) • Private Moscow (*with Adam Hamdy*) • Private Rogue (*with Adam Hamdy*) • Private Beijing (*with Adam Hamdy*) • Private Rome (*with Adam Hamdy*) • Private Monaco (*with Adam Hamdy*)

NYPD RED SERIES

NYPD Red (*with Marshall Karp*) • NYPD Red 2 (*with Marshall Karp*) • NYPD Red 3 (*with Marshall Karp*) • NYPD Red 4 (*with Marshall Karp*) • NYPD Red 5 (*with Marshall Karp*) • NYPD Red 6 (*with Marshall Karp*)

DETECTIVE HARRIET BLUE SERIES

Never Never (*with Candice Fox*) • Fifty Fifty (*with Candice Fox*) • Liar Liar (*with Candice Fox*) • Hush Hush (*with Candice Fox*)

INSTINCT SERIES

Instinct (*with Howard Roughan, previously published as* Murder Games) • Killer Instinct (*with Howard Roughan*) • Steal (*with Howard Roughan*)

THE BLACK BOOK SERIES

The Black Book (*with David Ellis*) • The Red Book (*with David Ellis*) • Escape (*with David Ellis*)

TEXAS RANGER SERIES

Texas Ranger (*with Andrew Bourelle*) • Texas Outlaw (*with Andrew Bourelle*) • The Texas Murders (*with Andrew Bourelle*)

STAND-ALONE THRILLERS

The Thomas Berryman Number • Hide and Seek • Black Market • The Midnight Club • Honeymoon (*with Howard Roughan*) • Sail (*with Howard Roughan*) • Swimsuit (*with Maxine Paetro*) • Don't Blink (*with Howard Roughan*) • Postcard Killers (*with Liza Marklund*) • Toys (*with Neil McMahon*) • Now You See Her (*with Michael Ledwidge*) • Kill Me If You Can (*with Marshall Karp*) • Guilty Wives (*with David Ellis*) • Zoo (*with Michael Ledwidge*) • Second Honeymoon (*with Howard Roughan*) • Mistress (*with David Ellis*) • Invisible (*with David Ellis*) • Truth or Die (*with Howard Roughan*) • Murder House (*with David Ellis*) • The Store (*with Richard DiLallo*) • The President is Missing (*with Bill Clinton*) • Revenge (*with Andrew Holmes*) • Juror No. 3 (*with Nancy Allen*) • The First Lady (*with Brendan DuBois*) • The Chef (*with Max DiLallo*) • Out of Sight (*with Brendan DuBois*) • Unsolved (*with David Ellis*) • The Inn (*with Candice Fox*) • Lost (*with James O. Born*) • The Summer House (*with Brendan DuBois*) • 1st Case (*with Chris Tebbetts*) • Cajun Justice (*with Tucker Axum*)• The Midwife Murders (*with Richard DiLallo*) • The Coast-to-Coast Murders (*with J.D. Barker*) • Three Women Disappear (*with Shan Serafin*) • The President's Daughter (*with Bill Clinton*) • The Shadow (*with Brian Sitts*) • The Noise (*with J.D. Barker*) • 2 Sisters Detective Agency (*with Candice Fox*) • Jailhouse Lawyer (*with Nancy Allen*) • The Horsewoman (*with Mike Lupica*) • Run Rose Run (*with Dolly Parton*) • Death of the Black Widow (*with J.D. Barker*) • The Ninth Month (*with Richard DiLallo*) • The Girl in the Castle (*with Emily Raymond*) • Blowback (*with Brendan DuBois*) • The Twelve Topsy-Turvy, Very Messy Days of Christmas (*with Tad Safran*) • The Perfect Assassin (*with Brian Sitts*) • House of Wolves (*with Mike Lupica*) • Countdown (*with Brendan DuBois*) • Cross Down (*with Brendan DuBois*) • Circle of Death (*with Brian Sitts*) • Lion & Lamb (with *Duane Swierczynski*) • 12 Months to Live (*with Mike Lupica*) • Holmes, Margaret and Poe (*with Brian Sitts*) • The No. 1 Lawyer (*with Nancy Allen*) • Eruption (*with Michael Crichton*) • The Murder Inn (*with Candice Fox*) • Confessions of the Dead (*with J.D. Barker*) • 8 Months Left (*with Mike Lupica*) • Lies He Told Me (*with David Ellis*) • Murder Island (*with Brian Sitts*) • Raised By Wolves (*with Emily Raymond*) • Holmes is Missing (*with Brian Sitts*) • 2 Sisters Murder Investigations (*with Candice Fox*)

NON-FICTION

Torn Apart (*with Hal and Cory Friedman*) • The Murder of King
Tut (*with Martin Dugard*) • All-American Murder (*with Alex
Abramovich and Mike Harvkey*) • The Kennedy Curse (*with Cynthia
Fagen*) • The Last Days of John Lennon (*with Casey Sherman and
Dave Wedge*) • Walk in My Combat Boots (*with Matt Eversmann
and Chris Mooney*) • ER Nurses (*with Matt Eversmann*) • James
Patterson by James Patterson: The Stories of My Life • Diana,
William and Harry (*with Chris Mooney*) • American Cops
(*with Matt Eversmann*) • What Really Happens in Vegas
(*with Mark Seal*) • The Secret Lives of Booksellers and
Librarians (*with Matt Eversmann*) • Tiger, Tiger • American Heroes
(*with Matt Eversmann*)

MURDER IS FOREVER TRUE CRIME

Murder, Interrupted (*with Alex Abramovich and Christopher
Charles*) • Home Sweet Murder (*with Andrew Bourelle and
Scott Slaven*) • Murder Beyond the Grave (*with Andrew
Bourelle and Christopher Charles*) • Murder Thy Neighbour
(*with Andrew Bourelle and Max DiLallo*) • Murder of Innocence
(*with Max DiLallo and Andrew Bourelle*) • Till Murder Do Us Part
(*with Andrew Bourelle and Max DiLallo*)

COLLECTIONS

Triple Threat (*with Max DiLallo and Andrew Bourelle*) • Kill or Be
Killed (*with Maxine Paetro, Rees Jones, Shan Serafin and Emily
Raymond*) • The Moores are Missing (*with Loren D. Estleman,
Sam Hawken and Ed Chatterton*) • The Family Lawyer (*with
Robert Rotstein, Christopher Charles and Rachel Howzell
Hall*) • Murder in Paradise (*with Doug Allyn, Connor Hyde and
Duane Swierczynski*) • The House Next Door (*with Susan DiLallo,
Max DiLallo and Brendan DuBois*) • 13-Minute Murder (*with Shan
Serafin, Christopher Farnsworth and Scott Slaven*) • The River
Murders (*with James O. Born*) • The Palm Beach Murders
(*with James O. Born, Duane Swierczynski and Tim Arnold*) • Paris
Detective • 3 Days to Live • 23 ½ Lies (*with Maxine Paetro*)

For more information about James Patterson's novels,
visit www.penguin.co.uk.